Michel de Certeau

Arts & Humanities
Research Council

Also available from Continuum:

Pierre Bourdieu: Agent Provocateur, Michael Grenfell

Michel de Certeau
Analysing Culture

Ben Highmore

continuum

Continuum International Publishing Group
The Tower Building   80 Maiden Lane
11 York Road   Suite 704
London SE1 7NX   New York, NY 10038

British Library Cataloguing-in-Publication Data
A catalogue record for this book is available from the British Library.

ISBN: 0-8264-6073-9 (paperback)

Library of Congress Cataloguing-in-Publication Data
A catalog record for this book is available from the Library of Congress.

Typeset by Servis Filmsetting Ltd, Manchester
Printed and bound in Great Britain by MPG Books Ltd, Bodmin, Cornwall

To listen is already to be open to and existentially disposed towards: one inclines a little to one side in order to listen.

Ranajit Guha

'Subjugated' standpoints are preferred because they seem to promise more adequate, sustained, objective, transforming accounts of the world. But *how* to see from below is a problem requiring as much skill with bodies and language, with the mediations of vision, as the 'highest' techno-scientific visualizations.

Donna Haraway

Practice is both the starting point and the testing ground of our conceptualization of the world. What is needed is not so much the recovery of practical philosophy as the recovery of the philosophy of practice.

Ngũgĩ wa Thiong'o

Contents

Abbreviations of works by Michel de Certeau

CP – *Culture in the Plural*, translated by Tom Conley (Minneapolis: University of Minnesota Press, 1997).
This was originally published in France in 1974 as *La culture au pluriel*. The English translation doesn't include the important essay 'The Beauty of the Dead' which can be found in English in *Heterologies*.

CS – *The Capture of Speech and other Political Writings*, translated by Tom Conley (Minneapolis: University of Minnesota Press, 1997).
The first part of this book consists of a pamphlet *La prise de parole* originally published in France in 1968, other materials date from 1976, 1983 and 1985.

H – *Heterologies: Discourse on the Other*, translated by Brian Massumi (Manchester: Manchester University Press, 1986).
There is no French equivalent to this book, though Michel de Certeau, *Histoire et psychanalyse entre science et fiction* (Paris: Gallimard, 2002) contains many of the same essays.

MF – *The Mystic Fable: Volume One – The Sixteenth and Seventeenth Centuries*, translated by Michael B. Smith (Chicago: University of Chicago Press, 1992).
This was originally published in France as *La Fable Mystique, XVIe–XVIIe Siècle* in 1982.

PEL1 – *The Practice of Everyday Life*, translated by Steven Rendall (Berkeley: University of California Press, 1984).
This was originally published in France as *L'invention du quotidien, I, arts de faire* in 1980.

PEL2 – Michel de Certeau, Luce Giard and Pierre Mayol, *The Practice of Everyday Life – Volume 2: Living and Cooking*, translated by Timothy J. Tomasik (Minneapolis: University of Minnesota Press, 1998).
This was originally published in France as *L'invention du quotidien, II, habiter, cuisiner*, in 1980.

PL – *The Possession at Loudun*, translated by Michael B. Smith (Chicago: University of Chicago Press, 2000).
This was originally published in France as *La Possession de Loudun* in 1970.

WH – *The Writing of History*, translated and introduced by Tom Conley (New York: Colombia University Press, 1988).
This was originally published in France as *L'écriture de l'histoire* in 1975.

The above initials will be used for referencing within the text. Where the above titles include work co-written with others (or editorial writing by translators and editors) this will be indicated by including the relevant name(s) after the page number(s). All other materials used, including other work by Michel de Certeau, are referenced in footnotes.

Preface and Acknowledgements

This book is written with a particular ambition in mind: to use the work of Michel de Certeau, not as an end in itself, but as a way of locating some methodological co-ordinates for studying culture – for cultural studies or cultural analysis. The 'cultural studies' that I have in mind is a disciplinary field (or interdisciplinary field) disabused of a certain self-regard. Cultural studies as a project has, in the past, thought of itself as a subversive and wily, non-disciplinary-discipline. If it had a flag of allegiance, that flag was more likely to be a political one than a methodological one. Always ready to launch a new intervention in the cultural terrain, cultural studies had to be flexible, not tied to particular ways of operating. In this way its tactic was to pilfer and retool methodologies fashioned elsewhere.

There are several things wrong with this self-understanding, the major one being that it now rings false (if, indeed, it ever rang true). In the first decade of the twenty-first century it seems clear to me that cultural studies is, *de facto*, a discipline, replete with a raft of dedicated journals, various international associations, and a whole panoply of undergraduate and graduate courses. The false heroics of imagining that cultural studies is some sort of academic subculture, always intervening on the side of the oppressed, must strike students as particularly odd, especially as they submit to the process of being schooled and judged by seasoned and not-so-seasoned professors. One sign of cultural studies' peculiar attitude to its own status is its constant anxiety about its beginnings. The stories cultural studies tells of itself are unrelenting in the way that they conjure a 'good' and radical project, which through a process of 'disciplinary' auto-critiques continues its radical mission. Such narratives always seem to begin with tales of radical interventions against the elitism of the 'establishment'. Yet now, in many ways, a loose cultural studies orientation *is* the academic establishment in much of the humanities and social sciences. Writers working in literary studies, for instance, are as likely to be writing about telegraphy or dust as about Shakespeare or Chaucer (and when they do write about Shakespeare and Chaucer the approach is rarely hagiographic). And they are likely to think of themselves as doing, however loosely, a version of 'cultural studies' (however averse they may be to some of the connotations of that denomination). Theoretical resources and named theorists are shared across any number of disciplines. For many, then, the term 'cultural studies' (in its most neutral guise) signals a general interdisciplinarity, a loosening up of borders, a questioning of the 'objects' of research (often coupled with an anti-canonical tendency) and a general openness to new approaches and perspectives (queer theory, postcolonialism and so on).

To mourn this situation as the 'death of a project' would, I think, seem churlish if we didn't at the same time recognize that it constitutes an extensive success. How cultural studies copes with the success of its more general project is, I think, a very real issue (even if, admittedly, it might not seem particularly urgent). If everyone is doing cultural studies (in art history departments, in sociology departments, in history schools and elsewhere) then what is the point in having a specific practice called 'cultural studies'? Surely if it is loose enough to accommodate such a variety of practices it has become a term that has simply been worn too thin to be useful, a term that signals in the same way that the term 'humanities' signals? In the other direction, though, a certain hardening of brand identity is emerging, often in the form of a parody that sees cultural studies declaring its radical political mission, while championing the latest craze associated with the culture industry. This, of course, is a caricature, assigned to cultural studies from outside – yet too often it seems uncannily to target a large chunk of what is most visible in cultural studies.

There is, I think, something far too comforting in seeing cultural studies' history as beginning in the 1960s as part of a project of the New Left. For a whole host of reasons it strikes me as peculiarly limiting and delusory to think in terms of such a narrow institutional base. More interesting, but much more messy, is to see cultural studies within a much longer and larger history; an inheritor of forces that made culture into an object that could be studied in the first place. An account of this aspect of cultural studies would need to link it to colonial encounters, to the so-called 'discovery of the new world', to the ethnology that emerged in the wake of these encounters, to the industrialization of culture and communication in the eighteenth and nineteenth centuries and so on. This is to imagine a form of cultural studies that, potentially at least, isn't blind to its unavoidable complicity with forms of cultural violence, cultural pacification and cultural management. Cultural studies is nowadays a sophisticated, politically sensitive, range of approaches to culture, yet for all that it is not a world away from the paternalism of folklore studies that were established in the nineteenth century. It is one of the great benefits of Michel de Certeau's work that he doesn't let cultural studies off the hook, but at every turn seems to ask how what we know (under the banner of modern liberal-humanism, for instance) differs (epistemologically, morphologically and so on) from what has been known and done in the name of 'studying culture' since the sixteenth century. At the same time de Certeau's work is far from falling completely on the side of critique. The reason for my interest in his work is that it constitutes a demand (an ethical, social, political demand) to generate new approaches, new ways of studying culture, that are responses (however tentative) to these critiques. The study of Michel de Certeau, I want to persuade you, is the study of inventive (and hopeful) methodologies in the face of epistemological doubt. What we can get from de Certeau is, partly, an ethical demand to go beyond critique, to offer substantive accounts of the world that are more inclusive, more attentive, more responsive to an alterity at the heart of culture.

This book could not have been written if it hadn't been for Wendy Bonner. Her love and humour (often in the face of a daily stream of minor catastrophes), and her camaraderie in the day-to-day business of getting on with getting on, is what drove this book. Zebedee and Molly, like small Zen teachers, helped me to see the beauty of the detail, and the value of the accidental. If at times I was a poor student, I was lucky enough to have patient and forgiving teachers. Encouragement and support for this book has come from many quarters. Tom Conley and Michael Sheringham have helped in all sorts of ways, not least by helping me to secure the funding that gave me the time, away from teaching, to write. For this I also need to thank the Arts and Humanities Research Council (UK), and the University of the West of England, Bristol, for releasing me from teaching for the academic year 2004–5. Luce Giard's enthusiastic support of my work on her friend, colleague and collaborator, Michel de Certeau, has been invaluable.

One of the most enjoyable aspects of working on this book has been the opportunity it has provided for meeting people who share similar preoccupa-tions; what was more unexpected was the level of conviviality that seemed to characterize all these meetings. In no particular order (apart from alphabetical) I want to acknowledge the following: Jeremy Ahearne, Stuart Allan, Caroline Bainbridge, Ian Buchanan, Gavin Butt, Tim Clark, Paola Di Cori, Mark Devenney, Rod Dickinson, Richard Fardon, Simon Gunn, Michelle Henning, Marie Theresa Hernández, Elizabeth Lebas, Nils Lindahl-Elliot, Jon Mitchell, Valentina Napolitano-Guayson, Wang Ning, Susannah Radstone, David Pratten, Alan Read, Gregory Seigworth, Gillian Swanson, Nigel Thrift and Joanna Zylinska. Scott McCracken and Greg Seigworth went, as always, far beyond the call of duty, and read and commented on the draft manuscript. Needless to say it is a better book for their involvement, even if I doubt that I have fully resolved the questions and problems that they put to me in response.

Mark Nowak gave me permission to reproduce my essay ' "Opaque, Stubborn Life": Everyday Life and Resistance in the Work of Michel de

Certeau', from *XCP: Cross Cultural Poetics* (7, 2000, pp. 89–99). Parts of this essay have been reworked and are included in Chapter 4. Taylor and Francis (www.tandf.co.uk), the publishers of *Strategies: Journal of Theory, Culture and Politics*, gave permission for me to reproduce 'Obligation to the Ordinary: Michel de Certeau, Ethnography and Ethics' (in *Strategies* Volume 14, No. 2, 2001, pp. 253–63). This essay has been much modified and bits of it are dispersed through the book. The argument animating Chapter 3 had its first airing at the 'Culture and the Unconscious' conference, London, 2003. Elements of Chapter 5 were presented at the 'Narrative Conference', Berkeley, 2003; the conference 'Cultural Studies: Between Politics and Ethics', Bath Spa University, 2001; the conference 'The Future of Literary Theory: China and the World', Beijing, 2000; and at the 'Reading/Writing the Contemporary' conference, University College of Ripon and York, St John, as far back as 1996. Part of Chapter 6 first saw the light of day at the 'Making Use of Culture' conference, Manchester University, 2005. The final impetus for the organization of this book came from the workshop, 'Michel de Certeau: Ethnographies of Everyday Life and Anthropological Returns of Histories', at Sussex University, 2005. I want to thank the organizers of these conferences and everyone who responded to my contributions.

While I was writing this book I received a letter from an anonymous reviewer, commenting on another book project I was planning (an edited collection of essays on Michel de Certeau's work). In the letter the reviewer wrote:

> In a field [cultural studies] overly enamored of the contemporary, de Certeau offers the historian's detailed appraisal of the past. In a field obsessed with the local, de Certeau offers itineraries to elsewheres. In a field where culture tends to be synonymous with the US model, de Certeau points to the other. In a field awash in the ordinary, de Certeau grasps the singular. In a field beset with nihilism, de Certeau evokes abiding faith in human history. In a field associated with celebrity stardom, de Certeau provides beguiling self-effacement.

These anonymous words, which I've taken the liberty of citing here, seem to me to vividly articulate the best reasons for studying de Certeau. At times I felt that the anonymous reviewer should have been writing this book instead of me: if I've come anywhere close to filling out the promise of this quotation I will be happy.

CHAPTER 1

Ways of Operating: Introducing Michel de Certeau's Methodological Imagination

For what I really wish to work out is a science of singularity; that is to say, a science of the relationship that links everyday pursuits to particular circumstances. And only in the local network of labor and recreation can one grasp how, within a grid of socio-economic constraints, these pursuits unfailingly establish relational tactics (a struggle for life), artistic creations (an aesthetic) and autonomous initiatives (an ethic). The characteristically subtle logic of these 'ordinary' activities comes to light only in the details. (PEL1: ix)

A SCIENCE OF SINGULARITY

'A science of singularity' is a phrase that haunts this book. Structurally a contradiction (isn't science concerned with the testable? the repeatable? surely its destination is in the opposite direction to the singular?), the phrase offers a seemingly impossible object. The phrase is the name of a project based on an oxymoron: a project 'naturally' destined to fail. But what if the two terms of the phrase were to alter, slightly, behind your back (so to speak), such that they weren't any longer so devoted to outdoing and undoing one another? What if they were to secretly reveal to each other another side of themselves – their hidden faces – a side that suddenly made communication and contact possible? It is such an alteration (and others beside) that I think Michel de Certeau's work performs. The subtle alteration of the conceptual and perceptual axioms that ground the study of culture is a key component of de Certeau's work and is characteristic of his way of operating. It is an operation that I would want this book to perform too. Or at least, if when reading this book you felt that certain words (not just 'science' and 'singularity', but also other terms like aesthetics, subjectivity, literature, history, voice and so on) were to undergo some sort of alteration, then this would be a mark of the book's success.

What kind of an alteration, though, could accommodate a phrase such as 'a science of singularity'? What would have to happen to 'science' to make it compatible and companionable with 'singularity', and what would 'singularity' need to do to become habitable for science? Is it a compromise that is needed? A little give and take, an inch here, a little concession there, so that then perhaps the terms can meet somewhere in the middle? In the face of an inherited intransigence (mainly from the nineteenth century) that would want to establish 'science' as a portal that would only be open to those ready to shrug off all that might taste of subjectivism, the entropy of compromise might well be a credible option. It might even signal a kind of inventiveness (albeit of a sheepish kind). But Michel de Certeau's alterations aren't, I don't think, of this order. Something else is going on. Science, as it moves to greet singularity, or subjectivity, or literature, does so, not on condition that it surrenders its desire to 'arrest the real', but rather, in a reversal of the function of compromise, a meeting is possible only because the desire for the real is increased, intensified. Communication and contact aren't the result of negating what is distinct and different in the various terms; rather, it is by insisting on difference and strengthening the desire of difference that communication is possible. In this way a binary logic is defeated (or sidestepped) by going 'round the back' – by increasing the peculiar desires that both terms might signal (often in opposition to the conventions that have congregated around them). To show my hand right from the start: it is when these two terms (science and singularity, but also others such as history and literature) are revealed as both striving for the real (a real which will always exceed attempts to circumscribe it) – in a shared quest (despite local rhetorical differences) – that a transformation of the study of culture is possible. And it is here, in the grip of this ambition, that this book is located.

Michel de Certeau's work – his practice – evidences a subtle imagination that seeks to alter the very meeting ground for attending to culture. This is a methodological imagination: an imagination that is concerned with method. And in this way 'method' is not the name of some 'tool-kit', some series of procedures or protocols to be performed when confronted with a set of objects, it is rather the name that we should give to the way we apprehend and comprehend the objects we attend to. By 'method' then, I don't want to suggest a plodding series of steps that will allow something to count as having being analysed, for instance. Instead I want to suggest that we use method and methodology to name the characteristics of our scholarly and intellectual contact with the world. How we make contact with the world, how we apprehend it and give it sense, I am going to argue, is not a matter of epistemological absolutes, but it is something that is, or should be, open to scrutiny in terms of ethics, as well as aesthetics and politics. Method falls on the side of form rather than content; it is what underwrites intellectual production. In the increasingly specialized and fragmented terrain of intellectual endeavour, methodology might be the one contact-zone that cultural writers and researchers share. While research objects can often seem more and more esoteric, research methods are something all those involved in writing about culture participate in, whether implicitly or explicitly. It is often what allows an essay or book to have a currency beyond its putative subject matter.

Method is process; it is the form of communication that a researcher adopts when she makes contact with a research object. Method is what is left after the vagaries of opinion have ceased to seem so important. It is a way of being in the world and in communication with the world. It is the core business of fashioning the world so as to be able to speak about it. In this fashioning we might find the seeds of a utopia – an ethics of 'open' communication and contact; a site where the connection between observing subjects and observed objects effects a change in both (where both bend a little way nearer to their other). But method might also fashion the world in more oppressive ways: think of some of the phrases that get used to describe methodological protocols – 'interrogating objects', 'rigorous criticism' and so on. Such approaches might suggest that the fashioning is mainly in one direction: that the world being attended to should be fashioned to the will of the researcher – or more precisely to the will of a method being deployed. A more open method would constitute itself around the mutual alteration of both subject and object. But how we judge the politics of method is not, I think, discernible by looking simply at results: 'radical' interpretations are not necessarily the outcome of radical procedures, any more than dominating methods will necessarily give voice to dominant and dominating meanings. But there is also a content of this form, one that is most vivid when texts or objects or practices are revealed as pedagogic. While an academic text book might explicitly teach the reader a range of facts or opinions, it also teaches implicitly or tacitly: it teaches by attuning the reader to certain *ways* of knowing, in a way similar to that of a swimming instructor attuning a body to a specific relationship with water. Method in the human sciences is often a form of tacit knowledge, learnt through trial and error, passed on through heavy exposure to exemplars.[1]

It is, though, hardly surprising if we tend to remember outcomes more readily than procedures. We live in a world where, as Marx forcefully argued, a product's glamour relies on the invisibility of its unglamorous (but often clamorous) production. Why should the human sciences be any different? We might remember Foucault telling us about the emergence of a medical gaze,[2] or a

---

[1] The classic discussion of 'tacit knowledge' can be found in Thomas Kuhn, *The Structure of Scientific Revolutions*, second edition (Chicago and London: University of Chicago Press, 1970), pp. 191–8.

[2] Michel Foucault, *The Birth of the Clinic: An Archaeology of Medical Perception*, translated by Alan Sheridan (London: Tavistock Publications, 1973); first published in France in 1963.

panoptic disciplinarity,[3] or regimens of care and self-regulation:[4] what seems to fade (and whether Foucault is complicit in this could be a subject for debate) is the production: the months, the years of sorting through dusty documents, of bringing an archive into being. In a different vein Freudian psychoanalysis might be remembered for lurid tales of 'sex-crimes' (Oedipal anxieties, castration complexes) and psychopathologies (masochism, scopophilia and so on). What might be harder to retain is a strong sense of the cryptic and speculative intuiting of dream analysis, or the simultaneously attentive and distracted listening that constitutes the analyst's role in the analysis (the other side of the 'talking cure').[5] The same is, I think, true of Michel de Certeau: a certain vividness pertains to ideas about 'strategies' and 'tactics', or cultural 'poaching', but what is much less vivid is what characterizes de Certeau's *practice* of studying culture. The irony here is that de Certeau's characteristic practice is, precisely, to attend to culture *as a practice*, as a field of practical operations. For instance, in his writing on historiography he works to draw attention to the material and institutional procedures for legitimating knowledge, and on the operations performed by the practical activities of writing history (moving documents from one place to another, and so on).

One result of a lack of explicit concern with production (process), coupled with the seduction of the product (outcome), is that the name 'theory' tends to designate an 'architecture of interpretation' rather than the 'form of attention' of a particular theorist. Of course in practice it is hard to separate out process and product (a content-free, pure-process piece of scholarly work would be hard to imagine – harder still to read); it is likewise epistemologically dubious to claim that description can be absolutely separated from interpretation (there is no neutral form of description, for instance). Yet we can talk about both the tendency of texts and the tendency of the *reception* of texts to favour outcome over process, interpretation over method and description. The danger of over-emphasizing the outcome of theoretical work is that it can establish a very specific pedagogic relationship between observer and observed – nowhere is this more obvious than in the practice of 'applied theory'. The application of theory

---

[3] Michel Foucault, *Discipline and Punish: The Birth of the Prison*, translated by Alan Sheridan (Harmondsworth: Penguin Books, 1982); first published in France in 1975.

[4] In particular, Michel Foucault, *The Uses of Pleasure: Volume 2 of The History of Sexuality*, translated by Robert Hurley (Harmondsworth: Penguin Books, 1986), published in France in 1984; and Michel Foucault, *The Care of the Self: Volume 3 of The History of Sexuality*, translated by Robert Hurley (Harmondsworth: Penguin Books, 1986), also published in France in 1984.

[5] It is telling, for instance, that when the publishers Penguin selected from Freud's complete works to produce their 15-volume Freud Library, Freud's various 'Papers on Technique' were mostly dropped, even though they would obviously be considered core texts for the practice of psychoanalysis. This point will be picked up again in Chapter 3.

is, in part, an application of ready-made interpretations, fabricated elsewhere and under very different processual circumstances, which are then attached to new objects. In teaching the application of theory, the learner gains a facility in manipulation, but this is traded in for a submissive role in the construction of what is applied. It is a situation which produces an outcome that is almost always known (within certain dimensions) in advance. Using a different set of terms Brian Massumi warns of the redundancy of an application model of theory:

> The first rule of thumb if you want to invent or reinvent concepts is simple: don't apply them. If you apply a concept or system of connection between concepts, it is the material you apply it to that undergoes change, much more markedly than do the concepts. The change is imposed upon the material by the concepts' systematicity and constitutes a becoming homologous of the material to the system. This is all very grim. It has less to do with 'more to the world' than 'more of the same'. It has less to do with invention than mastery and control.[6]

Massumi's complaint is that in the logic of application the object has to change to accommodate the theory: the world fits the theory, or is made to fit the theory, or else is rejected as non-viable. For Massumi (who, incidentally or not, translated the texts that make up de Certeau's *Heterologies*) the logic-of-application needs to be supplanted by a logic-of-invention – one that is based on intimate attention to the singular details of the example.[7]

A similar (though subtly different) argument is made by Shoshana Felman as she takes her distance from the dominant use of psychoanalysis for the study of literature – such 'cultural psychoanalysis' (which would also include disciplinary fields like film studies) is probably the field that has been most associated with the logic of application – and argues instead for a practice of implication, which is also a practice of imbrication:

> The traditional method of *application* of psychoanalysis to literature would here be in principle ruled out. The notion of *application* would be replaced by the radically different notion of *implication*; bringing analytical questions

---

[6] Brian Massumi, *Parables of the Virtual: Movement, Affect, Sensation* (Durham: Duke University Press, 2002), p. 17.

[7] Massumi is producing his own 'science of singularity': 'An example is neither general (as is a system of concepts) nor particular (as is the material to which a system is applied). It is "singular". It is defined by a disjunctive self-inclusion: a belonging to itself that is simultaneously an extendibility to everything else with which it might be connected (one for all, and all in itself).' *Parables of the Virtual*, pp. 17–18.

to bear upon literary questions, *involving* psychoanalysis in the scene of literary analysis, the interpreter's role would here be, not to *apply* to the text an acquired science, a preconceived knowledge, but to act as a go-between, to *generate implications* between literature and psychoanalysis.[8]

In this way the literary critic stages a meeting between the object and the body of theory and adjudicates as they rub against each other.

Michel de Certeau's work is nothing if not the refusal of the logic of application. Application is one example of the general pacification that certain forms of interpretation (academic and other) can perform on the world: and it is against such pacification that de Certeau's methodological imagination is set. Such pacification is relational: it establishes a passive relationship between object and method, learner and theory, the world and its writing. In a text that charts his intellectual awakening, de Certeau recognizes how disciplines can work to pacify and contain the sheer alterity of the objects they purport to study. His example, importantly, is the speech of the possessed (demonically or by the Holy Spirit) in the sixteenth and seventeenth centuries – speech to which various procedures of interpretation have been applied. De Certeau's intellectual awakening occurs when the object 'bites back':

> Normally, we domesticate the 'dear departed' so that they will not seem out of place in our shop windows or our thoughts; we preserve them under glass, isolate them, and deck them out so that they may edify us or serve as examples. All at once, however, these docile figures escaped my clutches. They *became* 'savages' to the extent that their lives and works seemed intimately connected with a bygone era.[9]

It is only when the singularity of the object (and in this sense all of history must be 'savage history' and all of the present 'a savage now') asserts itself that there is the possibility of productive knowledge.

Yet to reject, with de Certeau and others, a model of applied theory doesn't mean that there are going to be forms of attention that are either neutral (and won't thereby import ready-made interpretations) or are specific, *sui generis*, to the object. To imagine a form of observation that is entirely in the thrall of the object, with interpretations emerging *ex nihilo* from the object, is probably as

[8] Shoshana Felman, 'To Open the Question' in Shoshana Felman, ed., *Literature and Psychoanalysis – The Question of Reading: Otherwise* (Baltimore: Johns Hopkins University Press, 1982), pp. 8–9.

[9] Michel de Certeau, 'History and Mysticism' (1973) in Jacques Revel and Lynn Hunt, eds, *Histories – French Constructions of the Past: Postwar French Thought Volume I* (New York: New Press, 1995), p. 440.

wrong-headed as the 'applied theory' model. And this, I think, is where de Certeau's work will be particularly useful. It is de Certeau's refusal of the invitation to produce general theoretical interpretations (and there simply is no large-scale theoretical schema to be arrived at from de Certeau's writing), without thereby falling back on models of positivist empiricism and realism, that will make him relevant today.[10] As I want to show, the quality that de Certeau most productively exhibits is an inventive and generative approach to reading and observing that neither claims itself to be a form of realism ('it's just there, all you need to do is get it') nor imagines a general schema of meaning applicable to any number of examples. In this way de Certeau always finds the generative in critical engagement: what starts out as a problem becomes an opportunity – out of a critique of the claim that historiography is a science, for instance, there comes a practice aimed at increasing the truth content of historical works.

With de Certeau, then, we get a method that values the singularity of close attention to the specific, located object. But this method doesn't approach the specific object imagining itself free from centuries of philosophical problems and debates: it doesn't imagine that by just looking harder it will see what is there. Instead it recognizes that an alteration needs to be performed by the observing subject, and that this alteration needs to affect the very basis of perception and conception, to be able to see the object of observation outside of the frame that has already been made for it. To let the object bite back, to de-pacify the object, what is required is a disrupted and disrupting form of attention; a derailing of observation.

A BODY OF WORK

You can get a flavour of the range of de Certeau's work from a research application that he made towards the end of his life. Sketching out a project on the 'new world and narrative', de Certeau writes that it will continue work that he has already accomplished:

> Work undertaken in history (*mentalités* and spirituality in the sixteenth and seventeenth centuries; possession in the seventeenth century; religious thought and practices in the seventeenth century; Leibniz; linguistic policies

[10] In this, de Certeau's work might be compared to the work of deconstruction in general and Jacques Derrida in particular. While a comparison between Derrida and de Certeau is beyond the remit of this book, one place to begin such a comparison is suggested in Hent de Vries, 'Anti-Babel: The "Mystical Postulate" in Benjamin, de Certeau and Derrida', *MLN* 107, 1992, pp. 441–77.

and theories at the end of the eighteenth century) and in anthropology (possession; sorcery and mysticism; the concept of 'popular culture'; investigations conducted in Brazil, Chile and Argentina since 1966; the regular teaching of historical and cultural anthropology at the University of Paris VII since 1972; the foundation of DIAL, a centre for information on Latin America).[11]

This, though, is a far from exhaustive list of the areas in which de Certeau has contributed through research and publications. We would also need to include his contributions to (and interventions in) French and European cultural policy and his commentaries on and analysis of contemporary culture, society and politics, as well as his involvement in Lacanian psychoanalysis. But even leaving those aspects of his work aside, the above list still seems to be unswerving in its dedication to interdisciplinary work, and unnervingly diverse in its scope. Moving across forms of social activism and scholarly esoterica, the work seems too diverse to hold a connecting thread. At this general level, then, the question of the work's integrity, its wholeness, can arise: is there something holding all this work together? Is there a central project, an idea behind the various ideas on offer? Or should the work be thought of in discrete sections: religious history; a theory of historiography; political analysis; the ethnography of the near; social activism and so on?

The central argument to this book is that there is coherence in this work but it is not to be found at the level of objects of study or of theory – at least not at the level of theory as it is most often figured. It is at the level of method that de Certeau's work coheres (which is not to say that method is not theoretical). There is, then, a 'way of operating' that connects the scholarly writing on mystic and demonic possessions with work on the contemporary everyday; the work on the theory of historiography with his cultural-policy writing. The central ingredients of this method (which might be better described as 'metamethodology') centre on a critical epistemology and an ethical demand to respond to epistemological scepticism. So while de Certeau's work does seem unnervingly diverse there is, I think, a consistency to be found at the level of methodology – a metamethodology which is dedicated to encouraging heterogeneity and allowing alterity to proliferate (this is what de Certeau calls heterology). In the face of this diversity of research and consistency of method I've attempted to weave an argument through the various chapters that follow while also giving a sense of the rich diversity of the work. My main argument (as already suggested) is that de Certeau's work mounts a critique of the science claims to be found in

---

[11] Michel de Certeau, 'Travel Narratives of the French to Brazil: Sixteenth to Eighteenth Centuries', translated by Katharine Streip, *Representations* 33, 1991, p. 221.

classical versions of anthropology and history (like others who mount similar critiques, it is partly done by recognizing the necessary literary condition of cultural writing [ethnography, historiography and so on]), and which also subsist today. Yet rather than the literary condition of knowledge posing a limit on cultural science's ability to know the world, it is precisely through its literary condition that it can edge towards the real. This uncannily simple formula is one of the underlying features of de Certeau's work and it is both a form of liberation for scholarly work and an ethical obligation. It is a permission slip, if one were needed, for all sorts of scholarly experimentation, one where permission is granted not because 'anything goes' but because there is an obligation to find better ways of telling the past and telling the present.

Central to de Certeau's work, then, is an epistemological rupture that might account for the 'family resemblance' between the varied productions that go by the name of poststructuralism. Much of this work can seem aimed at stymying the business of 'telling it like it is' – it is, if nothing else, a fulsome critique of representational naturalism in its various guises. In historiographic work the bare bones of this critique can be demonstrated with ease – after all, we have no existential access to, or contact with, the past; we have to make do with shifting through texts, old film reels, people's reminiscences – all material that exist in the present, under present-day conditions, etc. Such an insistence on the refusal to let historical studies imagine that it provides access to the past (rather than to constructions that go by the name of 'the past') might well stymie those involved in it; after all, if there is no ultimate truth to be told of the past then what would be the point of just offering a version of it? One of the reasons that it doesn't stymie de Certeau is that as far as this goes historical work is no different from contemporary ethnographic work – there simply is no privileged access to the real. There is no choice but to work in a world of partial views. Not only is this one response to epistemological critique, it may also turn out to supply the kind of forms that are most adequate to registering our actuality.

In this, de Certeau's work looks quite similar to what Donna Haraway calls 'situated knowledge'. Haraway is a leading scholar within critical science studies, where the stakes of according 'truth' to knowledge are particularly high. But the critique of scientific objectivity is not only a powerful weapon against the interests that science can serve – the ability to critique the epistemological basis of science can just as well prove to be a 'double-edged sword', a liability, since being able to simply discredit knowledge out of hand (all knowledge is similarly 'untrue' – the sort of blanket epistemological claim that has gone by the name of 'relativism') is also useful to those who would, for instance, rather global warming wasn't a political issue. For Bruno Latour, the kind of epistemological scepticism that had been used by him and others to question the 'natural facts' of science is now routinely used by powerful business interests to question the knowledge of 'global warming' so as to protect those interests whose profits have been underwritten by environmental damage.[12]

Donna Haraway recognizes the essential difficulty facing critical science studies: how to maintain a robust epistemological critique without falling into a general indifference, where everything is equally untrue, unfounded and unnatural:

> So, I think my problem and 'our' problem is how to have *simultaneously* an account of radical historical contingency for all knowledge claims and knowing subjects, a critical practice for recognizing our own 'semiotic technologies' for making meanings, *and* a no-nonsense commitment to faithful accounts of a 'real' world, one that can be partially shared and friendly to earth-wide projects of finite freedom, adequate material abundance, modest meaning in suffering, and limited happiness.[13]

While de Certeau wouldn't have described his project in quite this way he is similarly navigating between two unacceptable positions: representational naturalism (a naive belief in the transparency of 'facts', 'images' and the like); and the 'total' critiques of representation (all is constructed, nothing has any epistemological foundation). As we will see, the way out of indifference, for de Certeau, is not in spite of epistemological doubt: rather, it is through epistemological doubt (by being responsive and responsible to epistemological doubt) that an antidote to indifference is found. Yet though de Certeau, I think, offers a different route out of indifference, his epistemology still looks similar to Haraway's:

> The alternative to relativism is not totalizing and single vision, which is always finally the unmarked category whose power depends on systematic narrowing and obscuring. The alternative to relativism is partial, locatable, critical knowledges sustaining the possibility of webs of connections called solidarity in politics and shared conversations in epistemology. Relativism is a way of being nowhere while claiming to be everywhere equally. The 'equality' of positioning is a denial of responsibility and critical enquiry. Relativism is the perfect mirror twin of totalization in the ideologies of objectivity; both deny the stakes in location, embodiment, and partial perspective; both make it impossible to see well.[14]

---

[12] Bruno Latour, 'Why Has Critique Run out of Steam: From Matters of Fact to Matters of Concern' in Bill Brown, ed., *Things* (Chicago: University of Chicago Press, 2004), pp. 151–73.

[13] Donna J. Haraway, 'Situated Knowledges', *Simians, Cyborgs, and Women: The Reinvention of Nature* (London: Free Association Books, 1991), p. 187.

[14] Haraway, 'Situated Knowledges', p. 191.

I need to inflect this term 'relativism' in a more nuanced way and suggest that it might be useful to distinguish between forms of 'absolute relativism' (the indifference of everything being equally untrue, for instance) and a 'relative relativism' which finds a method for making value judgements by *relating* one account to another. In this, the values underpinning judgement are not absolutes (for instance, the value of complexity, or the proliferation of difference, etc.) and can only be encountered in relative terms (x's account allows for more complexity than y's). Haraway is rightly attacking a form of absolute relativism and we might want to suggest that her alternative of 'situated knowledges' ends up promoting a form of critically relative relativism.

One of the main foci of this book is the activity of historiography, of writing history. Partly this is to reflect the weight of that activity within de Certeau's oeuvre. But it is also because it is in his thinking about the past and about the representation of that past that de Certeau attends to the epistemological problems and challenges that will inform his work on the history of the present and the social and cultural ethnography that he is probably most well-known for. To approach this work from the perspective of his critical historiography is, I hope, instructive: it certainly has deep consequences. One of the results of attempting to recognize the shared terrain of the historical work and the 'present'-directed work on cultural policy and sociology is that doing so challenges the 'special' character of the historian's field. For instance, the epistemological crisis facing historians – that they are only ever able to deal with traces of the past as they exist in the present and that their access to the actuality of the past is limited – seems less discipline-specific if we recognize that the same epistemological problems might actually characterize our contact with the present. And we can come to this recognition partly via an account of historiography.

For me the most useful aspect of de Certeau's work is the surprise it holds within it: what seems to be a critical impasse – a serious epistemological rupture that attacks many of the core values of historians and ethnographers – is grasped as the possibility and opportunity for production in those fields. The repercussions of such a position in the worlds of cultural policy, public art, contemporary ethnography, historical work – in the field of postcolonialism, for instance – provide the subject matter of this book. It is subject matter that necessarily has to move beyond the work of de Certeau and look to some of the urgent work that faces intellectuals now. To do this I have to disfigure de Certeau, displace his work with work by others.

My approach in this book has been to connect de Certeau to a host of other projects within the cultural sciences. The more usual route in books on a single author is to stick fairly closely to the theorist's work: the danger in following too many other leads is that you may lose some of the concentration on the work under consideration. This has been a danger I've had to entertain (and happily so). I'm following the logic, here, that the ideas that I want to explore – ideas that are found within de Certeau's work but which exist elsewhere as well – are best and most vividly exemplified by a range of works. At times the best examples of a way of operating favoured by de Certeau can actually be found in the works of others. This shouldn't be all that surprising – after all, the potential of a method or a metamethodology (if it is productive) is unlikely to be exhausted or even fully explored by one person. Indeed, the way that de Certeau explores historiographic dilemmas in seventeenth-century France may well connect to work done more recently in postcolonial historiography – in fact there is no reason not to assume that work done in the field of postcolonialism will have even more relevance for these issues than de Certeau's. Connecting de Certeau's work with other work, even to the point where the other work might displace de Certeau, is all to the good of this particular project. It allows the ideas to lose their 'ownership', their tie to an author-authority, while also strengthening (I hope) the weight being placed on method.

There is, I think, something similar taking place in de Certeau. When I've talked to people about their initial encounter with, for instance, *The Practice of Everyday Life*, several have told me how underwhelmed they were: they had expected the pyrotechnics of a 'French theorist' – outlandish claims, portentous prose. Instead what they find is a book of almost too sober reflection, that studiously footnotes a vast array of thinkers and artists who have preceded the work. The sense of an author is there but not one trumpeting their message from on high, rather one who in the more modest work of review, survey and synthesis is allowing something else to emerge – something not saturated by an ego. This something is not anyone's, but it is, I think, most recognizable, most productively portrayed in the work of de Certeau. And it is a something that should, I like to think, have serious consequences for the business of cultural studies and cultural analysis.

CULTURAL STUDIES AND MICHEL DE CERTEAU

For Ian Buchanan, writing in 1996, 'de Certeau's distinctive contribution to cultural studies has yet to be determined'.[15] For anyone familiar with cultural studies, especially with the genre of 'cultural populism' – a genre that seemed, at times, to indiscriminately champion the subversive potential to be found in corporate shopping malls, for instance, or in wearing the products of transnational companies – de Certeau's contribution to the field might seem to have been all

[15] Ian Buchanan, 'De Certeau and Cultural Studies', *new formations* 31, 1996, p. 175.

too determined.[16] Indeed as Simon During notes, 'Michel de Certeau, a Jesuit priest and historian of Christian mysticism, whose book, *The Practice of Everyday Life*, [was] translated into English in 1984, had an enormous impact on cultural studies in the late eighties and early nineties.'[17] Yet what Buchanan is suggesting is that cultural studies eschewed an encounter with de Certeau's form of attention, and instead opted to extract a number of theoretical interpretations – particularly the opposition 'strategies and tactics' as well as de Certeau's characterization of certain practices as poaching, and so on – and used these to bank roll its already established positions. As far as this goes, any sustained involvement with de Certeau's method was made more difficult precisely because of the seemingly easy success (and access) of what looked like packaged formulas, for instance: 'readers are travelers; they move across lands belonging to someone else, like nomads poaching their way across fields they did not write' (PEL1: 174). It seemed easy enough to use quotations like this within media studies, particularly by proponents of 'the active audience', without having to engage with the epistemological challenge of de Certeau. The odd sense in which de Certeau is insistently present within cultural studies (along with Foucault and Gramsci he is one of the most referenced writers in cultural studies writing) while simultaneously being eerily absent, is seen dramatically in the non-fit between the concerns and objects that cultural studies has been traditionally associated with and the focus of de Certeau's investigations. For Simon During:

[Cultural studies] has mainly directed itself to a particular set of cultural formations – those that connect most directly to its secular, middle-class, leftist, youngish (or wannabe young) more or less Eurocentric practitioners. Hence, it has tended to neglect, for instance, religion; food; sport; hobbysports such as fishing and train-spotting; middle-brow and 'kitsch' culture, especially that part which is family-based and of most interest to the middle aged such as home improvement and gardening. For different reasons it has neglected high culture itself.[18]

[16] For instance John Fiske, *Understanding Popular Culture* (London: Routledge, 1986) and Henry Jenkins, *Textual Poachers: Television Fans and Participatory Culture* (London: Routledge, 1992). There is a useful discussion of cultural populism in Jim McGuigan, *Cultural Populism* (London: Routledge, 1992); for the most vibrant and vociferous critique of cultural populism see Meaghan Morris, 'Banality in Cultural Studies' in Patricia Mellencamp, ed., *The Logics of Television: Essays in Cultural Criticism* (Bloomington and Indianapolis: Indiana University Press, 1990), pp. 14–43.

[17] Simon During, *Cultural Studies: A Critical Introduction* (Abingdon and New York: Routledge, 2005), p. 29.

[18] During, *Cultural Studies*, p. 7.

Interestingly many of the items on this list of non-topics have been central concerns for de Certeau: high culture and religion, for instance, are constant reference points, and the two volumes of *The Practice of Everyday Life* are much more concerned with the day-to-day life of young families, of the middle-aged and seniors, than with the exuberant subcultures of the young. In another vein, when there is mention of political struggle in de Certeau's work, the examples are usually the actual struggles of indigenous populations in Latin America, for instance, or ethnic minority groups in Europe, rather than political interpretations of the seemingly apolitical activities of fairly well-heeled Westerners.

My focus on Michel de Certeau, within the framework of cultural studies, is an attempt to do two things: to host a meeting between cultural studies and de Certeau's work so that the methodological relevance of de Certeau's practice is made evident; and in doing so to re-emphasise aspects of cultural studies that lie buried within it. And this requires a refiguring of cultural studies: a cultural studies with different beginnings. One of the characteristics of cultural studies has been its endless rehearsal of its paternity: the tale told of cultural studies' birth is usually focused on three books that appeared in the late 1950s and early 1960s in Britain. The books – Richard Hoggart's *The Uses of Literacy* (1957), Raymond Williams' *Culture and Society* (1958), and slightly later, E.P. Thompson's *The Making of the English Working Class* (1963) – are seen as creating a head of steam out of which emerges the first institutional setting for cultural studies at Birmingham University in 1964.[19] This is all well and good

---

[19] Richard Hoggart, *The Uses of Literacy: Aspects of Working-class Life With Special Reference to Publications and Entertainments* (London: Chatto & Windus, 1957); Raymond Williams, *Culture and Society: 1780–1950* (London: Chatto & Windus, 1958); E.P. Thompson, *The Making of the English Working Class* (London: Gollancz, 1963). For accounts of the emergence of cultural studies as a specifically named enterprise see: Dennis Dworkin, *Cultural Marxism in Postwar Britain: History, the New Left, and the Origins of Cultural Studies* (Durham and London: Duke University Press, 1997); Tom Steele, *The Emergence of Cultural Studies 1945–65: Cultural Politics, Adult Education and the English Question* (London: Lawrence and Wishart, 1997); Graeme Turner, *British Cultural Studies: An Introduction* (New York and London: Routledge, 1992). One of the aspects of cultural studies that any investigation of this particular formation should bring to light is the importance of historical research to cultural studies in the 1970s and 1980s. In the various publications of the Centre for Contemporary Cultural Studies we could note some of the following examples: John Clarke, Chas Critcher and Richard Johnson, eds, *Working Class Culture: Studies in History and Theory* (London: Hutchinson [in association with the CCCS, University of Birmingham], 1979); Mary Langham and Bill Schwarz, eds, *Crises in the British State 1880–1930* (London: Hutchinson [in association with the CCCS, University of Birmingham], 1985); Centre for Contemporary Cultural Studies, *Unpopular Education: Schooling and Social Democracy in England since 1944* (London: Hutchinson [in association with the CCCS, University of Birmingham], 1981); and Richard Johnson, Gregor McLennan, Bill Schwarz and David Sutton, eds, *Making Histories: Studies in History Writing and Politics* (London: Hutchinson [in association with the CCCS, University of Birmingham], 1982).

but it is hardly adequate for telling the larger story of how 'culture' (as social life, as complex representations) became something to study in the first place; and it doesn't begin to suggest what might happen to the notion of 'study' when its object becomes culture. I want to suggest two other beginnings to cultural studies – one a fairly awkward and idiosyncratic moment (though one with utopian potential), the other with a history that stretches back to colonial contact and conquest. I will start with the latter, partly because it is the larger story.

Across the itineraries of Michel de Certeau's diverse writings are to be found the co-ordinates of a central project: to map ethnology as it expands and mutates across the centuries from the 'discovery' of the New World to the present day. 'Ethnology' emerges in France as a named science in the 1830s,[20] and de Certeau works archaeologically to uncover the beginnings of ethnology *avant la lettre*, while at the same time tracing its formations and transformations in the present. Ethnology in the expanded sense that de Certeau gives the term is perhaps the single most important enterprise of the human sciences (in many ways it might simply be the human sciences). It is the business of writing human culture, a writing of culture in which the ordinary, the everyday, is simultaneously both inscribed and excised. It is cultural studies as a general and central project of Western culture (in particular), and of the world in general when its powerful groups coalesce and write about other, less powerful groups.

The 'discovery' of the New World presents de Certeau with a primal scene. In his 'Preface' to *The Writing of History*, de Certeau reads an allegorical etching (1619) by Jan Van der Straet of Amerigo Vespucci approaching a naked female 'native' lying in a hammock: 'An inaugural scene: after a moment of stupor, on this threshold dotted with colonnades of trees, the conqueror will write the body of the other and trace there his own history' (WH: xxv). De Certeau continues:

> What is really initiated here is a colonization of the body by the discourse of power. This is writing that conquers. It will use the New World as if it were a blank, 'savage' page on which Western desire will be written. It will transform the space of the other into a field of expansion for a system of production. (WH: xxv–xxvi)

Such writing invokes a double movement: on the one hand a repression and on the other an inscription of power. In a similar vein to the work of writers such as Gayatri Chakravorty Spivak and Edward Said, the colonial scene of writing is seen as premised on the West's perception of its other as a *tabula rasa* that

---

[20] de Certeau, 'Travel Narratives of the French to Brazil', p. 224.

requires writing (or 'worlding' in Spivak's words).[21] In a pivotal chapter of *The Writing of History* ('Ethno-Graphy – Speech, or the Space of the Other: Jean de Léry'), de Certeau reads the autobiographical account of Jean de Léry's journey to Brazil in the 1550s. A French Calvinist, Léry flees France for Geneva, and from there heads to Brazil. After three months in Brazil his route is reversed: 'At the end of his journey, after all the comings and goings, the Savage is invented' (WH: 213). What marks this as a 'primal scene in the construction of ethnological discourse' (WH: 211) is partly a spatial displacement: while Léry encounters the other 'over there' (in Brazil, amongst the Tupis Indians), he writes the encounter 'over here' (in France) some 20 years later. For de Certeau:

> A structure already appears to be in place. From festive, poetic, ephemeral speech are delineated the tasks of conserving, of verifying, and of conquering. A will to power is invested in its form. . . . The multiplicity of procedures in which 'declarations' of this will are written elaborates the space of an organization around the *same*, which extends without undergoing any modification. These are scriptural organizations, commercial, scientific, and colonial. The 'paths of writing' combine a plurality of itineraries with the singularity of the place of production. (WH: 217–8)

For de Certeau the 'ordinary' culture of the other falls on the side of orality and heterogeneity. Such culture is ordered and normalized in the act of writing (or what de Certeau will refer to as an inscription within a scriptural economy). In this operation the culture of the other is remaindered. For de Certeau the other – 'the Indian, the past, the people, the mad, the child, the Third World' (WH: 3) – is transformed: 'invented', 'repressed', 'changed' by a writing located elsewhere (the West, the Academy, the State, etc.).

This moment of combining repression (erasure) with power (inscription) is a consistent object of de Certeau's attention. Writing about Abbot Grégoire's report 'On the necessity and means of annihilating patois and of universalizing the use of the French language', written towards the end of the eighteenth century (in the wake of the Revolution), de Certeau emphasizes how local (French) dialects and patois are catalogued, 'preserved' and mummified at the same time as they are policed with a view to their obliteration (H: 122–3, with Julia and Revel).[22] Similarly, in writing about Charles Nisard (an under-secretary in the

[21] Gayatri Chakravorty Spivak, 'The Rani of Sirmur', *Europe and Its Others: Volume One*, Francis Barker, Peter Hulme, Margaret Iversen and Diana Loxley, eds, (Colchester: University of Essex, 1985), p. 133; Edward Said, *Orientalism* (London: Routledge and Kegan Paul, 1978).

[22] The study was a group project and resulted in a book: Michel de Certeau, Dominique Julia and Jacques Revel, *Une politique de la langue. La Révolution française et les patois: l'enquête de Grégoire* (Paris: Gallimard, 1975).

French Ministry of Police who wrote one of the first histories of popular culture),
de Certeau finds an 'unavowed operation': 'Before being studied, it [popular cul-
ture] had to be censored' (WH: 119 with Julia and Revel).[23] For de Certeau 'the
birth of studies devoted to street literature (the inaugural book is Nisard's, published in 1854) is tied to the social censorship of their object' (WH: 119 with
Julia and Revel). As we move from the nineteenth century into the present,
popular culture, everyday life and the ordinary-other remain objects for a scriptural economy that continually finds new ways of erasing and inscribing ordinary culture. The forms of attention given to everyday life expand enormously:
from the varied academic attention it receives (from sociology and anthropology
to all sorts of cultural studies courses dedicated to forms of 'popular culture' –
sport, reading, media studies, audience studies, etc.), to the massive expansion
of the media's interest in the ordinary (newspapers, radio phone-ins, 'real-life'
documentaries, 'fly-on-the-wall' TV, web-cams on the Internet, etc.), to the
commercial and state forms of market research and polling. For de Certeau the
description of the media's re-presentation of an everyday actuality might work as
a general leitmotif for an expanded scriptural economy:

> Today it [the 'Voice of the people'] is 'recorded' in every imaginable way, nor-
> malized, audible everywhere, but only when it has been 'cut' (as when one
> 'cuts a record'), and thus mediated by radio, television, or the phonograph
> record, and 'cleaned up' by the techniques of diffusion. (PEL1: 132)

An expanded ethnology of the present re-presents the ordinary in a 'clean and
proper' space, without the noise and 'wild orchestration' of the heterogeneous
everyday.

What are we to make of a cultural theory that claims that all forms of inscription (writing, picturing) remainder the very object they seek to retain? What
possibilities are there for an ethnography of the ordinary if everyday life 'cannot
be captured in a picture' or 'circumscribed in a text' (PEL1: 102)? What future
could ethnography have when its operations necessarily instigate repression?
Here it is important to heed de Certeau's own description of his project. Calling
his approach 'polemological' (PEL1: xvii), de Certeau forces theory to recognize
its own limits. A polemological approach works on the side of the heuristic,
where 'theory' and 'method' are put into crisis as they encounter the everyday
world. Such an approach can't be measured in terms of descriptive realism but
should be judged in terms of its ability to generate new possibilities in an
encounter with the ordinary. De Certeau's polemological approach exaggerates

---

[23] This essay, 'The Beauty of the Dead: Nisard', which was written with Julia and Revel, was first
published in *Politique Aujourd'hui* in December 1970.

elements within a practice so that its operations can be 'played out'. What this results in is an ethical provocation that would ask any ethnography (audience research, subcultural studies, etc.) to account for its distance and proximity from the primal scene of ethnological encounter. When faced with such ethnological expansion, de Certeau's ethical provocation is both clear and self-implicating:

> The Bororos of Brazil sink slowly into their collective death, and Lévi-Strauss takes his seat in the French Academy. Even if the injustice disturbs him, the facts remain unchanged. This story is ours as much as it is his. In this one respect (which is an index of others that are more important), the intellectuals are still borne on the backs of the common people. (PEL1: 25)

If such a 'scene of ethnology' is unavoidable (where repression is the very condition of ethnology) then a practice that avoids repression and power is impossible.

And this is the context in which to situate cultural studies. Or rather; this is another context in which to situate cultural studies, one that undoes some of the damage caused by too many stories of its radical heritage, one that recognizes that cultural studies is constituted by a structural complicity with colonial ethnology. This is not a condition that can be simply shrugged off, once and for all: it is the larger ground upon which attempts are made (by those working in cultural studies and elsewhere) to make less complicit studies of culture, to allow other voices to be heard.

My second beginning for cultural studies is a methodological beginning.[24] In the winter of 1936–7, a group of filmmakers, poets, journalists, anthropologists and others got together to suggest a form of, what they called, Mass Observation.[25] This group, closer to the status of amateurs than academic professionals, set out to establish a new domain: the ordinary life of ordinary people as recorded by ordinary people. In a pamphlet published in 1937, which was also an invitation to join in the process, the group set out their project and indicated the sort of ideas that were informing their approach. Marx and Freud provided central co-ordinates, as did the social anthropology that was at the time the core methodology for British approaches to the living aspects of culture (even if these cultures had to be far away from London to require such scrutiny). One of the promises that Mass-Observation made at this point was to suggest that for the new objects of attention (and for that matter the new subjects

---

[24] In thinking about the multiple possible beginnings for cultural studies, and how these various beginnings determine multiple trajectories, I am drawing on Edward Said, *Beginnings: Intention and Method* (New York: Columbia University Press, 1985 [1975]).

[25] For an account of Mass-Observation see my *Everyday Life and Cultural Theory: An Introduction* (London and New York: Routledge, 2002), Chapter 6.

providing the attention) 'such a framework as this will be most useful to us as a starting point. As we proceed it will be developed, modified and supplemented until it becomes unrecognisable'.[26]

Mass-Observation here make a similar point to that made by Massumi above, namely that in the process of open investigation the conceptual apparatus must be altered – the investigation of new objects, new subjects and new worlds should make traditional forms of attention unrecognizable. It is the promise of an approach to new objects (or new amalgams of objects, or old objects newly conceived) of scrutiny that will, in the process of being scrutinized, transform the business of scrutinizing. And if cultural studies (or 'interdisciplinarity') is going to offer something new, and something substantive, then it will need to be in the business of transforming the business of scrutiny. Mass-Observation recognized that observation isn't a neutral process and that it is necessary to establish certain initial frameworks for observation: but the logic again is not one of application, it is one of alteration.

Such a process and such a problem need to be set at the heart of cultural studies. Without it, cultural studies will remain forever looking for what it has already found; it will propagate a form of attention that will carry on finding what it already knows, what it has already known, in the various objects and processes it is studying. In the work of Michel de Certeau the disfigurement of bodies of theory is a central component – it is the process of altering the meeting ground of culture and theory writ large. It is the process of making, of inventing. There is, for instance, little in de Certeau's work that could be called psychoanalysis – yet psychoanalysis is a key discipline and association for de Certeau. What has happened is that by taking psychoanalysis out of the analyst's consulting room into the mass singularities of culture, de Certeau has refused to apply the interpretations of Freud and Lacan. What has happened is that psychoanalysis has been made unrecognizable; it has been disfigured. But in doing this, I will argue, de Certeau works in a way that is both truer to psychoanalysis and truer to the objects of study than any applied psychoanalysis could ever be (see Chapter 3). If cultural studies is going to have a meaningful role in intellectual life such forms of disfigurement will need to be constitutive of its methods.

THE SHAPE OF THINGS TO COME

This book moves from the past to the present, from epistemological problematics to a politics of hope, from abstractions to practices – but it doesn't do so

---

[26] Mass-Observation, *Mass Observation*, introduction by Julian Huxley (London: Fredrick Muller, 1937), p. 58. The pamphlet was written by Charles Madge and Tom Harrisson.

evenly. There is, I hope, always an emphasis on practice, always a sense of ethics infiltrating epistemological inquiry. The next chapter sets out to explain the critical ground that de Certeau shares with thinkers such as Hayden White and Roland Barthes in the field of historiography. It rehearses the arguments that were made in the late 1960s and early 1970s regarding the necessary rhetorical condition of 'history' (as text). But it shows that de Certeau arrived at his critical epistemological position, not by looking at abstract absolutes (the past is necessarily mediated through language, for instance) but by looking at the practical and material conditions of knowledge. As such de Certeau seems much more ready to contemplate alternatives to epistemological critique, and in this his work as a historian has a good deal of similarity to the anthropologically inflected historiography produced in the name of cultural history. I look, particularly, at *The Possession at Loudun* as an example of what I am calling de Certeau's 'interstitial practice'.

Chapter 3 is dedicated to the psychoanalytic aspect of de Certeau's work. This is probably the central chapter as far as theoretical methodology goes, but it is also the most tentative one. De Certeau was heavily involved in Lacanian psychoanalysis and on a few occasions wrote explicitly about psychoanalytic issues. For the most part, though, psychoanalysis is not a resource that is particularly visible in de Certeau's work. My argument here is that it is so fundamental to de Certeau's practice that it is rarely explicitly drawn on – and that it is also altered (sometimes beyond recognition) to become a form of psychoanalytic cultural studies. In something of a counter-intuitive move I suggest that the way for psychoanalytic cultural studies to move away from its dependency on the interpretative archive that was fashioned in 'clinical' circumstances is actually to return to psychoanalysis as a practice, a form of attention. This means treating it as a practice of listening, of allowing voices to speak, of establishing a scene of communication that allows the unconscious to signify. I want to argue that de Certeau's work is aimed at replicating and making social the communicative conditions of psychoanalysis, and that this is not just a feature of his historiographic work (where references to Freud and Lacan are most numerous) but is implicit in his work on contemporary culture (cultural commentary and cultural-policy work). To demonstrate this I use his commentary on May 1968, *The Capture of Speech*, as an example of an analysis based on a form of psychoanalysis altered as it inhabits the conditions of culture.

Chapter 4 begins by returning the discussion to the problems of historiography, more particularly the problem of writing history from 'subjugated standpoints'. In history this often means writing about material that archival practices either haven't deemed worthy of retention, or else have become archival material because 'subjugated lives' are precisely those lives that fill the courtrooms, the medical wards, and so on, but have no literary production of their own. The problem is both epistemological and ethical: how to write about what is least present (what de Certeau called the 'zones of silence'), coupled with the obligation to listen to those voices that have been silenced. In this the central theme becomes most visible: namely that de Certeau's work can most productively be seen as a metamethodology that requires the study of culture to fulfil an ethical obligation *as* a response to epistemological doubt. The work of the Subaltern Studies group of historians is used to show a comparable set of ethical, political and epistemological preoccupations and to offer examples of various attempts at fashioning a practice that answers this problematic. De Certeau's later, ethnographic work on everyday life is used to show how this ethical epistemological challenge is always future-orientated and requires different kinds of archives to be imagined and made. The interviews and studies of local, ordinary culture are taken as practices that respond to a situation made most explicit in historiographic work.

Chapter 5 continues the theme of practice. If practice, for de Certeau, is the response (both responsive and responsible) to the epistemological and ethical challenge he articulates, it is necessarily literary in form and social in orientation. Chapter 5 pursues the literary condition; Chapter 6 the social. In Chapter 5 I look at de Certeau's understanding of narrative and its relevance for understanding everyday life as practical life. In this I try to move the discussion away from 'power and resistance' to look at the work of memory and desire as organizing themes for narrative and the daily. One of de Certeau's favoured novelists was Marguerite Duras, and I use her work to show another way of thinking about everyday life and narrative in regard to memory and desire. Because I'm interested in thinking about de Certeau's work as providing suggestions (practical ones) about how to write better accounts of culture – more vivid, visceral, complex accounts of the past and the present – I show how this discussion is not simply about life as material practice, or about the appreciation of literature, but about how writing culture necessitates an embracing of the literary possibilities of all writing. I look at the work of two historians of queer culture: Martin Duberman and Samuel Delany. In their literary approach to the past they are, to my mind, two of the best examples of writers reacting to the epistemological problematic of the past in a way that is responsive and responsible. Their literary-ness is 'worn on their sleeve' not because they don't believe in historical truth, but because they are committed to historical truth, to understanding the past – a past that always exceeds them. As gay men living in a heteronormative culture they know the stakes of words like 'truth' and 'reality' better than many: as courageous witnesses to culture, they are prepared to go beyond critique and to tell the past and the present with a voice that is distinctive, and speaks in the plural.

Chapter 6 shows the way that de Certeau's approach is aimed at social ends. Although he worked consistently for various government research agencies, this social aim is not simply to be found here, in the preparation of policy directives. More fundamentally I want to suggest that de Certeau's methodology (his meta-methodology) is itself social, in that it performs a way of connecting to the world that values a form of communication that is radically 'inclusive' and open to the culture of the other. This is not the neo-liberal version of multicultural-ism whereby a sense of 'diversity' becomes a brand identity for selling a cultural package that is mainly open to commerce. For de Certeau 'diversity' is the fun-damental operation of alteration in the face of those that are other than you: it is the welcome that refuses to preach 'acculturation' or 'assimilation' – it is the hospitality that will alter its laws in its dynamic changing culture where immi-gration is not something to be 'dealt with' but is the life-blood of culture itself. As a way of showing how this might be used to fashion cultural practices I will look at de Certeau's cultural-policy suggestions and show how various artists, especially those engaged with ideas of immigration and globalization, can be seen as particularly relevant as models for cultural policy.

I end with a conclusion that returns us to my initial project: how might cul-tural studies engage with the work of de Certeau and what would it be like if it did? In other words, what would cultural studies look like if it chose to be a 'sci-ence of singularity'? The answer for me would be a practice that is grounded by a metamethodology based on a critical epistemology and an ethical demand to alter culture in the interests of subjugated lives and knowledges.

CHAPTER 2

An Epistemological Awakening: History and Writing

What is a theory, if not the articulation of a practice? And what is an epistemology, if not a discourse that elucidates that relationship? [1]

Envisaged then as a 'discipline,' historiography is a science which lacks the means of being one. Its discourse undertakes to deal with what is most resistant to scientificity (the relation of the social to the event, to violence, to the past, to death), that is, those matters each scientific discipline must eliminate in order to be constituted as a science. But in this tenuous position, historiography seeks to maintain the possibility of a scientific explanation through the textual globalization produced by a narrative synthesis. (H: 219–20)

SPEAKING WITH THE DEAD

What gets called 'history' (a school subject, a professional practice, a type of television programme and so on) consists of ordering and commenting on documents. It is often, if not always, the practice of writing about writing – it is re-writing. There is no direct contact with the past, of course, only commerce with its traces. This is common knowledge, yet somehow it seems peculiarly hard to make this knowledge count for much: what are historians meant to do with such a truth? To try to make this condition more evident some professional historians would urge us to call this 'history' what it really is – historiography (history-*writing*) – leaving the word 'history' to signify the unreachable terrain of the past.[2] Yet even the most careful historian (or historiographer) slips, and ends

---

[1] Michel de Certeau, 'A Transitional Epistemology: Paul Veyne' (1972) in Jacques Revel and Lynn Hunt, eds, *Histories – French Constructions of the Past: Postwar French Thought Volume I* (New York: New Press, 1995), p. 313.

[2] 'In current usage "history" connotes both a science and that which it studies – the explication which is *stated*, and the reality of *what has taken place* or what takes place. Other disciplines are not burdened with this ambiguity: French does not refer to "physics" and "nature" with the same name.' (WH: 21)

up calling an account of the past simply 'history'. This slippage, which seems almost impossible to guard against, is more than intellectual negligence, it tells us something. Historians desire the dead; they want the unattainable – what else would drive them (us) to spend so many hours amongst the dusty remains of the past? As Stephen Greenblatt states at the start of his book *Shakespearean Negotiations*, 'I began with the desire to speak with the dead'.[3] Desire, though, faces an epistemological limit: what there is of the past (its documents) exists for the historian only in the present. Speaking with the dead gets replaced with speaking for the dead – a heady mixture of necrophilia and ventriloquism.

Michel de Certeau wrote history and he wrote about the writing of history. This dual historiographic orientation – a production and a commentary on production – generated a historiographic practice that was self-reflexive, critical, and yet still maintained the desire to 'speak with the dead'. Like others writing about the status of knowledge generated by historians (historiographic epistemology), de Certeau's position is most immediately understood as a critique of historiographic positivism. It refutes a world where truth and knowledge are seen as readily accessible through the reconstruction of the past, by the exhaustive (and exhausting) amassing of facts. De Certeau's critical historiography is clearly suspicious of the objectivist claims of Western historiographic practice, most vividly signalled by Leopold von Ranke's statement that his historical writing 'merely seeks to show the past as it once was' or 'how it essentially was' [*wie es eigentlich gewesen*].[4] Ranke was writing in 1824 and by the time de Certeau was addressing the issue of historiographic theory and practice the discipline consisted of a wide variety of positions few of which would uncritically uphold a Rankean practice. Yet the value of 'science', of gathering and sifting objective facts, remained and remains a value that underwrites historiographic practice. But it is not primarily as a critic of objectivism that de Certeau should be read (such criticisms are available in many other places besides), rather it is the generative potential of his critical position that should, I think, guide our reading.

De Certeau's historiographic practice, which was also a meta-historiographic practice, can be best seen as an antidote to much of the *perceived* relativism that has been associated with the anti-objectivist 'linguistic turn' in historiographic thinking and in the human sciences more generally. This, it seems to me, is the

---

[3] Stephen Greenblatt, *Shakespearean Negotiations: The Circulation of Social Energy in Renaissance England* (Berkeley: University of California Press, 1988), p. 1.

[4] Leopold von Ranke, *Geschichten der romanischen und germanischen Völker* (1824), cited in Reinhart Koselleck, *Futures Past: On the Semantics of Historical Time*, translated by Keith Tribe (Cambridge: MIT Press, 1985), p. 31. It is worth noting that this is from Ranke's first book and that 'scientific objectivity' is presented here as a fairly modest claim designed to distance the study of history from the more ambitious (and clearly *more* epistemologically problematic) task of planning the future on the basis of understanding the past.

strength and the originality of the work: it is a sustained explication of a textual-ist position, yet rather than this resulting in abandoning notions of reality, or truth, de Certeau allows them to return, altered – now, less complacent than before, filled with doubt and anxious about their status, yet still there, opera-tive, desirous of truth, reality, actuality. In de Certeau's work the 'speaking with the dead' encounters the linguistic condition of historiography without con-ceding the desire for the past:

> Paper has long since lost its power to resurrect the dead, but this open secret is no reason to veer off into subjectivism or relativism. It simply suggests that the relation of the text to the real is necessarily a relation with death. Historiography is a form of writing, not of speech. It assumes a vanished voice.[5]

The recognition that the past is dead, and that the historian relates to what is no longer in existence (particularly the orality of the past), should guard against the false value of historical 'immersion' in a period. De Certeau's position allows us to re-read the critical positions staked by the likes of Hayden White (the name most often associated with the linguistic turn in Anglophone historiography), not as stymying the desire to produce more 'scientific' or 'accurate' accounts of the past, but as the necessary conditions for activating and actualizing such a desire. Against what many critics of so-called 'postmodern'[6] historiography tend to think, de Certeau allows us to fully face the fact that the past is unrecoverable except as a deathly writing *without* abandoning the will to know the past more completely, more distinctly. With de Certeau absolute relativism is resisted; what returns, recoded as a critical practice, is a non-categorical evaluation. Absolutism is avoided and in its place appears a relative relativism that needs to be under-written by an ethics, an aesthetics and a politics.

Michel de Certeau provides historiographic thought, not just with an epis-temological crisis or an epistemological undoing (which might be one reading of Hayden White's approach), but with an epistemological awakening that

---

[5] Michel de Certeau, 'History and Mysticism' (1973) in Revel and Hunt, eds, *Histories*, p. 441.

[6] Within the field of Anglophone academic historiography 'postmodernism' is most often used as a 'portmanteau' word into which can be thrown all sorts of theoretical and critical approaches. Thus, for a seemingly large number of historians, Michel Foucault is a postmod-ernist as is Hayden White. The refusal amongst many historians to distinguish between theor-etical accounts of historiography and then to provide a misleading category for these varied accounts is one symptom of a lack of engagement with the epistemological possibilities as much as the epistemological limits of critical historiography. It is becoming increasingly clear to me that the term 'postmodernism' lacks *any* characteristics that would allow it to be a useful cat-egory in these debates.

results in a re-grounding of the science of history. The 'literary-ness' of historiography becomes the opportunity for historians to become (more) 'scientific'
in their commerce with the past. Rather than treating 'literature' and 'the
science of history' as antithetical, de Certeau's practice suggests a new cosmology of historiography, such that the becoming-literary of historiography coin-
cides with the desire to produce 'better' histories of the past. If critical
historiography has been accused of ushering in a form of relativism that would
give any account of the past equal status (thereby allowing it to be epistemologically vulnerable to Holocaust deniers, for instance), here relativism insists
on critical evaluation – which is, significantly, an anti-relativist operation. If
there are no absolute guarantees to knowledge, no final jury that would arbitrate
on the 'facts', it is even more crucial to make relative judgements, such that one
account is judged as relatively better than another on account of a set of values
(the ability to present complexity, say) that historians defend. Foregrounding
the poetics of historical knowledge becomes the basis for fashioning new poetics, not on the grounds that 'anything goes' but on the grounds that such work
is essential to the production of 'better', more valuable and valid, accounts of
the past.

FOUNDATIONAL CHALLENGES

One of the factors that most insistently works to challenge the delusion that
historiography is the activity of retelling the past, 'as it once was', is the historicity of historiography. As de Certeau notes: 'although this is a patent truth,
we should recall that any reading of the past – however much it is controlled
by the analysis of documents – is driven by a reading of current events' (WH:
23). Thus the difference between a historiographic account of Joan of Arc written in mid-nineteenth-century France and one written at the end of the twentieth century in the US couldn't be explained merely in terms of new evidence
coming to light, for instance; it would have to take into account changes of a
much more general and historical nature (genre changes in scholarly practice,
changes in the role of women, the specificity of the writer's situation and so on).
One of the most succinct formulations of this idea is offered by Walter
Benjamin:

> The events surrounding the historian, and in which he [*sic*] himself takes
> part, will underlie his presentation in the form of a text written in invisible
> ink. The history which he lays before the reader comprises, as it were, the
> citations occurring in this text, and it is only these citations that occur in a
> manner legible to all. To write history thus means to *cite* history. It belongs

to the concept of citation, however, that the historical object in each case is torn from its context.[7]

The existential condition of historical writing, which will be part of what will make de Certeau conceive of his historiography as 'broken' and as 'interstitial' (existing between the pressing conditions of the present and the alterity of the past), is joined with a more insistent challenge that has been dubbed 'the linguistic turn'. In effect, the concern with the existential condition of historiography becomes focused solely on its linguistic, material condition.

Towards the mid to late 1960s and into the 1970s a number of theorists produced vigorous critiques of the foundations of conventional historiographical thought and practice. Amongst these, the ones that reverberated most widely were: Hayden White's 'Burden of History' in 1966,[8] leading to his sustained work *Metahistory: The Historical Imagination in Nineteenth-Century Europe* in 1973;[9] Roland Barthes' 'Discourse of History' in 1967;[10] and Paul Veyne's 1971 *Writing History: Essay on Epistemology*.[11] Michel de Certeau's 'The Historiographical Operation' (included in *The Writing of History*), which was initially published as the opening chapter to Jacques Le Goff and Pierre Nora's edited three-volume *Faire de l'histoire* of 1974 (which positioned itself as the collection of the 'new history'), might well be seen as the culmination of this flurry of theoretical ground clearing.[12] But alongside its critique of the epistemological and processual basis of dominant historiographical practice, de Certeau's long essay is also a subtle invitation to a practice that can accommodate such a critique at the same time as it inventively and sensitively offers another approach to the business of 'making and doing history'. To get a sense of the way this moment of critique challenged the conventions of historiography (its Rankean aspirations, if not its Rankean practice) it is worth looking briefly at Roland

[7] Walter Benjamin, *The Arcades Project*, translated by Howard Eiland and Kevin McLaughlin (Cambridge, Mass. and London: Harvard University Press, 1999), p. 476 [N11,3]. This unfinished project was worked on from 1928 until his death in 1940.

[8] Hayden White, 'The Burden of History', *History and Theory*, vol. 5, no. 2, 1966, pp. 111–34, reprinted in Hayden White, *Tropics of Discourse: Essays in Cultural Criticism* (Baltimore and London: Johns Hopkins University Press, 1985), pp. 27–50.

[9] Hayden White, *Metahistory: The Historical Imagination in Nineteenth-Century Europe* (Johns Hopkins University Press, 1973).

[10] Roland Barthes, 'The Discourse of History', in *The Rustle of Language*, translated by Richard Howard (Oxford: Blackwell, 1986), pp. 127–40 – this was first published in France in 1967 in the journal *Information sur les sciences socials*.

[11] Paul Veyne, *Comment on écrit l'histoire* (Paris: Seuil, 1971), translated by Mina Moore-Minvolucri as *Writing History: Essay on Epistemology* (Manchester: Manchester University Press, 1984).

[12] Jacques Le Goff and Pierre Nora, eds, *Faire de l'histoire* (Paris: Gallimard, 1974).

Barthes' contribution to the 'linguistic turn' in his essay 'The Discourse of History' and where necessary drawing connections with the work of Hayden White and Paul Veyne.

The initial salvo against the historian's claim to objectivity is for Barthes to question the distinction that might be made between historiography and literature:

> The narration of past events, commonly subject in our culture, since the Greeks, to the sanction of historical 'science', placed under the imperious warrant of the 'real', justified by principles of 'rational' exposition – does this narration differ, in fact, by some specific feature, by an indubitable pertinence, from imaginary narration as we find it in epic, the novel, the drama?[13]

If, as Barthes supposes, it is the narrative element of historiography that determines what counts as history, and this makes it indistinguishable from those forms of discourse that are works of imagination, then the epistemological ground of historical science (and here science equals objectivism) begins to seem particularly shaky.

Hayden White, in his almost contemporaneous 'The Burden of History', points out that historiography's claim to be both objective and interpretative and to position itself between science and art (sharing what is best in both) begins to look like a category mistake: '[the] supposedly neutral middle ground between art and science which many nineteenth-century historians occupied with such self-confidence and pride of possession has dissolved in the discovery of the common constructivist character of both artistic and scientific statements'.[14] The task that White set himself in *Metahistory* was to show just how determining the constructivist or linguistic aspect of historiography is:

> Through the disclosure of the linguistic ground on which a given idea of history was constituted, I have attempted to establish the ineluctable poetic nature of the historical work and to specify the prefigurative element in a historical account by which its theoretical concepts were tacitly sanctioned.[15]

In this, poetics isn't the ornamental casing of the historian's account of the past, its decorative finish; it actually determines the content of the account (it determines what is recountable) – or, as he would show in the title of a later book,

---

[13] Barthes, 'The Discourse of History', p. 127.
[14] White, 'The Burden of History', p. 28.
[15] White, *Metahistory*, p. xi.

there is a content to form.[16] For White this position requires the total evacuation of the epistemological ground of historiography: 'the best grounds for choosing one perspective on history rather than another are ultimately aesthetic or moral rather than epistemological'.[17]

There is, I think, a polemical point to this, but it is a difficult one to take absolutely seriously mainly because it seems to deny the epistemological possibilities of literature. Seen from a reverse angle you would also need to counter the novelist's belief (if it exists) that theirs is the work of pure imagination, when clearly the majority of the content of novels is based on a world made up of known elements that are familiar to us all and which unproblematically reference reality. As Antony Easthope points out, 'it is hard to find a novel in which Paris is not the capital of France'[18] – it is even harder to find novels where water isn't wet, for instance. The polemic works partly because of the low epistemological status of literature: the trouble is that such a polemic also helps sustain this low status. Michel de Certeau, as we will see, is more open to the epistemological possibilities of history, not because he has a less assured critique of historiographic objectivism, but because, importantly, he will allow aesthetic materials (literature and art, but also history) to have relatively high epistemological value. In this de Certeau's position is closer to Paul Veyne's:

> For history is an art, like engraving or photography. To affirm that it is not science, but that it is an art (a minor art), is not to sacrifice to an annoying commonplace or to clear the ground: it would be, if it were affirmed that history, whatever one does, will be a work of art in spite of efforts it makes to be objective, the art being an ornament or incompressible margin. The truth is a little different: history is a work of art *by* its efforts toward objectivity . . .[19]

For de Certeau and Veyne (and at times for White) the epistemological crisis is turned into an *awakening* by recoding the poetic condition of historiography as the very condition of its claim to objectivity. Not only does this rescue historiography as a project based on the premise of producing knowledge, it also allows common cause to be made between history and literature. The 'being literary' of history is not the most damning indictment that can be levelled at it, rather it is its most challenging potential for knowing the past.

[16] Hayden White, *The Content of the Form: Narrative Discourse and Historical Representation* (Baltimore and London: Johns Hopkins University Press, 1987).

[17] White, *Metahistory*, p. xii.

[18] Antony Easthope, 'Romancing the Stone: History Writing and Rhetoric', *Social History* 18, 2, 1993, p. 239.

[19] Paul Veyne, *Writing History*, p. 229.

But if history is essentially a literary form, then for critical theorists like White and Barthes one of the problems with conventional historiography was that it took its literary form only from the nineteenth-century realist novel, and then simply stuck to it, unchanging. As far as this goes historiography's production of 'objectivity', or more pointedly 'illusionistic naturalism', was an effect of genre – an effect produced by inhabiting the genre of naturalism:

> On the level of discourse, objectivity – or lack of signs of the 'speaker' – thus appears as a special form of image-repertoire, the product of what we might call the *referential illusion*, since here the historian claims to let the referent speak for itself. This illusion is not proper to historical discourse; how many novelists – in the realistic period – imagine they are being objective because they suppress signs of the *I* in the discourse![20]

'Image-repertoire' is the term Barthes uses to designate the foundational tropes and conventions of a genre or discourse, and here he uses it to point to one of the effects of hiding the writing subject. The genre of conventional historical writing in Barthes is not objective – but it does produce the effect of objectivity, or the illusion of objectivity, by hiding its condition as discourse:

> Hence, we arrive at that paradox which governs the entire pertinence of historical discourse (in relation to other types of discourse): fact never has any but a linguistic existence (as the term of discourse), yet everything happens as if this linguistic existence were merely a pure and simple 'copy' of another existence, situated in an extra-structural field, the 'real'.[21]

For Barthes this suggests that as well as appearing similar to nineteenth-century novels, the historian's discourse is also uncannily similar to the psychotic's:

> We might say that, in a sense, 'objective' discourse (this is the case with positivist history) joins the situation of schizophrenic discourse; in either case, there is a radical censorship of the speech-act . . . a massive reflux of discourse towards statement and even (in the historian's case) towards the referent: no one is there to assume the statement.[22]

Psychotics and (some) historians behave as if their words emanated from an elsewhere and an else-when: for some what emanates is the voice of God.

---

[20] Barthes, 'The Discourse of History', p. 132.
[21] Barthes, 'The Discourse of History', p. 138.
[22] Barthes, 'The Discourse of History', p. 135.

Given the long love affair of modernist art with forms of psychological derangement, it might seem odd to see critical theory's engagement with historiography as often simply championing the modernist canon. The argument is partly that a turn towards more self-consciously textual forms of literature would allow the linguistic construction of historiographic discourse to be evident. In this regard Antony Easthope can write for many when he declares that:

> Contemporary history-writing was developed essentially in the Victorian period with a mode of discourse very like that of the nineteenth-century realist novel. A way forward might be for history-writing to take on board some of the principles, insights and techniques associated with Modernist fiction, to move away from George Eliot and become a bit more like James Joyce.[23]

James Joyce or Virginia Woolf are offered as the antidote to the illusionistic conventions of the realist form.[24] Hayden White suggests a more varied perspective when he suggests that:

> When many contemporary historians speak of the 'art' of history, they seem to have in mind a conception of art that would admit little more than the nineteenth-century novel as a paradigm. And when they say they are artists, they seem to mean that they are artists in the way that Scott or Thackeray were artists. They certainly do not mean to identify themselves with action painters, kinetic sculptors, existential novelists, imagist poets, or *nouvelle vague* cinematographers.[25]

At times this invocation of modernisms seems nothing more than an admonishment to historians that they are missing out on the latest in the way of styling that is available. And I think it is useful to position Michel de Certeau against this blandishment – not because he is content with the conventional forms of historiographic work (he clearly wasn't), but because he refuses to generalize at this level, to pitch realism against modernism in this way, or, more fatuously, to pitch postmodernism against realism. It is only at an epistemological level that this argument amounts to anything. And at an epistemological level arguments need to be mounted through the specificity of texts and their productivity. Modernism or realism works to chaperone and protect specific writing practices from epistemological scrutiny.

[23] Easthope, 'Romancing the Stone', p. 248.
[24] See Jacques Rancière, *The Names of History: On the Poetics of Knowledge*, translated by Hassan Melehy (Minneapolis: University of Minnesota Press, 1994), p. 100.
[25] White, 'The Burden of History', p 42.

In later chapters I will show how the epistemological capacities and capabilities of literary-history (the name for the common cause of literature and historiography to attend to the past) can only be assessed case by case. While it won't be possible in the space available here, it will ultimately, I think, mean distinguishing between the epistemological potential of Virginia Woolf and James Joyce (and any other canonical and non-canonical author) rather than in tying them together. For now though I need to proceed with distinguishing and connecting de Certeau's work with this meta-historiographic moment, and to spend some time rehearsing the arguments he makes in his essay 'The Historiographical Operation'.

THE HISTORIOGRAPHICAL OPERATION

One of the keys to de Certeau's methodology is signalled in the title of 'The Historiographical Operation': it is by treating forms of knowledge as practices, as operations, that de Certeau performs a practical criticism that is materialist and grounded in the possible. Treating historiographical production as a practical operation allows de Certeau to attend to the material practices of shifting through archival sources (in regional libraries and national archives, for instance); and to the way that institutions such as universities are used to vouchsafe historical knowledge (through peer assessment and the allocation of financial resources by funding bodies, for instance); and to the practices of writing that materially produce knowledge (the genre conventions of organizing narratives around the chronological unfolding of events, for instance). In contrast to the often epistemological abstractions and critical negations of Barthes and White, de Certeau offers a theoretical approach that is aimed at generating historiographic practice, rather than simply stymying conventional approaches:

> But only a theory which articulates a practice can be accepted, that is, a theory which on the one hand opens the practices to the space of a society, while on the other it organizes the procedures belonging to a given discipline. On a necessary limited scale, envisaging history as an operation would be the equivalent to understanding it as the relation between a *place* (a recruitment, a milieu, a profession or business, etc.), analytic *procedures* (a discipline), and the construction of a *text* (a literature). (WH: 57)

While the linguistic turn has focused fairly exclusively on the textuality of historiography, de Certeau accompanies this focus with attention to the processual protocols of 'the historian's craft' and on the spatial setting of the historian (her and his institutional situation). One of the outcomes of such an approach is, as I mentioned in the previous chapter, to produce a form of critical discourse that understands all knowledge (including its own) as situated (limited, interested, etc.).

The attention to place is a constant orientation in de Certeau's work and can be thought of as a 'geography of knowledge' if we see mobility as a crucial aspect of this geography. For de Certeau, 'all historiographical research is articulated over a socio-economic, political, and cultural place of production' (WH: 58). Places permit and prohibit. Anyone, for instance, working in a British university (and I would guess it would be the same in many other countries) knows that research is encouraged as long as it follows a prescribed pattern. My research, which culminated in this book, was funded and made possible because one institution agreed to employ me as a teacher and allow me to apply for research leave, another contracted me as an author, while another paid for my time away from teaching. An interlinked network of universities, national funding bodies and publishers are involved in *permitting* such research (a state of affairs that is usually discoverable by a quick glance at the acknowledgements pages of most academic books). This book, then, is located across this network of institutions, which simultaneously permit and prohibit: 'research is circumscribed by the place that a connection of the possible and impossible defines' (WH: 68). In other words had I not gained the number of 'permissions' needed (for instance, not found employment as a teacher, which then provides an academic legitimation) the research would not have taken place; and the contours of what is possible and what is impossible are constantly being reasserted through the social and cultural practices of academic 'places'. Within the context of UK academic work 'research' is a euphemism; what it really means is 'publication' – production: a fact spatially sustained through items like funding-application forms that couple ideas about 'value for money' with outcomes (books, articles and the like), which is then linked back to more financial resources through the auditing of research based on published output, on the basis of which institutional funding is then allocated.

In relation to the production of 'history' (historiography), an emphasis on the material places of production (places of permission and prohibition) allows de Certeau to make the first in a number of moves that shift the terms of critique away from an absolutist account of epistemology, to one immediately more material and more generative (the option of producing historiography 'outside of space' is, of course, not an option):

> Before knowing what history says of a society, we have to analyse how history functions within it. The historiographic institution is inscribed within

a complex that permits only one kind of production for it and prohibits others. Such is the double function of the place. It makes possible certain researches through the fact of common conjunctures and problematics. But it makes others impossible; it excludes from discourse what is its basis at a given moment; it plays the role of censor with respect to current – social, economic, political – postulates of analysis. (WH: 68)

The act of excluding, of interdicting, is an activity that shapes and signifies, just as much as the act of permitting and promoting. The 'language' that history speaks is therefore both a social and a spatial one: 'history is defined entirely by a relation of language to the (social) body, and therefore by its relation to the limits that the body assigns either in respect to the particular place whence one speaks, or in respect to the other object (past, dead) that is spoken about' (WH: 68–9).

Places (ones you can enter and ones you can't) are the hosts of practice, and it is history as a material practice that is de Certeau's next topic:

[Historians] work on materials in order to transform them into history. Here they undertake a practice of manipulation which, like others, is subject to rules. A comparable manipulation would be the manufacturing of goods made of already refined matter. First transforming the raw material (a primary source) into a standard product (secondary source), the work of the historian carries it from one region of culture ('curiosities', archives, collections, etc.) to another (history). (WH: 71)

'History', then, is already determined by the activities of conserving and archiving: 'In history everything begins with the gesture of *setting aside*, of putting together, of transforming certain classified objects into "documents"' (WH: 72). What the production of historiography does is constantly move documents from one place to the other, not just altering the context for these documents, but altering their 'composition'. Crucially this movement, and its attendant decompositions and recompositions, does not access the past: what it does is access materials that are constituted by their interpretation of the past. In this sense there are no 'raw' or 'primary' sources that could speak immediately for the past: as Nietzsche had already ascertained, the historian is in the business of interpreting interpretations (as is the anthropologist). For de Certeau, the epistemological fact that historians are trading in 'refined matter' doesn't invalidate the attempt to write history, in many ways it becomes the condition of possibility for writing anything of value – whether it is about the past or the present. In this his position is similar to the anthropologist Clifford Geertz when he writes that 'what we call our data are really our own constructions of other people's constructions of what they and their compatriots are up to'.[26] There is no material that is useable by cultural studies (and in this I include history, anthropology and other forms of cultural science) that isn't already 'refined', already marked.

While the movement of documents is often recoverable through footnotes, acknowledgement pages, and so on, what de Certeau seems to be suggesting here is that some forms of historiography seem to transfer documents from one place to another under the cover of darkness. So historiography involves the movement of interpretative forms from a national archive, say, into a scholarly monograph. Archives are constituted by such practices while also determining them: 'the origins of our National Archive already imply, in effect, the combination of a *group* (the "erudite"), *places* ("libraries"), and *practices* (of copying, printing, communication, classification, etc.)' (WH: 73). What is crucial within de Certeau's meta-historiography is that such a movement is both inevitable and open to all sorts of possibilities: from the almost complete veiling of sources (as if the past 'speaks for itself') to the inclusion of archival mobility as a focus of the historiographic account (which is a characteristic of de Certeau's practice). When historiography embraces this aspect of production, the changing history of an event, the mutability of its meaning, can become the object of reflection. A vivid example of this is Shahid Amin's *Event, Metaphor, Memory: Chauri Chaura 1922–1992*, which recounts the events of February 1922, when a police station in North India was attacked by supporters of Gandhi, and then follows the history of this historical event as it is constantly reinterpreted and remembered.[27]

The third area of 'The Historiographical Operation', and the one more familiar within the terms of the 'linguistic turn', is de Certeau's concern with writing. Yet even here (or perhaps especially here) the concern is not abstractly epistemological but epistemological within the terms of material practices. Thus, for instance, he can show how writing works antagonistically to the business of research by necessarily producing discrete and bounded accounts:

> While research is interminable, the text must have an ending, and this structure of finality bends back upon the introduction, which is already organized by the need to finish. Thus the whole is presented as a stable architecture of

---

26 Clifford Geertz, *The Interpretation of Cultures: Selected Essays* (London: Fontana Press, 1973), p. 9. For a more sustained enquiry into the consequences of this for cultural history see my *Cityscapes: Cultural Readings in the Material and Symbolic City* (Houndmills: Palgrave Macmillan, 2005), pp. 16–21. For an argument that wants to insist on the difference between de Certeau and Geertz see Chapter 4 of Ian Buchanan's *Michel de Certeau: Cultural Theorist* (London: Sage, 2000).

27 Shahid Amin, *Event, Metaphor, Memory: Chauri Chaura 1922–1992* (Berkeley and Los Angeles: University of California Press, 1995).

elements, rules, and historical concepts which form a system amongst themselves, and whose coherence is owing to a unity designated by the author's
proper name. Finally, in order to maintain itself by means of some few examples, scriptural representation becomes 'full'; it fills or obliterates the lacu-
nae that are to the contrary the very principle of research, for research is
always sharpened through lack. (WH: 86–7)

Here writing isn't simply a constructivist architecture that produces the past; it
is more characteristically directed against research, interning the past in variously ornate mausoleums:

> Writing speaks of the past only in order to inter it. Writing is a tomb in the
> double sense of the word in that, in the very same text, it both honours and
> eliminates. Here the function of language is to introduce through *saying*
> what can no longer be *done*. Language exorcises death and arranges it in the
> narrative that pedagogically replaces it with something that the reader must
> believe and do. (WH: 101)

This position, though, comes perilously close to the kind of absolutist stance
that the essay seems to have studiously refused: if all writing simply instils a
deathly cover over the endless possibilities of research, what possibility is there
for a more productive engagement with historiography? I will come back to
de Certeau's understanding of writing and speech in following chapters. For
the moment though I want to suggest that while this seems like a form of
absolutism there are always various possibilities for writing, some relatively
more death-like than others, and some relatively better able in allowing a range
of voices to circulate. In Chapter 4 this argument will have to be more finely
tuned as the stakes become particularly high in the context of historians trying
to write the histories of people who have effectively been excised from the
archives.

   For the moment though I want to end this section by claiming that what is
distinctive about de Certeau's meta-historiography as well as his historiography
(as we will see) is that while it is as forcefully argued as Barthes' and White's critical positions it is constantly aimed at the epistemological practicalities and possibilities. More than this though, the nature of the critical moves he makes
suggests the possibility of other 'relatively' better practices, relatively more productive, more liberatory, ways of making and doing history. In this sense (and
this is, I think, the most important aspect of de Certeau's work) epistemological
critique provides the opportunity and the means for generating better accounts
of the past. So while institutions might legitimate knowledge and police what
will count as knowledge, de Certeau, rather than suggesting the illusionary

non-space of non-institutional knowledge, suggests a way of working at the limits of what is allowable in a place. Similarly, rather than refusing to participate in the recomposition of documents as they travel from one place to another, de Certeau wants such travelling to become part of the varied stories historiography can tell. And lastly, rather than imagining a pure writing unsullied by death, he wants to imagine a form of writing less in control of the voices that circulate within in it: less a mourning and more a haunting.

So, for instance, de Certeau can imagine within the institutions that produce history other forms of historiography:

> The historian comes to circulate *around* acquired rationalizations. He or she works in the margins. In this respect the historian becomes a prowler. In a society gifted at generalization, endowed with powerful centralizing strategies, the historian moves in the direction of the frontiers of great regions already exploited. He or she 'deviates' by going back to sorcery, madness, festival, popular literature, the forgotten world of the peasant, Occitania, etc., all these zones of silence. (WH: 79)

Because he writes primarily as a historian – not simply as a philosopher of history – his critical position is able to offer generative possibilities as the very basis of theory. De Certeau is writing as a historian amongst historians, as part of a community who are not straightforwardly tied to the forms of nineteenth-century historiography, but who are dedicated in various ways to a 'new history', to exploring the zones of silence that are, ultimately, historiography's operative territory and should, most productively, be the focus of its ethical obligation.[28] To pursue de Certeau's historiographic epistemology, then, we need to enter the murky world of historiographic *practice*, attending to the various kinds of historical work that seem to participate in this epistemological position. The 'new historicism' that has emerged in literary studies might be one place to go: another is the cultural and ethnographic history that is emerging alongside, but independently of, de Certeau's theoretical discourse.

THICKENING THE TEXT: 'HISTORY IN THE ETHNOGRAPHIC GRAIN'

Attention to the meta-historiography of de Certeau can provide a rapprochement between the theory and practice of historiography in a way that might

---

[28] His critique of Barthes' 'The Discourse of History' is that it 'too easily' relies on 'examples nearest to narrative but quite distant from current practice' (WH: 41).

allow a more fruitful reflection on the methodological and epistemological principles informing current practices. The need for this rapprochement is most evident when viewing the field of history from outside. Two seemingly contradictory 'facts' seem almost immediately to come into view. The first is that the discipline of history (especially in Anglophone culture) is peopled by academics peculiarly resistant to theory. Thus Dominic LaCapra, an intellectual historian, could write in 1985 that:

> Historians tend to pride themselves on their immunity to the wormlike doubt and self-reflexive scrutiny that have appeared in other areas of inquiry, notably those infiltrated by recent French thought. Far from seeing recent critical initiatives as holding forth the angelic promise of reformation or even a renaissance in historical studies, many historians have been seized with what might almost be called a counter-reformational zeal in reasserting orthodox procedures.[29]

And it is true that you don't need to look particularly far to find examples to confirm this view.[30] Yet the other 'fact', to my mind, is the mass of new and inventive approaches to historical writing that have emerged since the 1960s and 1970s.[31] The new cultural history, to borrow a title from one characteristic collection,[32] is hardly an exemplification of orthodoxy, even if it still maintains faith in the ability of historians to account accurately for the past. Thus LaCapra can go on to claim:

> If one were to generalize somewhat rashly about prominent trends in the [historian's] profession, one might list the following: an inclination to rely on a social definition of context as an explanatory matrix; a shift toward an interest in popular culture; a reconceptualization of culture in terms of collective discourses, mentalities, world views, and even 'languages'; a redefinition of intellectual history as the study of social meaning as historically constituted; and an archivally based documentary realism that treats

---

[29] Dominic LaCapra, *History and Criticism* (Ithaca and London: Cornell University Press, 1985), p. 46.

[30] One of the most notorious examples of this 'counter-reformational zeal' is Arthur Marwick, 'Two Approaches to Historical Study: The Metaphysical (Including "Postmodernism") and the Historical', *Journal of Contemporary History*, 30, 1995, pp. 5–35. The essay is notorious mainly because it extols the virtues of precision and the historian's responsibility 'not to get it [the past] wrong', while being full of imprecision and inaccurate accounts of various theorists.

[31] For an overview of the range of approaches see, for example, Peter Burke, ed., *New Perspectives on Historical Writing* (Cambridge: Polity Press, 1991).

[32] Lynn Hunt, ed., *The New Cultural History* (Berkeley: University of California Press, 1989).

artefacts as quarries for facts in the reconstitution of societies and cultures of the past.[33]

LaCapra has in mind Carlo Ginzburg's *The Cheese and the Worms: The Cosmos of a Sixteenth-Century Miller*,[34] but any number of books would have done just as well. Ginzburg's book is, amongst other things, a form of micro-history, and is best understood as part of a gradual emergence of cultural history, dedicated to ethnographic understandings of the past. This is historiography that appears to be more informed by theories associated with anthropology and literary studies than by the specific critiques of historiography mounted by Roland Barthes and Hayden White. The theorists that seem to inform historians like Natalie Zemon Davies, for instance, are literary historians like Mikhail Bakhtin, anthropologists like Victor Turner and Mary Douglas, and 'theorists' like Roger Caillois.[35] This ethnographic history is not non-theoretical even if it eschews a head-on collision with the epistemological problems elucidated by White and Barthes.[36]

There is a vital tendency within the contemporary cultural sciences that readily connects with de Certeau's approach to the study of culture, and has a currency that crosses between a number of disciplines, particularly history, literary studies and anthropology. De Certeau's 'science of singularity' can, in the field of historiography (but elsewhere as well), be seen as part of a general shift towards what Perry Anderson usefully calls the 'micro-archival'. Anderson, in an essay that is an audit of intellectual force-fields in British culture from the 1960s to the late 1980s, points to a shift in historiography that was also taking place more generally in Europe and in North America. 'It was the late sixties,' writes Anderson, referring to the work of Lawrence Stone and others, 'which saw the zenith of the kind of radical history, informed by and attached to the ideals of the social sciences – structural explanation of the broadest human processes . . . by contrast the ensuing twenty years witnessed the progressive retreat and erosion of this model of historiography, the reassertion of the particular and the piecemeal, the contingent and the episodic'. The relationship

[33] LaCapra, *History and Criticism*, p. 46.
[34] Carlo Ginzburg, *The Cheese and the Worms: The Cosmos of a Sixteenth-Century Miller*, translated by Anne and John Tedeschi (Baltimore: Johns Hopkins University Press, 1997) – first published in Italian in 1976.
[35] Natalie Zemon Davies, *Society and Culture in Early Modern France* (Stanford: Stanford University Press, 1975).
[36] For a stunning critique of how 'theories' can become Theory, and endlessly caught chasing its anti-essentialist, social-constructivist tail, see Eve Kosofsky Sedgwick and Adam Frank, 'Shame in the Cybernetic Fold: Reading Silvan Tomkins' in Sedgwick, *Touching Feeling: Affect, Pedagogy, Performativity* (Durham: Duke University Press, 2003), pp. 93–121.

between sociology and history was, for Anderson, in 'contraflow': 'just as sociology finally discovered the macro-historical, history itself was going increasingly
micro-archival.'[37] Writing about a similar situation in France during roughly the
same period, the cultural historian Roger Chartier could describe how the drift
of advanced historiography moved from a concern with the *longue durée* to a
belief in quantitative history (the historian Emmanuel Le Roy Ladurie would
claim, in 1968, that 'historians will either be [computer] programmers or they
will no longer exist'[38]), but then moved towards a historiographic practice more
anxious about the very condition of meaning of the documents and practices of
the past:

> A cultural history that, once emancipated from the traditional definition
> of the history of mentalities, came to pay more attention to the modalities
> of appropriation than to statistical distributions, more to processes for con-
> structing meaning than to the unequal circulation of objects, and more to
> seeing connections amongst practices and representation than to inventory-
> ing mental tools.[39]

This movement (from confidence in the large-scale to what might be called
'micro-puzzling') describes tendencies to be found in advanced historiography,
even if they don't correspond to a more general sense of practice.[40] This partial
shift can be read in a number of ways: positively, as an attempt to get to grips
with the experiential conditions of a past whose alterity or epistemological problems come to light alongside a number of other historical issues (second-wave
feminism, the success of decolonization and so on); and more negatively as a
failure of nerve, as a loss of faith in emancipatory projects like Marxism, with
its ambition to offer complete explanations of the course of history, for instance.
In this context, de Certeau's insistence on the detailed example and on a close-
reading of the document is nothing out of the ordinary – it is synchronized in
relation to a number of tendencies within historiography that start to privilege
the 'textuality of the text', start to move towards an anthropological and culturalist historiography.

Robert Darnton's essay 'Workers Revolt: The Great Cat Massacre of the Rue
Saint-Séverin', from his 1984 collection, *The Great Cat Massacre*, can be taken

---

[37] Perry Anderson, 'A Culture in Contraflow', in *English Questions* (London: Verso, 1992), p. 282.
[38] Revel and Hunt, eds, *Histories*, p. 329.
[39] Roger Chartier, *On the Edge of the Cliff: History, Language, and Practices*, translated by Lydia
   G. Cochrane (Baltimore and London: Johns Hopkins University Press, 1997), p. 2.
[40] For instance it should be noted that Perry Anderson's account is clearly a confident macro-
   history and that 'standard' histories of nations and periods continue to be produced during this
   period and probably constitute the mainstay of historical publishing.

as a fitting example of the micro-archival approach of historiography, or as Darnton calls it, 'history in the ethnographic grain'. It is a piece of self-declared anthropological historiography that emerged, as the author states in his preface, out of a graduate seminar that he co-taught with Clifford Geertz in the 1970s at Princeton: 'the ethnographic historian studies the way ordinary people made sense of the world. He [*sic*] attempts to uncover their cosmology, to show how they organized reality in their minds and expressed it in their behavior.'[41] Darnton's essay is also useful as it was critically scrutinized by Chartier – for not being micro-historical enough. The essay concerns the ritual massacre of cats by a couple of apprentice printers in Paris in the 1730s. This was a riotous massacre that was, according to Darnton, a complex 'joke'. It was a cultural performance that successfully allowed the apprentices to undertake a number of actions: they could perform the massacre as a symbolic revenge against the owners of the printing shop, 'the bourgeois' and his wife, whose cherished cat was one of the victims; they could do this safely free from reprisals (the bourgeois asked the apprentices to cull the cats); and it allowed them cultural entry into the world of the printer journeyman that they were on their way to becoming (the other printers enjoyed the joke and its burlesque retellings). But what is particularly interesting is the way that Darnton constructs this reading from an account written by one of the apprentices:

> The only version of the cat massacre available to us was put into writing, long after the fact, by Nicolas Contat. He selected details, ordered events, and framed the story in such a way as to bring out what was meaningful for him. But he derived his notions of meaning from his culture just as naturally as he drew in air from the atmosphere around him. And he wrote down what he had helped to enact with his mates. The subjective character of the writing does not vitiate its collective frame of reference, even though the written account must be thin compared with the action it describes.[42]

Darnton is, as we would expect, dealing in refined material. What is complexly staged here though is the possibility of this text for 'doing history'. First of all Darnton is eager to stage his 'doing history' as a *reading* of this text: already it seems closer to certain versions of literary history than to the illusionist naturalism that can most often be found in the narratives of macro-history. But it is a reading that situates itself around a problem and a paradox. On the one hand the account is ethnographically thin: the culture that it belongs to has codified

---

[41] Robert Darnton, *The Great Cat Massacre, and Other Episodes in French Cultural History* (Harmondsworth: Penguin, 1991), p. 11.

[42] Darnton, *The Great Cat Massacre*, p. 99.

it in ways that mean it isn't transparent or in any way 'full' in terms of meaning. This is something that Darnton will explain in a further essay:

> Although we can trace Contat to an actual printing shop and confirm many of the details in his narrative, we cannot be sure that everything happened exactly as he said it did. On the contrary, we must allow for stylized elements in his text. It belongs to a genre of working-class autobiography . . . and it includes elements from two other genres: the *misère*, or burlesque lament about the hard life of the workers in certain trades, and the technical manual, a variety of 'how-to' literature popular amongst printers. Because Contat shaped his text according to generic constraints, we cannot treat it as if it were a window, which provides an undistorted view of his experience.[43]

Yet it is precisely because it is already culturally marked (and how could it not be?) that it can potentially be the basis for thick description. In other words the text, however truncated it seems, is potentially thick because its generic truncations point it to a world of cultural (rather than simply social) meaning. It is precisely because it is stylized and not transparent that it leaks cultural meaning. In this sense the object of cultural history is not really the raw actuality that now only exists in opaquely coded representations; it is the code itself, the opacity, that is the object.

Cultural history, then, has to be close to literary analysis because it is through the analysis of generic conventions that it can perform history in the ethnographic grain:

> The anthropological mode of history has a rigor of its own, even if it may look suspiciously like literature to a hard-boiled social scientist. It begins with the premise that individual expression takes place within a general idiom, that we learn to classify sensations and make sense of things by thinking within a framework provided by culture. It therefore should be possible for the historian to discover the social dimension of thought and to tease meaning from documents by relating them to the surrounding world of significance, passing from text to context and back again until he has cleared a way through a foreign mental world.[44]

What Darnton's essay performs is this 'passing from text to context and back again' – and each time we return to the scene of the massacre it appears a little bit thicker, more culturally dense, more plural in terms of its outcomes.

---

[43] Robert Darnton, 'The Symbolic Element in History', *Journal of Modern History* 58, 1986, p. 227.
[44] Darnton, *The Great Cat Massacre*, p. 14.

Darnton's essay on the cat massacre is clearly directed at the local, detailed world of Parisian printers via a close reading of a specific text. In its aims, its commitments and self-understanding it would seem a world away from the kind of historical ambition that animated Fernand Braudel's landmark book of 1946 – *The Mediterranean and the Mediterranean World in the Age of Philip II*[45] – with its desire to tell a macro-history of a region and a time. Yet in terms of the kind of complex temporal dimension that the space is studied through, both Braudel and Darnton produce similar durational orchestrations. Where Braudel famously designated three durational levels (geological time, social time and event time) for studying the Mediterranean, Darnton performs a similar contextualization for the cat massacre. The contexts that are detailed begin with an amalgam of social and event time: this is the context of changes in the print industry at this time, and crucially changes in the role of print masters as they became owners of the shops, making it nearly impossible for journeymen to become masters of shops. The next context, which has greater duration to it, is formed by the ritualistic elements of print culture, more particularly the cultural rights-of-passage by which an apprentice might move into the world of the journeymen. Third (and most problematically from the perspective of Roger Chartier), is the trans-cultural, trans-historical symbolic and connotative world of 'cats' (vernacular references to female genitalia being the most insistent). While the increasing length of the durations is designed to thicken the ethnographic possibilities of Contat's account (to move it into anthropological time) it is here that the historicity of the text can be lost. For Chartier the singularity of the historical performance must always be kept to the forefront, and rather than relay a text into the a-historical time of symbolic culture, historiography must constitute itself by its attempt:

> To define the instances of behaviour and the rituals present in the text on the basis of the specific way in which they are assembled or produced by original invention, rather than to categorize them on the basis of remote resemblances to codified forms amongst the repertory of Western folk-culture.[46]

In Chartier's argument the 'ethnographic grain' of Darnton's historiography favours the *longue durée* of symbolic culture (though, for Darnton, this is clearly

---

[45] Fernand Braudel, *The Mediterranean and the Mediterranean World in the Age of Philip II*, translated by Siân Reynolds (Berkeley, Los Angeles and London: University of California Press, 1995) – this was first published in France in 1946.

[46] Roger Chartier, 'Text, Symbols and Frenchness: Historical Uses of Symbolic Anthropology' (1985) in *Cultural History: Between Practices and Representations,* translated by Lydia G. Cochrane (Cambridge: Polity Press, 1988), p. 109.

not a static culture); while for Chartier the cultural is more closely associated with the limited agency of historical individuals:

> The fundamental object of a history that aims at recognizing the way social actors make sense of their practices and their discourse seems to me to reside in the tension between the inventive capacities of individuals or communities and the constraints, norms, and conventions that limit (more or less strongly according to their position within relations of domination) what it is possible for them to think, say, and do.[47]

Whatever the disagreements that exist between Chartier and Darnton it seems clear that the original document (Contat's text) is not something 'full' or thick with the past; nor is it in any sense 'raw' material. It is, as Geertz would say about ethnographic work, 'somebody's interpretation about what they think they are up to', and because that interpretative context is now gone (the world of journeymen and artisan printers slaughtering cats) it is going to need thickening to make any sense of. Darnton does this by filling in a sense of context, but it is worth noting how mutable this sense of context is and how the process of 'thickening' is related to the pluralizing of the possible contexts that can be provided for understanding the cat massacre. It is this cross-stitching, between text and a range of possible contexts, that seems to characterize the operation of cultural history, and which Darnton describes as follows:

> We can read a text like Contat's not to nail down all the whos, whats, wheres, and whens of an event but rather to see what the event meant to the people who participated in it. Having worked out a tentative interpretation, we can go to the other documents – contemporary collections of proverbs, folklore, autobiographies, printing manuals, and *misères* – to test it. By moving back and forth between the narrative and the surrounding documentation, we should be able to delineate the social dimension of meaning – to 'get' the cat massacre.[48]

Historiographic understanding, for cultural historians like Darnton, Chartier and de Certeau, is not about providing a single context for making sense of a historical document. Rather it is the never-completed (or complete-able) task of multiplying the contexts, of thickening the perspectives, to arrive at fuller accounts of the past. Such thickening offers fuller accounts of the past while, *at the same time*, increasing epistemological doubt.

---

[47] Roger Chartier, *On the Edge of the Cliff: History, Language, and Practices*, translated by Lydia G. Cochrane (Baltimore: Johns Hopkins University Press, 1997), p. 20.

[48] Darnton, 'The Symbolic Element', p. 228.

Before showing how de Certeau inhabits this historiographic territory it is worth making two points. First, whether we opt for Chartier over Darnton or vice versa, when we look at historiography as a collective endeavour (rather than the work of sole authors) it is precisely this kind of discussion that characterizes it. So inasmuch as historiography is the name we give to a field, a series of institutions and the dialogues that take place within them, then historiography is essentially unfinished and constantly in the business of pluralizing contexts. Second, though, in relating to Chartier and Darnton's dialogue, we need to draw a distinction between 'specificity' (and particularity – which is what they are discussing) and singularity: singularity is irreducible, something of it will always outstrip understanding, whereas the specific suggests a knowable, definable phenomenon that can then be related to more general social and cultural contexts. For de Certeau the singularity of historical events can't simply be 'known': singularity requires multiple sidelong approaches and circling. In this there is no text–context relationship: rather the singular consists of the multiple contexts (that are also texts) that are the traces of singularity.

THE THEATRE AT LOUDUN: AN INTERSTITIAL PRACTICE

An 'event' of even greater opacity than the cat massacre was the topic of Michel de Certeau's first substantial historiographic monograph. It concerned the demonic possession of Ursuline nuns in the provincial town of Loudun, France, that first reveals itself in September 1632. In 1634 the local Father, Urbain Grandier, who it turned out was a womanizer, overly-eloquent for his social station, and seemed to have a knack for making powerful enemies, was convicted of the sorcery that had led to the possession. He was executed by incineration. The possessions, though, didn't stop with Grandier's death. Loudun became a theatre for these spectacular possessions: it showcased bravura exorcism, filled with erotic suggestion and generally aimed at tormenting the nuns; an endless procession of 'professionals' who come and go; and a hermeneutic duel between medicine and religion, science and theology, competing for control of the possessions. The whole scene could, at times, seem like a tawdry sideshow attraction. De Certeau could write bitingly as the show became shopworn:

The diabolical was becoming commonplace. It was gradually becoming profitable . . . The horror was transformed into a spectacle, the spectacle into a sermon. True, there was still weeping and wailing during the exorcisms that continued to be carried out after the execution of 'the sorcerer,' Urbain Grandier, but that did not prevent the serving of snacks to the spectators who filled the churches. (PL: 3)

As the possessions carried on, and as doctors and theologians flexed their discursive muscles over the bodies of the nuns, two protagonists of the possessions
emerged, united by an affection for one another that found its form in a long
correspondence, part of which had been edited by de Certeau in an earlier
work.[49] One protagonist is the practitioner of mystics[50] Jean-Joseph Surin, who
takes the devils into himself so as to free the nuns of torment. He is, for de
Certeau, at the heart of his studies on mystics. Surin's writings, his words, are
exemplary of mystic speech. The other protagonist is Jeanne des Anges, the chief
nun who will make a career out of her torments.

Stephen Greenblatt provides an overview of the impact of the event of the
possessions, and how they can be read as a prism refracting deep cultural
changes:

> The whole complex, interlocking structure of French society in this period
> was touched, lightly but decisively, by the writhings of a group of young
> cloistered women in a small provincial town. And linked to these individu-
> als and these institutions are obscure but momentous changes that de
> Certeau brilliantly evokes: a glacial shift in the relation between the sacred
> and the profane; a last, perversely theatrical manifestation of a certain form
> of ancient faith; a closing of the borders between the natural and the fantas-
> tic; a murderous rearguard action against an epistemological transformation.
> (Greenblatt in PL: x-xi)

De Certeau's book is not, I think, as categorical as Greenblatt makes out.
There is no ultimate epistemological victor in de Certeau's account that could
erase an opponent (even though de Certeau's conclusion seems to suggest a version closer to Greenblatt's). One way of describing de Certeau's practical theory
and theoretical practice is as interstitial: instead of operating in relation to categorical imperatives (an event or practice is either on the side of hegemony or
resistance; it is either avant-garde or conventional) de Certeau suggests a practice
that finds a place to the side of such categories. But to get a fuller sense of de
Certeau's practice we need to get more of an inkling of the formal priorities that
de Certeau pursues, get a feel for the kind of historiography that he fashions.

One of the defining characteristics of *The Possession at Loudun* is the vast
amount of textual space that is given over to quotation. At times the book resembles a montage of archival documents (letters from Grandier to his mother, legal

---

[49] Jean-Joseph Surin, *Correspondance*, edited and introduced by Michel de Certeau (Paris: Desclée
de Brouwer, 1966).

[50] De Certeau uses the term 'mystics' in a similar way to the term 'physics', i.e. to designate an
arena of knowledge, investigation and discourse. Crucially it needs to be distinguished from
'mysticism' (as a 'degraded' belief) and a nominated person (a mystic).

minutes from the Bibliothèque Nationale and so on) punctuated by de Certeau's commentary. In many chapters the documents make up half of what is written, often being allowed to continue undisturbed across three or four pages. In effect *The Possession at Loudun* is partly a dossier, and seems similar to the dossiers that Michel Foucault would go on to edit in the 1970s.[51] The inclusion of archival materials in more unadulterated forms than is usual in historiographical work performs in a number of competing and conflicting ways. In one way it allows for a polyphonic text to be produced: it is not a text that consists of a single voice (the author, historiographer) that frames and saturates the words of any other author who might get quoted. Here voices clash and disturb one another, producing a form that forcefully disallows a single assured knowledge of the past. As the title of de Certeau's introduction has it: 'History is Never Sure'. And yet these other voices don't allow us access to a past, they are not the signs of a more 'authentic', a more historical historiography. In this, as in Darnton, the uncommented document, the unadulterated archival voice doesn't produce thickness or historical communication. Wim Weymans has recently shown how *The Possession at Loudun* refuses the false lure of 'the real' that historical documents can at times offer:

> The historian and his or her sources are continually alternated. Perhaps contrary to expectations, however, the source material does not bring the reader into a more direct contact with the past. Precisely because the sources are simply presented without immediate interpretation, it becomes clear just how far from 'obvious' they can be. They often contradict each other, sometimes they are broken off, and frequently they raise questions. Only by confronting these unruly source materials with the contemporary historian's attempt to understand them can the absent past become visible.[52]

By consistently invoking and insisting on the absence of history (of any sure knowledge, of any 'place' to produce such a knowledge) a more engaged and engaging historiography is produced. This is a practice that moves documents

[51] Michel Foucault, ed., *I, Pierre Rivière, having slaughtered my mother, my sister, and my brother . . .: A Case of Parricide in the 19th Century*, translated by Frank Jellinek (Lincoln and London: University of Nebraska Press, 1975), published originally in France in 1973, and Michel Foucault, ed., *Herculine Barbin: Being the Recently Discovered Memoirs of a Nineteenth-Century French Hermaphrodite*, translated by Richard McDougall (New York: Pantheon Books, 1980), published originally in France in 1978. These 'Foucault' books, which play a very marginal part in the mass of commentary on Foucault, are the product of a collective practice: they are the work of the seminar. In this they are again related closely to de Certeau's proclivities towards more collective practices of historiographic and ethnographic work.

[52] Wim Weymans, 'Michel de Certeau and the Limits of Historical Representation', *History and Theory*, 43, 2004, p. 166.

from one place to another in the light of a sun that doesn't so much illuminate as make evident a productive lack.

An insistence that historiography deals in documents, rather than in 'the past', produces what de Certeau will call an 'interspace' and what I want to call interstitial history:

> History books begin with a present. They are constructed on the basis of two series of data: on the one hand, the 'ideas' we have about the past, ideas that are still conveyed by old material, but along pathways blazed by a new mentality; on the other hand, documents and 'archives', remains saved by chance, frozen in collections that attach meanings to them that are also new. Between the two, a difference makes it possible to disclose a historical distance . . . It is within that 'interspace' that this book on Loudun was formed. It is cracked from top to bottom, revealing the combination, or the relation, that makes history possible. Divided between commentary and archival sources, it refers to a reality that once had a living unity, and *no longer is*. It is, in short, broken by an absence. (PL: 7–8)

Such an interstitial history isn't merely unsure about where the past can be found (in the accounts of the nuns, or the doctors, perhaps the exorcists?) but also *when* the past can be found. All history has its history: a state of affairs that often exists in the work of an historian to show how inadequate previous attempts have been in setting the record straight about a period or an event (and which in professional practice is often, confusingly, referred to as 'historiography' – as if the writing of history isn't always historiographic). For de Certeau, though, the production of discourse is the historical focus and refuses to allow 'events' to have a discrete temporal dimension.[53] The 'event' of possession is produced excessively and continually from the 1630s in the form of a myriad of booklets (PL: 210–11), through to Jules Michelet's *La Sorcière* of 1862 on to Aldous Huxley's *The Devils of Loudun* of 1952 and on to de Certeau's own account. Such a lineage is not a teleology that can be accounted for in relation to the development of better scientific instruments for 'doing history': it is the mark of the hold these events have over us and of our complicity in the production of deviltry.

Such a production works systematically to refuse the lure of progress. And it is a difficult lure to refuse. It is easy enough for a historian to remind readers of the continued savagery that exists even now in so-called civilization; it is hard for an author not to distance herself or himself from such base matters, to seem

---

[53] For an example of a recent work that refuses the temporal discreteness of the 'event' (though it is a book that is critical of de Certeau) see Kristin Ross' excellent *May '68 and its Afterlives* (Chicago: University of Chicago Press, 2002).

wise to such horror and to talk implicitly from the side of progress. 'Progress' is what *The Possession at Loudun* is 'about', it is what this theatre stages – and it is performed with all due savagery, as it continues to be:

> Bound to a historical moment – that is, to the passage from religious criteria to political ones, from a cosmological and celestial anthropology to a scientific organization of natural objects ordered by the scrutiny of man – the possession of Loudun opens out also onto the strangeness of history, the reflexes triggered by its alterations, and the question that arises the moment there loom before us – different from the deviltries of former times but no less troubling – the new social figures of the other. (PL: 228)

The Possession at Loudun is an example of interdisciplinary cultural history that consists of a 'weaving together of Christian mysticism, strenuous political and sociological analysis, psychoanalysis, and scrupulous attentiveness to the voice of the Other' (Greenblatt in PL: xi). In many ways it is a reply to the 'hermeneutics of suspicion' that would ask: 'once we recognize that there can be no explanatory horizon which is not itself implicated in the field we wish to explain, how do we justify the task of interpretation?'[54] The answer to this is a practice of plural, unfinished, yet fastidiously detailed analysis:

> Analyze initially how a diabolic 'place' – a diabolic scene – was organized through the play of social, political, religious, or epistemological tensions, and how this composition of place, this production of theatrical space, enabled a reclassification of social representation to function as shifts in frames of reference. (WH: 245–6)

The Possession at Loudun is the interstitial practice that is a reply that anticipates the authors of *Telling the Truth about History*, who want to find a way out of the opposition of objectivity and subjectivity:

> Nineteenth-century philosophy so overdichotomized the difference between objectivity and subjectivity that it is difficult, when using their terms, to modify the absolute doubt that springs from the recognition that human minds are not mirrors and recorders. Denying the absolutism of one age, the doubters, however, seem oblivious to the danger of inventing a new absolutism based upon subjectivity and relativism.[55]

[54] Claire Colebrook, *New Literary Histories: New Historicism and Contemporary Criticism* (Manchester: Manchester University Press, 1997), p. viii.
[55] Joyce Appleby, Lynn Hunt and Margaret Jacob, *Telling the Truth about History* (New York: W. W. Norton, 1994), p. 247.

Read alongside *The Possession at Loudun*, de Certeau's important essay 'The Historiographical Operation' reads as an epistemological explanation of his historiographic practice. *The Possession at Loudun* provides access to a practice articulated by a theory (the singularity of the event; the plurality and mutability of context; the long uneven and unending work of modernization; the continuation of belief into modernity and so on). 'The Historiographical Operation' allows us to know how such a theoretical practice works, to know how theory articulates practice. It is the elucidation of that relationship that constitutes de Certeau's epistemology: 'what is a theory, if not the articulation of a practice? And what is an epistemology, if not a discourse that elucidates that relationship?'[56]

The epistemological and theoretical architecture that underpins this practice has a central but invisible heart. Psychoanalysis is a continued reference point in de Certeau's work. But it would be hard to find any scholar in France in the second half of the twentieth century who didn't include a familiarity with psychoanalysis as part of their armoury of erudition. With de Certeau, though, psychoanalysis doesn't make for a display of erudition; nor is it a diagnostic practice that de Certeau articulates. It is because psychoanalysis lies buried in de Certeau, as a structural yet de-structuring ingredient, that it is so important for an understanding of his work. And it is because his work as a historian insists that history deals fundamentally in death that it is fundamentally psychoanalytic:

> What characterizes a work as 'historical,' what allows one to say that one is 'making history' (we 'produce' history as we manufacture automobiles), is not the conscientious application of established rules (although such rigor is necessary). It is rather, the operation that creates a space of signs proportionate to an absence; the structures the reconnaissance of the past not in the manner of a present possession or yet another science but in the form of a *discourse structured by a missing presence*; that, through its processing of materials presently dispersed in our own time, opens up a place in language and a reference unto death . . . [57]

Psychoanalysis is a central ingredient for de Certeau's work, not because his work shares the same symbolic economy as psychoanalysis (it doesn't), but because psychoanalysis transforms epistemological critique (the difficulty of knowing the past, or the unconscious in any direct way) into an opportunity for producing thicker, more replete knowledge.

---

[56] de Certeau, 'A Transitional Epistemology: Paul Veyne', Revel and Hunt, eds, *Histories*, p. 313.
[57] de Certeau, 'History and Mysticism' in Revel and Hunt, eds, *Histories*, p. 440.

CHAPTER 3

The Oceanic Rumble of the Ordinary: Psychoanalysis and Culture

Normally, strange things circulate discreetly below our streets. But a crisis will suffice for them to rise up, as if swollen by flood waters, pushing aside manhole covers, invading the cellars, then spreading through the towns. It always comes as a surprise when the nocturnal erupts into broad daylight. What it reveals is an underground existence, an inner resistance that has never been broken. This lurking force infiltrates the lines of tension within the society it threatens. Suddenly it magnifies them; using the means, the circuitry already in place, but reemploying them in the service of an anxiety that comes from afar, unanticipated. It breaks through barriers, flooding the social chamber and opening new pathways that, once the flow of its passage has subsided, will leave behind a different landscape and a different order. (PL: 1)

PRACTITIONERS OF THE UNCONSCIOUS: EXTRA-MURAL PSYCHOANALYSIS

Auditors of the unfinished business of the twentieth century should leave a little space to note the unrealized potential of psychoanalysis for the study of culture. In this note they might want to point to Michel de Certeau's work as a valiant and yet unfinished attempt to make psychoanalysis unrecognizable, to set about altering it, and in doing so make it into a science of culture rather than maintain it as a science of the subject that can then be applied to culture and society. De Certeau was a founder member of the *École freudienne de Paris* (EFP), a psychoanalytic school established by Jacques Lacan as a response to the persistent exclusion of Lacanian psychoanalysis from the International Psychoanalytic Association.[1] As Jacqueline Rose and Moustafa Safouan have argued, the

---

[1] For a detailed account of the various internecine struggles in French psychoanalysis see Elisabeth Roudinesco, *Jacques Lacan & Co.: A History of Psychoanalysis in France 1925–1985*, translated by Jeffrey Mehlman (London: Free Association Books, 1990) and Elisabeth Roudinesco, *Jacques Lacan: An Outline of a Life and a History of a System of Thought*, translated by Barbara Bray

institutional form of this school, its attempt to find a psychoanalytic forum for its members, was a central part of the school's project.[2] De Certeau remained a member from its inauguration in June 1964 (performed by Lacan via a tape-recorded message) to its acrimonious dissolution in 1980 (precipitated in part by Michèle Montrelay's insistence that the school provide space for discussing feminist issues – a position actively supported by de Certeau[3]). The EFP consisted of many analysts and trainees from a previously Lacanian-orientated school (*Société française de psychoanalyse*), as well as a raft of new members that included Michel de Certeau, Michèle Montrelay, Luce Irigaray, Félix Guattari, François Roustang and Cornelius Castoriadis. Though most of these members either were, or would become, practising psychoanalysts, the EFP was not closed to those who, like de Certeau, were interested in Lacanian psychoanalysis for other reasons.

In 1968 Serge Leclaire (a psychoanalyst and member of the EFP) worked to establish a psychoanalytic enclave within the experimental *Universitaire de Vincennes-Paris VIII* (a university that was formulated in the general fallout of the May events of that year). This enclave was within the philosophy department and consisted of a number of 'free electives' (courses students could take which were not constitutive of their 'majority', for instance, philosophy or literature).[4] Seminars were taught exclusively by members of the EFP – by Michel de Certeau, and others – in 'a space in the university reserved for practitioners of the unconscious, as far removed as possible from psychology'.[5] The seminars at Vincennes 'established for the first time in a French university a psychoanalytic teaching stripped of any debt to medicine or psychology'.[6] While psychoanalysis had always been amenable to disciplinary migration, the EFP at Vincennes institutionalized psychoanalysis as a science that could drift free of its moorings in medicine and psychology and set up shop as a branch of philosophy, literary analysis, historiography and so on. At the same time, and even more controversially, the EFP was concentrating (as perhaps the term 'school' implies) on instituting a number of changes to the way psychoanalytic training

(Cambridge: Polity Press, 1997). These two books offer the most thorough treatment of the French national context of psychoanalysis and the charismatic figure of Jacques Lacan. For a shorter account see Sherry Turkle, *Psychoanalytic Politics: Jacques Lacan and Freud's French Revolution* (New York: Basic Books, 1978).

[2] Moustafa Safouan, *Jacques Lacan and the Question of Psychoanalytic Training*, translated and introduced by Jacqueline Rose (Houndmills: Macmillan, 2000).

[3] Roudinesco, *Jacques Lacan & Co.*, p. 651.

[4] It would later become 'The Department of Psychoanalysis', achieving relative autonomy within the university.

[5] Roudinesco, *Jacques Lacan & Co.*, p. 553.

[6] Roudinesco, *Jacques Lacan & Co.*, p. 552–3.

was conceived, as well as altering the condition of the analytic session (the 50-minute hour).

For all his considerable involvement and commitment to psychoanalysis, there are not in de Certeau's work the psychoanalytic signposts that we might expect to find. There is, for instance, a marked refusal to use the diagnostics of psychopathology to explain and characterize situations or individuals (a practice that is most insistently seen in Anglophone film studies in the late 1970s and 1980s where relationships, including the relationship between the abstracted spectator and the screen characters, were constantly defined in terms of narcissism, masochism and so on). Nor is the technical vocabulary of psychoanalysis more generally put into play. The mystery of the absence (in the work) of a presence (institutional commitments) is broached by de Certeau in *The Mystic Fable*:

> Seventeen years of experience at the École freudienne de Paris have not produced a competency that it would suffice merely to 'apply' to historical cases, but rather an awareness of theoretical procedures (Freudian and Lacanian) capable of bringing into play what the language of the mystics had already articulated and capable of displacing and amplifying its effects. (MF: 9)

The phrasing is slightly disingenuous: it is not competency that is lacking (as Wlad Godzich notes in his foreword to *Heterologies*, de Certeau had advanced training in a range of disciplines, including psychoanalysis), but a belief that 'application' is not the appropriate (or the theoretically productive) recourse for a psychoanalytically orientated approach to the study of culture. We have, then, an inkling of how psychoanalysis might be directed in the study of culture: as a theoretical procedure; or as a processual awareness.[7] And here, de Certeau starts to articulate a position in regard to what is one of the crucially unanswered questions of the twentieth century – namely – what might become of psychoanalysis once it is addressed to the communal, social and virtual realm we call culture, rather than to the monadic individual of classical analysis? Of course, there is no lack of possible answers here (many of them supplied by Freud) – but what might make these answers unsatisfying is that they often seem simply to extend the purview of psychoanalysis while maintaining the same interpretative moves: now a whole society is narcissistic rather than an individual.[8] The game remains the same, while the board is considerably extended.

---

[7] See also Verena Andermatt Conley's essay 'Processual Practices', *South Atlantic Quarterly* 100, 2, 2001, pp. 483–500.

[8] An easy target here would be a book such as Christopher Lasch's *The Culture of Narcissism: American Life in an Age of Diminishing Expectations* (New York: Norton, 1979).

What makes cultural psychoanalysis 'unfinished business' is precisely the lack of transformation as it moves from the realm of the individual to the social. In part the unaltered continuation of psychoanalysis, as it moves from the 'couch' into 'culture', is due to the assumed universalism that attaches itself to psycho-analytic concepts, and makes it easy for psychoanalysis to inhabit the study of culture 'wholesale':

> In both ethnology and history, certain studies demonstrate that the general use of psychoanalytical concepts runs the risk of blossoming into a new rhetoric. The concepts are thus transformed into figures of style. Recourse to the death of the father, to Oedipus or to transference, can be used for any-thing and everything. Since these Freudian concepts are supposed to explain all human endeavour, we have little difficulty driving them into the most obscure regions of history. Unfortunately, they are nothing other than dec-orative tools if their only goal amounts to a designation or discreet obfusca-tion of what the historian does not understand. They circumscribe what cannot be explained, but they do not explain it. They avow an unawareness. They are earmarked for areas where an economic or a sociological explan-ation forcibly leaves something aside. A literature of ellipsis, an art of expounding on scraps and remnants, or the feeling of a question – yes; but a Freudian analysis – no. (WH 288–9)

For de Certeau, this aspect of the cultural life of psychoanalytic terms is another form of cultural pacification (it follows the logic of application): it marshals oth-erness and difference and corrals them into conformity.

In pointing to the success psychoanalysis has found in exporting concepts like 'the death-of-the-father' into the study of history and literature, de Certeau acknowledges what is, I think, the central structural tension in the possibility of cultural psychoanalysis. On the one hand psychoanalysis, through case studies, through theorizing, has found time and again the same forms: here castration, there envy, for instance. The accumulative weight of these formulations is enor-mous and seems to spread unconditionally – could there have been a time when a boy-child's path into manhood wasn't structured according to the myth of Oedipus? Because certain Freudian concepts seem eternal they seem generally applicable and endlessly exportable. On the other hand what is profound in both Freudianism and Lacanianism is the determined necessity of refusing a cul-tural stability between word and meaning, symbol and symbolism, that could allow for the export of generally valid formulations. Writing in 1968 Serge Leclaire would suggest that semiotic instability (an instability not only putting in crisis the relationship between signifier and signified, but also the relation-ship between sign and referent) was at the heart of psychoanalysis:

One and the same text, or better yet one and the same letter, both constitutes and represents unconscious desire. In its ultimate aim, psychoanalysis
thereby puts into question the common and convenient distinction between
a term of reality and representation. This may be surprising even to those
most familiar with psychoanalysis.[9]

Not only are the 'things' found in dreams – trains, tunnels, cigars, etc. – not
part of a lexicon that could allow them to be simply substituted for sexual
organs, for instance, they can also simply be bits of the material real world. But
the real world in all its manifest 'there-ness' is also a virtual realm where 'things'
can generate and convey all sorts of psychical investments. For Leclaire this
means that:

One may thus see the double requirement imposed on the psychoanalyst:
on the one hand, he [*sic passim*] must have at his disposal a system of reference, a theory that can permit him to order the mass of material he gath-
ers without prior discrimination; on the other hand, he must set aside any
system of reference precisely to the extent that adherence to a set of theories necessarily leads him, whether he likes it or not, to privilege certain
elements.[10]

Thus knowledge needs to be set aside even if it can be called on at a moment's
notice. Leclaire's 'double requirement' though is an impossible trick to institute: how would you suspend interpretative schemas (whilst simultaneously
being informed by them) such that you could hear the singularity of the
other? But it is this 'double requirement' – to be theoretically informed while
simultaneously letting go of theories – that is necessary for attending to the
singular.

To stop cultural psychoanalysis trading in clichés, in ossified diagnostic forms
(psychopathology, most crucially), it needs to reclaim what Jean Laplanche
insists is the profound anti-hermeneutics of psychoanalysis. For Laplanche this
is the essence of the psychoanalytic project and its greatest challenge. This is
psychoanalysis when it is conceived of as a methodological imagination dedicated to the practice of free association, designed to make a space for the unconscious to speak. Laplanche shows how the refusal of a hermeneutic 'key' is crucial
to Freud's *Interpretation of Dreams* and how his 'analysis' of a specimen dream

---

[9] Serge Leclaire, *Psychoanalysing: On the Order of the Unconscious and the Practice of the Letter*,
translated by Peggy Kamuf (Stanford: Stanford University Press, 1998), p. 38 – first published
in France in 1968.
[10] Leclaire, Psychoanalysing, pp. 14–15.

(his own dream of 23–24 July 1895 – the dream of 'Irma's Injection'[11]) works precisely against developing an interpretative grid for future dream-works:

> Here Freud presents us with twenty pages of association, of deciphering – but without any codes, certainly without the one-to-one correspondences; twenty pages of unbinding (*Entbindung*) operating on a more or less coherent narrative of the dream. The associative pathways are followed, the points of intersection noted, but no synthesis is proposed.[12]

The ambitiousness of de Certeau's project becomes clear if it is seen as offering an unbinding of culture similar to Freud's unbinding of the dream. Freud's revolutionary understanding of the dream-work emerged from a simple refusal to supply a general lexicon of dream symbols. Recognizing the dream as both opaque and singular, Freud refused to 'treat dreams as a kind of cryptography in which each sign can be translated into another sign having a known meaning, in accordance with a fixed key'.[13] Opting instead for an approach that insists that 'all the material making up the content of a dream is in some way derived from experience',[14] Freud is faced with the impossibility of a general interpretation of dreams. Freud takes as his remit, not the general meanings of dreams (each one is too particular), but the general rules of combination and substitution by which a dream can be seen as meaningful in the first place. He offers a poetics of the dream-work (a logics of dreaming) that allow the forms of figuration that orchestrate dreaming to become apparent. Pointing out the figural operations of condensation and displacement (which famously get translated into metaphor and metonym in Lacan's language-centred psychoanalysis), the dream is seen as a rebus that can only be understood in relation to a complexity of history and desire. Here the dream content is always singular, unrepeatable, while the dream form is posited as common to the material practice of dreaming.

But if the mobilising of psychoanalytic interpretations (or its extended analogies) is to be studiously avoided, what is left? What precisely is left of psychoanalysis once its interpretative architecture (a Freudian analysis) is jettisoned? Can a practice of studying culture be considered 'psychoanalytic' if it eradicates the interpretative economy of 'castration', 'Oedipus' and so on? What, in this context, would be 'the feeling of a question'? What sort of a question could this be? In this context and as a useful descriptor of de Certeau's practice it might be that psycho*analysis* needs to be thought of in the light of unbinding rather than

---

[11] Sigmund Freud, *The Interpretation of Dreams* (1900) translated by James Strachey (Harmondsworth: Penguin, 1976), pp. 180–99.

[12] Jean Laplanche, 'Psychoanalysis as Anti-Hermeneutics', *Radical Philosophy* 79, 1996, p. 8.

[13] Freud, *The Interpretation of Dreams*, p. 171.

[14] Freud, *The Interpretation of Dreams*, p. 69.

interpretation and that, as we shall see, this is best thought about in relation to the actual analytic session.

Laplanche, in his 1987 book *New Foundations for Psychoanalysis*, works to reposition what he calls 'extra-mural psychoanalysis' to a central position within the psychoanalytic project itself. His examples of extra-mural psychoanalysis are those works of Freud dealing with religion, civilization, taboos, art and so on. By calling this writing 'extra-mural' Laplanche wants to draw a distinction between a psychoanalysis immersed in questions of culture and a psychoanalysis that is applied, like a ready-made, to the cultural. This is Laplanche's characterization of extra-mural psychoanalysis: 'in works on so-called extra-mural psychoanalysis, *psychoanalysis invades the cultural*, not only as a form of thought or a doctrine, but as a *mode of being*.'[15] It is this mode of being, or less mysteriously, this characteristic way of operating, that I want to examine here. By distinguishing doctrinal and interpretative positions from operational ones, Laplanche opens up a space for rethinking the possibilities of cultural psychoanalysis. And it is in this space that I think Michel de Certeau can most productively be seen – and in a way that could allow us to reconceive a relationship between psychoanalysis and culture; a relationship which leaves neither of these terms untouched. It is part of the larger project of de Certeau and part of the insistence that a logic of alteration supersedes a logic of application.

While Laplanche's characterization of extra-mural psychoanalysis is designed to designate work that emerges from psychoanalysis itself, it is worth expanding on within a more culturalist context – even if this means pushing in a direction that Laplanche himself doesn't follow. The form of cultural studies that does deploy a range of ready-made psychopathologies for diagnosing cultural forms and forces should necessarily be questioned as to the migration of psychoanalysis from the clinical to the cultural. What, after all, is at stake when someone diagnoses a culture as narcissistic? What is the status of 'culture' in such a designation? And what would happen to psychoanalysis if we were to conceive of the cultural in a way that is not amenable to such diagnostics? What if we insist that it is unproductive or even foolhardy to use a lexicon fashioned for describing and explaining a monadic subject for diagnosing the heterogeneous plurality of practices that gets called culture? What, then, would be the point of psychoanalysis' engagement with culture? Perhaps this is just another way of asking what is a psychoanalytic mode of being? What, in other words, would be left over if psychoanalysis didn't have immediate recourse to its hardwon conceptual and interpretative frameworks? Or, to put it more starkly, what could psychoanalysis *be* if not its doctrines and forms of thought?

---

[15] Jean Laplanche, *New Foundations for Psychoanalysis*, translated by David Macey (Oxford: Blackwell, 1989), p. 12. Italics in the original.

This is where de Certeau's writing has to be clearly distinguished from the writing associated with the cultural psychoanalysis that can be seen in the work of the Frankfurt School, or Julia Kristeva, or Cornelius Castoriadis, or Slavoj Žižek.[16] There is not space here to discuss all the very many strands of cultural psychoanalysis, but it might be worth very briefly looking at Žižek's position – partly because Žižek appears as the brightest star in a firmament of cultural psychoanalysis as it is presently being imagined. Over the last 20 years Žižek has produced a vast array of texts that mobilize commercial culture (in the main) to elucidate the importance of Lacanian psychoanalysis for understanding modern life, and more particularly why we appear to desire our own domination, or at least why we seem incapable of shrugging off such domination.[17] In words he's borrowed from the German cultural critic Peter Sloterdijk, Žižek is interested in how people believe what they believe, and act how they act, not when they are in the grip of false consciousness, for instance, but when 'they know very well what they are doing, but still they are doing it'.[18] Žižek's is a politicization of Lacanianism inasmuch as he mobilizes psychoanalysis so as to understand present-day racism (anti-Semitism is a theme he frequently returns to). Important and difficult though this work is, here I just want to look at the way Žižek sets up a contact between psychoanalysis and his 'cultural' examples (jokes, Hitchcock's films, the novels of Ruth Rendell and so on).[19]

The most uncharitable reading of Žižek from this perspective would claim him as merely a proselytizer of Lacanianism, someone who simply deploys commercial, familiar culture to effect the best possible take up of Lacan's ideas. In

---

[16] For the Frankfurt School and psychoanalysis see Martin Jay, *The Dialectical Imagination: A History of the Frankfurt School and the Institute of Social Research 1923–1950* (London: Heinemann, 1973) – Chapter 3; and Joel Whitebook, *Perversion and Utopia: A Study in Psychoanalysis and Critical Theory* (Cambridge: MIT Press, 1996). For Julia Kristeva the quickest route to her cultural psychoanalysis is probably by going to Ross Mitchell Guberman, ed., *Julia Kristeva Interviews* (New York: Columbia University Press, 1996). For Castoriadis the classic text is *The Imaginary Institution of Society*, translated by Kathleen Blamey (Cambridge and Oxford: Polity Press, 1987) – first published in France in 1975; but see also his collection *World in Fragments: Writings on Politics, Society, Psychoanalysis, and the Imagination*, translated by David Ames Curtis (Stanford: Stanford University Press, 1997).

[17] There is a burgeoning secondary literature on Žižek. For a useful introduction which also includes an extensive bibliography of Žižek's work (though such bibliographies are usually out of date within months – such is the publishing output of Žižek) see Sarah Kay, *Žižek: A Critical Introduction* (Cambridge: Polity, 2003).

[18] Slavoj Žižek, *The Sublime Object of Ideology* (London: Verso, 1989), p. 29. The formula is from Peter Sloterdijk, *Critique of Cynical Reason*, translated by Michael Eldred (London: Verso, 1988) [published in Germany in 1983], who titles his first chapter 'Cynicism: The Twilight of False Consciousness'.

[19] See Slavoj Žižek, *Looking Awry: An Introduction to Jacques Lacan through Popular Culture* (Cambridge: MIT Press, 1991).

this he is simply a psychoanalytic theorist concerned with explanations of the subject, using cultural texts for exemplification (in the same way that Freud, for instance, would use E.T.A. Hoffmann to discuss the uncanny). What this suggests is that psychoanalytic theory (its interpretative architecture) will always take precedence over other cultural work, so much so that it is hard to imagine Žižek being interested in cultural materials unless they *already* articulate the themes central to Lacanian psychoanalysis. On the other hand it is clear that Žižek at least treats these cultural texts seriously as articulators of psychical forces rather than as objects in need of theoretical (psychoanalytic) interpretation (in this his position is similar to the one that de Certeau adopts). As far as this goes Žižek's cultural psychoanalysis manages to steer a path away from a logic of application: he doesn't analyse popular culture by applying psychoanalysis. Instead, texts are chosen because they can explicate psychoanalytic theory, which also means that the cultural is never in a position where it could alter psychoanalysis – in many ways it is used simply to buttress ideas already staked out in psychoanalytic theory.

What distinguishes the cultural psychoanalysis of Žižek from the more buried psychoanalysis of de Certeau is also what allows de Certeau's work to be potentially more productive for generating a culturally orientated approach for unbinding the communal, material and virtual realm that is culture. Because in the end Žižek is dedicated to explaining the social via a theory of the subject he is inevitably held in the grip of, an 'identity' model of culture (though one that is subtle and interestingly provocative). Michel de Certeau's work is not, by comparison, based around a theory of the subject, and, as Ian Buchanan notes, it also resolutely refuses to be based around notions of identification.[20] When something like the unconscious speaks in de Certeau's books (say in *The Possession at Loudun*[21]) it is neither the unconscious that *belongs* to particular social agents and binds them to their personal history, nor is it a general unconscious that stretches across time and cultures that might be found in Jung. It is the unconscious in its multiform singularity that precisely doesn't belong to anyone but animates the peculiar binds and unbindings that hold us and reject us in the name of culture (in all its historicity). As far as this goes the unconscious, in the study and analysis of culture, is precisely that which doesn't belong to any*one* – it is multitudinous, unstoppably plural.

---

[20] Ian Buchanan, 'De Certeau and Cultural Studies', *new formations*, 31, 1996, p. 182.

[21] For Dominick LaCapra 'de Certeau's powerful and insufficiently recognized *Possession at Loudun*', is where he 'undertakes perhaps his most compelling attempt to relate history and psychoanalysis in a micrological study of the past' (Dominic LaCapra, *History in Transit: Experience, Identity, Critical Theory* [Ithaca and London: Cornell University Press, 2004], p. 3).

PSYCHOANALYSIS AND HISTORIOGRAPHY

The relationship between Michel de Certeau and psychoanalysis is at its most intriguing when we remember that de Certeau's main production is in the realm of historiography and when we note the evident antipathy that psychoanalysis seems to have for history (as a production that insists on the *changing* nature of the world). Dylan Evans, in a useful essay on Lacan and historicism, suggests that:

> In most of Freud's writings, for example, it is as if the dimension of history had been suspended, so that it is easy to see the model of the ego, the id and superego as an eternal Platonic form, a shining jewel invulnerable to the vagaries of time. In so far as history is discussed, it is always in terms of a myth of origins which anchors the unchangeability of the psyche in a primal crime of biblical proportions.[22]

Indeed it could be argued that psychoanalysis in its most classical and familiar form simply negates anything that might be called historical: 'if we employ psychoanalysis in its most pristine state, its most traditional form, we run the risk of eliminating history in the name of studying it. That is because the two classical psychoanalytic approaches to history (however modified more recently) are the *Totem and Taboo* and the individual-psychopathological models.'[23]

As a historical narrative Freudian psychoanalysis begins on the edge of prehistory with the first 'known humans' being defined by the sort of social-sexual organization that is still found today. In the very first words of *Totem and Taboo* we read:

> Prehistoric man, in the various stages of his development, is known to us through the inanimate monuments and implements which he has left behind, through the information about his art, his religion and his attitude towards life which has come to us either directly or by way of tradition handed down in legends, myths and fairy tales, and through the relics of his mode of thought which survive in our own manners and customs. But apart from this, in a certain sense he is still our contemporary.[24]

[22] Dylan Evans, 'Historicism and Lacanian Theory', *Radical Philosophy* 79, 1996, p. 35.

[23] Robert Jay Lifton, 'Whose Psychohistory?' in Peter Brooks and Alex Woloch, eds, *Whose Freud? The Place of Psychoanalysis in Contemporary Culture* (New Haven and London: Yale University Press, 2000), p. 222.

[24] Sigmund Freud, 'Totem and Taboo' (1913), *The Penguin Freud Library 13: The Origins of Religion* (Harmondsworth: Penguin, 1990), p. 53.

For a historian interested in dynamic and detailed changes in society and culture the presumed eternal state of castration anxiety, for instance, might seem the very essence of a non-historical attitude. More amenable to a historical sensitivity would be Žižek's position: 'historicity proper involves a dialectical relationship to some historical kernel that stays the same – not as an underlying Essence but as a rock that trips up every attempt to integrate it into the symbolic order.'[25] A dialectic between the tenacity of 'the age-old' and the shifting ground of the 'now' might well furnish a useful historical attitude; yet there is no reason why psychoanalytic historiography should simply rest with this duality of durations and why it couldn't be more hospitable to a fuller orchestration of different temporalities.

It might, at this stage, be useful to distinguish four types of psychoanalytical historiography. First would be the historiography that comes from 'extra-mural' psychoanalysis proper, and tells either 'eternal' history or a sort of pre-historical history: e.g. the establishing of incest taboos, the birth of religion, the primary repression that constitutes society and so on.[26] Here historical change *can* (just) be imagined, but such change becomes impossible to recover or effectively imagine. Thus Lacan can write:

> Think about the origin of language. We imagine that there must have been a time when people on this earth began to speak. So we admit of an emergence. But from the moment that the specific structure of the emergence is grasped, we find it absolutely impossible to speculate on what preceded it other than by the symbols which were always applicable. What appears to be new thus always seems to extend itself indefinitely into perpetuity, prior to itself. We cannot, through thought, abolish a new order. This applies to anything whatsoever, including the origin of the world.[27]

Second would be the historiographical work that 'applies' psychoanalysis to explain the choices made by social and historical agents. This has mostly taken the form of the extended case history where historical figures (Leonardo da Vinci, for instance) or more contemporary public figures are scrutinized *as*

[25] Slavoj Žižek, *The Metastases of Enjoyment: Six Essays on Women and Causality* (London: Verso, 1994), p. 199.

[26] The key texts from Freud are: *Totem and Taboo* (1913); *The Future of an Illusion* (1927); *Civilization and its Discontents* (1929–30); *Moses and Monotheism* (1934–8) and can be found in the *Penguin Freud Library Volumes 12* and *13* (Harmondsworth: Penguin, 1990 and 1991).

[27] Jacques Lacan, *The Seminar of Jacques Lacan: Book II, The Ego in Freud's Theory and in the Technique of Psychoanalysis, 1954–1955*, translated by Sylvana Tomaselli (Cambridge: Cambridge University Press, 1988), p. 5.

though they were an analysand (a client, patient, etc.).[28] Third we could situate a more cultural psychoanalysis where a psychoanalytic approach is used to explain specific social forms (say urban racism in the nineteenth century). A prime example of this is the way that Julia Kristeva's psychoanalytic notion of abjection has been used for the purpose of cultural history.[29] Fourth, and for my purposes most importantly, are the works that 'do history' with a psychoanalytic interest and where the process of combining the two leaves both substantially altered. It is in this group I'd want to place de Certeau, but to give a flavour of its possibilities I want to mention, briefly, another historian who has done much to alter the terms for the commerce between history and psychoanalysis.

Carolyn Steedman's *Landscape for a Good Woman: The Story of Two Lives* is an attempt to tell the story of her mother and her mother's 'affective politics' – the cultural and social envy that seemed to drive a working-class woman to holding Conservative political affiliations.[30] One thing worth mentioning straight away is that Steedman's reference to psychoanalysis is not the determining instance of her project: she is not doing history so as to understand psychoanalysis. Initially and profoundly psychoanalysis is used operationally. It allows Steedman to begin by recounting a dream she had of her mother and to ask what kind of historical evidence this is. For positivist historians, of course, this would be the ultimate example of unreliable evidence, but for someone interested in historicizing the affective histories of class and gender, say, the way that hatred, fear, enjoyment, shame get mobilized in people's lives, then a dream might be extremely fertile historical testimony. (Dreams might also be thought of as providing privileged access to the cultural in that they are peculiarly coded forms, and as suggested in the last chapter, such opacity rather than impeding cultural history should be considered cultural history's object.) Similarly it takes Steedman into an epistemological realm where her mother's lies about her early life, rather than disbarring her as an informant of oral history, become key elements in building up a picture of a historically located person, whose very complexity spilt out into other histories (the history of domestic service, for instance).

[28] Again sticking with Freud, the classic works would include the 'case studies' (particularly *Psychoanalytic Notes on an Autobiographical Account of a Case of Paranoia* [1910]) and the writings on Leonardo and Michelangelo. But also see Sigmund Freud and William C. Bullitt, *Thomas Woodrow Wilson, Twenty-Eighth President of the United States: A Psychological Study* (London: Weidenfeld and Nicolson, 1967) for this approach at its most problematic.

[29] Julia Kristeva, *Powers of Horror: An Essay on Abjection*, translated by Leon S. Roudiez (New York: Columbia University Press, 1982) – which has been the theoretical resource for more specifically historical works such as Peter Stallybrass and Allon White, *The Politics and Poetics of Transgression* (London: Methuen, 1986) and Mary Russo, *The Female Grotesque: Risk, Excess and Modernity* (London and New York: Routledge, 1994).

[30] Carolyn Steedman, *Landscape for a Good Woman: The Story of Two Lives* (London: Virago Press, 1986).

So one way of describing Steedman's project in *Landscape for a Good Woman* is that it sets out with an epistemological problem: how to go about knowing those aspects of the past that seem most recalcitrant to documentation: the world of affects and emotions. Here psychoanalysis is not the epistemological answer (the science that solves the dilemma of recovering historical affect). Rather psychoanalysis is relevant and useful because it too shares the epistemological dilemma of knowing the truth about a realm where truth (or testability) seems to be the least operable value.

For de Certeau history and psychoanalysis must meet under conditions that entail epistemological upheavals, which will alter the field of both psychoanalysis and historiography. In an essay on the history of psychoanalysis ('Psychoanalysis and Its History') de Certeau most clearly elaborates the convergences and divergences between the two fields:

> Psychoanalysis and historiography . . . have two different ways of distributing the *space of memory*. They conceive of the relationship between the past and the present differently. Psychoanalysis recognises the past *in* the present; historiography places them one *beside* the other. Psychoanalysis treats the relation as one of imbrication (one in the place of the other), of repetition (one reproduces the other in another form), of the equivocal and of the *quiproquo* (What 'takes the place' of what? Everywhere, there are games of masking, reversal, and ambiguity). Historiography conceives the relation as one of succession (one after the other), correlation (greater or lesser proximities), cause and effect (one follows from the other), and disjunction (either one or the other), but not both at the same time). (H: 4)

Here psychoanalysis provides a different model of time and space – it is not based on either–or (either here or there) but on and–and (here and there, then and now). In many ways, then, psychoanalysis can disturb the smooth surety of linear time and produce more uncomfortable and productive notions of time for history – ones more imbricated with the criticism of conventional history (discussed in the last chapter).

Psychoanalysis and (new) historiography face the same field of problems: 'to elaborate (how? where?) different ways of thinking, and by so doing overcome violence (the conflicts and contingencies of history), including the violence of thought itself' (H: 5). Psychoanalytic historiography, then, is not (necessarily) history that applies a barrage of psychoanalytic interpretations to the field of history (psycho-history). At its most productive psychoanalytic historiography is the temporal orientation and sensitivity that is responsive to the epistemological conditions of writing history (writing the dead). It offers a different way of imagining the past in relation to the present: a relationship where imbrication and equivocation take the place of fixed lines of causality and movement.

For de Certeau a historiography that could be imbricated with psychoanalysis would be intimately familiar with the history of psychoanalysis, not simply as a changing conceptual field, but more interestingly as a changing institutional and practical field, as a clinical field:

> A psychoanalysis of history must adopt an inward orientation, accepting the necessary work of elucidating the meaning of the gaps in the theory on the following points: a) the relations of transference and the conflictual ones upon which analytic discourse is constructed, b) the functioning of Freudian associations or schools, for example their forms of licensure and the nature of the power inherent in 'holding' the position of analyst, and c) the possibilities of establishing analytic procedures within psychiatric institutions, where psychoanalysis, after emerging from its offices dedicated to a privileged clientele, would come into contact with the administrative alliances of politics and therapy, as well as the popular murmur of madness. (H: 14)

De Certeau asks historians to engage in psychoanalysis not as a dynamic field of explanation, but as a clinical field (that is, ultimately, as an operational field), and the reason he does this, I want to argue, is because it is here that the possibility of a different relationship between writing and speaking is being imagined, that a utopian space is being opened up for communicating differently, for listening to the communicating vessel otherwise.

A FEELING FOR A QUESTION: LISTENING OTHERWISE

Jacques Lacan's formulation that the unconscious, as it reveals itself in analytic phenomena, 'is structured like a language' can be seen as a Copernican revolution (of sorts), bringing together Freud and the insights of linguistic philosophers and theorists such as Roman Jakobson.[31] In this light psychoanalysis becomes a linguistically-based science: 'Psychoanalysis should be the science of language inhabited by the subject. From the Freudian point of view man is the subject captured and tortured by language.'[32] The linguistic impulse of Lacanianism probably did much to make it habitable for text-based forms of

---

[31] Jacques Lacan, *The Psychoses: The Seminar of Jacques Lacan, Book III, 1955–56*, translated by Russell Grigg (London and New York: Routledge, 1993), p. 167.
[32] Lacan, *The Psychoses*, p. 243.

cultural enquiry (literary studies, film studies),[33] and Lacan's dense, allusive (and for many, illusive) style of writing probably seemed more approachable to those more used to studying Mallarmé than to those for whom Freud's crisply erudite 'after-dinner-speech-ness' was a model for psychoanalytic writing. The Lacanian world was filled with even more new technical terms than Freud and his colleagues had managed to generate, which Lacan then cocooned in a network of algebraic formulations, mathematical frameworks and thickly poetic figurations.[34] The allure of the Lacanian vocabulary (its esotericism) has worked, I think, to marginalize consideration of Lacanian psychoanalysis as a clinical and pedagogic *practice*.[35]

What is most often lost, as psychoanalysis migrates into other disciplines, is the nature of its practice – its means and mode of production. What migrate are 'concepts', ready-made interpretations (interpretations of interpretations; over-refined matter) that can only follow the logic of application as they connect to social and cultural materials. What is left behind is a 'form of attention'.[36] In the 1960s, the more everyday aspects of Lacanianism – its clinical and pedagogic practice, within the institutional context of the EFP – were just as important as the conceptual architecture of Lacanianism as a mode of thought. The presentations by members of the EFP of clinical case studies were a key element of pedagogic and clinical practice and take the emphasis away from Lacan himself as the sole voice of Lacanianism.[37] Psychoanalysis has always had a radical

[33] Lacan is adamant, though: claiming that the unconscious is structured like a language is not claiming that the unconscious is only expressed in discourse.

[34] For two very different 'insider' accounts of Lacanianism see: Catherine Clément, *The Lives and Legends of Jacques Lacan*, translated by Arthur Goldhammer (New York: Columbia University Press, 1983); and Stuart Schneiderman, *Jacques Lacan: The Death of an Intellectual Hero* (Cambridge: Harvard University Press, 1983). Both books provide vivid examples of the charismatic cult of Lacanianism – though Clément's account is the more sceptical of the two.

[35] The best lexicon of Lacanianism is now Dylan Evans, *An Introductory Dictionary of Lacanian Psychoanalysis* (London and New York: Routledge, 1996). Still invaluable is Jean Laplanche and Jean-Bertrand Pontalis, *The Language of Psychoanalysis*, translated by Donald Nicholson-Smith (London: Hogarth Press, 1983). The latter was first published in France in 1967, so while it is Lacanian in orientation it does not attend to the later formulations of Lacan.

[36] Frank Kermode's short book *Forms of Attention* (Chicago and London: University of Chicago Press, 1985) is a scintillating discussion of the way different forms of attention produce their cultural objects. The phrase 'form of attention' is, I think, a particularly useful way of discussing method as it equally stresses the formalism that is at the heart of any method (however empiricist), while also emphasizing that method is always perception (both attention and inattention, perception and imperception).

[37] A flavour of clinical Lacanianism and the practice of 'case presentation' is provided by Stuart Schneiderman, ed. and trans., *Returning to Freud: Clinical Psychoanalysis in the School of Lacan* (New Haven and London: Yale University Press, 1980) – though a couple of the case studies in the collection are older than the EFP.

pedagogic mission (or a mission that is always able to radically alter pedagogy) and in Lacanianism this aspect of psychoanalysis is central and insistently controversial. One place where the radical alteration of pedagogy was experienced (and not as a form of liberal reform) was in the 'pass' (*la passe*). For those younger members of the EFP who wanted to establish themselves as psychoanalysts the new 'pass' (introduced in 1967), by which an analyst-in-training has to get witnesses to present an account of her or his training analysis to a board who may or may not agree to 'pass' the candidate, was a controversial and innovative aspect of 'official' Lacanianism.[38] While it was voluntary, it was also a visible sign of a successful analysis. It was a form of examination or judgement where the submitting analyst had no right of reply (judgements couldn't be called into question, though training analysts could submit themselves to be judged again), and where success or failure (or completed or incomplete analysis) was determined by a form of communication that didn't need the subject's presence. While this might seem to present a particularly opaque form of power, it also suggests a model of communication whereby the insistence of the unconscious could pass across solitary agents of language. And it is here that the unconscious seems least tied to notions of identity and of personal ownership, and most like a social register of communication that is (for the most part) culturally occluded.

Alongside this there was the ongoing controversy around Lacan's short sessions: sessions that could be just ten minutes long (sometimes less). While the psychoanalytic establishment felt that it brought clinical practice into disrepute, Lacanians saw it as crucial:

> The combined pressure of the shortness of the sessions and the unpredictability of their stops creates a condition that greatly enhances one's tendencies to free-associate. When things come to mind they are spoken almost immediately, with spontaneity, for there is no time to mull them over, to find the nicest formulation. The analysand is encouraged, rather unsubtly, to get to the point, not to procrastinate or beat around the bush or even to prepare the analyst to hear disagreeable comments. Almost by definition the ego can never be master of the short session.[39]

Such practices along with Lacan's regular seminar suggest that while the interpretative schemas that Lacan's work seems to give rise to are no doubt important, we might be missing something crucial if we don't recognize these other, operational aspects of Lacanian practice. Seen from this perspective it is the

---

[38] On the practice of the 'pass' see Roudinesco, *Jacques Lacan & Co.*, pp. 443–61.
[39] Schneiderman, *Jacques Lacan*, pp. 133–4.

more clinical side of Lacanianism that feeds into its cultural potential, precisely because it isn't interpretation that is to the fore, but the possibility of communicating differently (via free association, for instance, or the pass). This context, whereby the clinical becomes the model for the study of culture, precisely because it is where interpretation is not established in advance, and because it is an experimental art of communication, is the one that has most to offer for an understanding of Michel de Certeau's work.

Firstly then, to understand the role of the cultural analyst who wants to adopt and adapt a psychoanalytic way of being, we would need to look at the role of the psychoanalyst and the method and form of attention that has been at the heart of psychoanalysis, namely the 'analytic session' – the scene of the 'talking cure'.[40] In one place, stereotypically recumbent on a couch, lies the analysand (the putative 'patient') encouraged to speak of everything, to freely associate from one point or memory to the next. In the other place sits the listening analyst, sagely encouraging speech ('go on', 'you said you felt . . .'), quietly allowing silences to be filled, gently unblocking communication (from the unconscious to the conscious). And it is here in this meeting between voice and ear, between sound and silence, that you can find the deep structure of de Certeau's psychoanalytic 'form of attention'.

A Freudian–Lacanian psychoanalyst is first and foremost a listener: one who listens to another:

> The psychoanalyst is nothing by himself [*sic passim*]. His function resides in the fact of his representing something that transcends him infinitely. His true place is that of the listener. He is the one through whom the analysand addresses himself to the other in order to have the truth of his message recognized and to have it translated there where it hides in the cipher-language of discourse. His powers as a translator are conferred upon him by the linguistic structure inherent in the unconscious. It is by virtue of his participation in the world and in culture that the analyst has a role.[41]

[40] Hubert Damisch imagines a kind of 'clinical setting' in his attention to art works: 'I think that we have to face the fact that due to psychoanalysis we are working with the work of art differently. Speaking for myself now, I am no longer interested in working *on* the work of art. I am no longer interested in applying any tool *upon* or to the work of art. I am interested in working *with* the work of art, in exactly the same way that an analyst works with an analysand.' Hubert Damisch, in discussion, in Peter Brooks and Alex Woloch, eds, *Whose Freud? The Place of Psychoanalysis in Contemporary Culture* (New Haven and London: Yale University Press, 2000), p. 134. While much of Freud's breakthrough work was via self-analysis, this can still be thought of as a talking–listening practice, even if what is being listened to is 'inner-speech', dream-works, slips, jokes and so on.

[41] H.-T. Piron, *et al.*, *La Psychanalyse, science d'homme* (1964), cited in Anika Lemaire, *Jacques Lacan*, translated by David Macey (London: Routledge & Kegan Paul, 1977), p. 217.

This notion of 'translator' can sound as though there is a master dictionary that might reveal the truth of the other's unconscious – an application of code-breaking – but one of the reasons why Lacanians prefer the duality analyst/analysand, over analyst/analysed, is to refuse the notion that the analysand is being analysed by the analyst. The communicative situation distributes analytic labour more evenly: the analysis must always be a self-analysis, even if it has been facilitated by another. We have already shown how psychoanalysis only has real potential for cultural analysis when it is seen as anti-hermeneutic, when it is recognized as refusing the language of translation and seen instead as a plur-alizing of contexts.

To return to Freud, the analytic session isn't about one person curing another, but presents a scene in which the unconscious can emerge, and which allows a certain awareness to be available to those involved so that they may have more knowledge of the forces determining their lives. Freud describes the process as a form of attention and inattention:

> The technique, however, is a very simple one. As we shall see, it rejects the use of any special expedient (even that of taking notes). It consists simply in not directing one's notice to anything in particular and in maintaining the same 'evenly-suspended attention' (as I have called it) in the face of all that one hears. In this way we spare ourselves the strain on our attention which could not be kept up for several hours daily, and we avoid a danger which is inseparable from the exercise of deliberate attention. For as soon as anyone deliberately concentrates his attention to a certain degree, he begins to select from the material before him; one point will be fixed in his mind with particular clearness and some other will be correspondingly dis-regarded, and in making this selection he will be following his expectations or inclinations.[42]

For Freud the attitude of the analyst was crucial to the possibility of psychoanalysis. The attitude can best be termed a distracted attention attuned and attuning itself to the speech of another. The attitude that Freud wants analysts to adopt is neither passive nor concentrated. It is an actively distracted listening which encourages unconscious processes to take part in the session:

---

[42] Sigmund Freud, 'Recommendations to Physicians Practising Psycho-Analysis' (1912), *The Standard Edition of the Complete Psychological Works of Sigmund Freud, Volume XII*, edited by James Strachey (London: Hogarth Press and the Institute of Psycho-Analysis, 1958), pp. 111–12 (partially cited in Leclaire, *Psychoanalysing*, p. 12).

To put it in a formula: he [the psychoanalyst] must turn his own unconscious like a receptive organ towards the transmitting unconscious of the patient. He must adjust himself to the patient as a telephone receiver is adjusted to the transmitting microphone.[43]

But as two pairs of ears (the analyst's and the analysand's) bend to hear the voice of the unconscious, the unconscious they hear is not that which belongs to the one or the other (they are not bending towards each other in the nature of a compromise). In this sense psychoanalytic listening is both peculiar and a foundational form of communication. As Roland Barthes suggests:

Listening, then, involves a risk: it cannot be constructed under the shelter of a theoretical apparatus, the analysand is not a scientific object from whom the psychoanalyst, deep in his armchair, can project himself with objectivity. The psychoanalytic relation is effected between two subjects. The recognition of the other's desire can therefore not be established in neutrality, kindliness, or liberality: to recognize this desire implies that one enters it, ultimately finding oneself there. Listening will exist only on condition of accepting the risk . . .[44]

Listening is the process of adjustment necessary for a new form of communication to take place that could hear the voice of the other: a voice that is neither yours nor mine – but potentially both yours and mine.

As far as this goes de Certeau can be seen as continuing a train of enquiry that is central to so-called poststructuralism, the investigation of otherness:

On the modern stage the oral trajectories are as individual as the bodies and as opaque to meaning, which is always general . . . Even philosophy, from Deleuze's *Anti-Oedipus* to Lyotard's *Libidinal Economy*, has labored to hear these voices again and thus to create auditory space. This is a reversal that is leading psychoanalysis to pass from a 'science of dreams' to the experience of what speaking voices change in the dark grotto of the bodies that hear them. (PEL1: 162)

The sound of the other needs to alter the disposition of the hearer: remain the same and you will miss what is being said. And it is here, in this utopian space

---

[43] Freud, 'Recommendations', pp. 115–16.
[44] Roland Barthes (with Roland Havas), 'Listening' (1976) in *The Responsibility of Forms: Critical Essays on Music, Art, and Representation*, translated by Richard Howard (New York: Hill and Wang, 1985), p. 256.

of communication, where two enunciating performances open up to one another and adapt to the other of what is being said, that de Certeau's approach to culture suggests an ethics of communication.[45]

It is this scene that also allows for the most productive understanding of de Certeau's constant figuring of speech ('voice', 'sound' and so on) in relation to writing (what he will call in *The Practice of Everyday Life*, 'the scriptural economy'). Speech exists within writing in a way analogous to the way repressed materials exist within the unconscious: they are there but they aren't recoverable in any straightforward fashion. As a historian de Certeau deals with writing, but he also knows that much of what is stored in archives, and much of what has been produced in the name of scholarship, or law, or sociology, or cultural studies, is a form of writing that bears a deathly relationship with orality. Court secretaries transcribe the voices of the poor, the dispossessed, the mad, the dangerous, and turn it into writing. Anthropologists, ethnologists, sociologists, go into the field and turn the sounds of others into words on a page, indistinguishable from other words, saturated by other intentions. There is something inevitable in this process and something that will make us all complicit in our own repression, yet while it is inevitable it is not inexorable. Psychoanalytic cultural studies would be dedicated to the possibilities of speech being allowed to be heard in this writing. As we will see in the next chapter, 'listening' becomes a form of attention central to those trying to recover the lives of those written out of history. As the Subaltern Studies historian, Ranajit Guha, puts it: 'to listen is already to be open to and existentially disposed towards: one inclines a little to one side in order to listen.'[46]

But listening to sounds that have effectively been excised by the scriptural economy requires either sensitivity to the smallest of lexical vibrations or a form of writing able to echo the sounds that are missing from the scriptural order. For de Certeau the scriptural practices that overwrite the voices they contain mean that 'these voices can no longer be heard except in the interior of the scriptural

---

[45] There is, of course, more that could be said here about the way that auditory culture is positioned within cultural theory and culture more generally. I will return later to the notion of voices, and particularly voices in texts; for the moment though it is worth pointing out that there is an emerging study of auditory culture in cultural history and cultural studies, see for instance: Steven Connor, 'The Modern Auditory I' in Roy Porter, ed., *Rewriting the Self: Histories from the Renaissance to the Present* (London: Routledge, 1997), pp. 203–23, and Connor's viscerally vivid phenomenological description of vocalizing in the first chapter (in particular) of *Dumbstruck : A Cultural History of Ventriloquism* (Oxford: Oxford University Press, 2000). See also Jonathan Rée, *I See a Voice: Deafness, Language and the Senses – A Philosophical History* (New York: Metropolitan Books, 1999).

[46] Ranajit Guha, 'The Small Voice of History' in *Subaltern Studies IX: Writings on South Asian History and Society*, edited by Shahid Amin and Dipesh Chakrabarty (Delhi: Oxford University Press, 1996), p. 9.

systems where they recur. They move about, like dancers, passing lightly through the field of the other' (PEL1: 131).[47] To listen to this textual sound means paying attention to the sonority of the lexical performance:

> [The] valorization of sound, the key to paranomases, alliterations, rhymes, and other phonic games, seeds an oral transgression through the semantic organization of the discourse, a transgression which displaces or cuts the articulated meanings and which renders the signifier autonomous in relation to the signified. This sonorous wave spreads across the syntactic landscape; it permeates it with leeways, charms, and meanderings something unknown. The analyst's ear practises precisely on hearing the murmurs and the games of these other languages. It makes itself attentive to the poetics which is present in every discourse: these hidden voices, forgotten in the name of pragmatic and ideological interests, introduce into every statement of meaning the 'difference' of the *act* which utters it. (H: 53)

Such sonority, then, is not just to be found in texts specifically attuned to a poetics of vocal cadences, it will be found in all discourse.

And it is here that we can most clearly see the topography of de Certeau's thought: voices are simultaneously absent and present within writing. This is because for de Certeau the real (the unmanageable, polyphonic excess of life) is what constitutes discourse, even if discourse is what remainders and manages it. In this way the cultural unconscious that provides an access to the real is not something that is outside discourse and is repressed by discourse: rather, it is in discourse (constitutionally) but is not reducible to discourse. The swarming sonority of culture escapes direct representation in discourse (there is no pure voice to be reclaimed), while its hum is ever present. So the topography that de Certeau is thinking with is not made up of fixed and bounded territories. This is why he can write that certain uses of culture (his example is the way colonized peoples use the culture of colonialists against the grain) 'escaped it [the dominant social order] without leaving it' (PEL1: xiii). This suggests a topography that is not physical (either inside or outside) but is more fluid, where the real saturates discourse but is not given presence there where the real pokes through discourse (and the saturation becomes visible) at its

---

[47] The distinction between speech and writing is not materially essentialist. In this way you can have a form of writing that is vocal: see Michel de Certeau, 'Vocal Utopias: Glossolalias', *Representations* 56, 1996, pp. 29–47. This essay was first published in France in 1980 in a journal called *Traverses* (a research review published by the Centre Pompidou) – concerned with cultural space, the journal was edited by Michel de Certeau, Louis Marin, Jean Baudrillard, Paul Virilio and others. For more on this journal see Verena Andermatt Conley's essay 'Processual Practices'.

points of tension. Tom Conley offers a useful gloss on de Certeau's relationship with the real:

> For de Certeau, it appears that the *réel* . . . is a 'nature' always in dynamic relation with 'culture', glimpsed in its points of strain, or heard in its silences. The historian apprehends it in the gaps that knowledge cannot rationalize. It appears on the edges of systems of intelligibility or seeps through lapses where discourses from one period cannot be assimilated into those of others. (Conley in WH: xvii)

To get a sense of how psychoanalytic listening might inform the practice of cultural analysis, how it might apprehend the real as it seeps into discourse, I want to return to an essay I have already mentioned in Chapter 1, above: 'Ethno-Graphy – Speech, or the Space of the Other: Jean de Léry'. De Certeau's approach in this essay is an example of psychoanalytic historiography. His description of Jean de Léry's writings as a 'primal scene' of ethnology should alert us to the importance of psychoanalysis here. The centrality of the Freudian notion of the 'return of the repressed' is, for de Certeau, a compelling aspect of both historiography and psychoanalysis: historiography, like consciousness, 'is both the deceptive *mask* and the operative *trace* of events that organise the present' (H: 3). Just as the operations of the ego and consciousness repress traumatic material, only to find such material returning (as symptoms, coded in dreams, etc.), so the lived-ness of everyday life (the overflowing everyday), managed by the mechanisms of the official writing of culture, spills out surreptitiously in fragments and traces. For de Certeau ethnological texts need to be mined in a similar way to dreams:

> In this respect the reading of texts has much to do with an interpretation of dreams; texts form discourses about the other, about which we can wonder what is actually told *there*, in those literary regions that are always drawn from what is really occurring. (WII: 211)

While the ethnological text offers a particular view of the other, and in so doing inscribes its 'will to power', it also leaves traces, remainders that point to an excess, an overflow, out of which the ethnographic text is fashioned. So alongside the analysis of the inscription of power and desire, comes another job: to recover such traces as the signs of an excess, as the seepage of the real. In his reading of Jean de Léry's journey to Brazil, de Certeau suggests that 'something remains over there, which the words of the text cannot convey; namely, the speech of the Tupis' (WH: 213). While the text can't convey it (literally, carry it back) 'the *voice* can create an *aparté*, opening a breach in the text and restoring a contact of body to body' (WH: 235). The breach in Léry's text occurs precisely when he tries to recount his experience of hearing the collective voices of a Tupi assembly:

> Such a joy it was hearing the beautifully measured rhythms of such a multitude – and especially the cadence and refrain of the ballad, all of them together raising their voices to each couplet, saying: *heu, heuaüre, heüra, heüraüra, heüra, heüra, oueh* – that I remained completely ravished. But moreover, every time the memory comes back to me, my heart throbs, and it seems as if their music still rings in my ears. (Jean de Léry quoted in WH: 213)

Speech [the 'Voice of the people'] becomes the other in writing, and acts as a disruption within writing: 'these voices can no longer be heard except within the interior of the scriptural systems where they recur' (PEL1: 131) [this reading of Léry is picked up again on p. 91]. And thus 'orality insinuates itself, like one of the threads of which it is composed, into the network – an endless tapestry – of a scriptural economy' (PEL 1: 132). The opposition of speech to writing needs to be thought of as an imbrication. Here speech doesn't signify authenticity or self-presence, but the disruption of the self-confidence of a scriptural economy. In a culture literally governed by vision and writing, other senses and forms of production become, potentially at least, destabilizing. For de Certeau the privileging of speech is a crucial tactic for insinuating the other in the place of writing. Elsewhere, especially in the second volume of *The Practice of Everyday Life*, de Certeau and his research colleagues similarly privilege smell, taste and the haptic (gestures, ways of walking, etc.).

We are faced with an economic architecture that is structured across four trajectories. First off there is an originary plenitude of ordinary culture, marked by an unmanageability of heterogeneous voices. Here the everyday overflows in its plurality. Secondly there is the fabrication of the social text, fashioned out of this overflowing plenitude, where this culture is 'tamed', made to signify within a system of writing. Accompanying this, and indissociable from it, is the inscription of a desire, a will to power. Lastly there are the traces, the remainders of this overflowing unmanageability that erupt within representation. The problem here is the same problem that psychoanalysis faces: the real never shows itself directly, and in full. Ordinary, everyday culture only comes to signification as a fragment that points to something else that is un-recordable. Insisting on this continues de Certeau's work of ethical provocation, short-circuiting any claims to the adequacy of representation. De Certeau's polemical inclusion of all cultural writing within a repressive economy should leave us sceptical about any privileging of an authentic voice of the 'people', of the 'popular', of the 'everyday' (who, for instance, could speak in the name of the everyday?). But more than this, it works as an invitation to generate new forms of reading and writing. In the end the question is less about the limitations of writing and picturing and more about the possibilities for registering the overflow of everyday life. As de Certeau writes at the start of *The Practice of Everyday Life*, the project's 'goal will be achieved if everyday practices, "ways of operating" or doing things, no longer appear as merely the obscure background of social activity, as if a body of theoretical questions, methods, categories, and perspectives, by penetrating this obscurity, make it possible to articulate them' (PEL1: xi).

How, then, to negotiate this contradictory demand? How would you go about recording something that is un-recordable? Given that what practitioners of cultural studies do is write and sometimes picture, then what are the possibilities for ethno-graphic practice? De Certeau suggests a range of possibilities: to foreground and make vivid the absence and occultation of the everyday; to recover the textual remainders of everyday life; and to search out and generate forms for registering the everyday that are less tied to a scriptural economy. From this it might be necessary to treat ethnographic texts as dream-works at the same time as restoring purposefully unscientific forms (novels, artworks, etc.) to the status of ethnographic and theoretical texts. Both of these are approaches that de Certeau employs. For instance, in *The Practice of Everyday Life* de Certeau enthuses about a social history museum in Vermont:

> The display includes innumerable familiar objects, polished, deformed, or made more beautiful by long use; everywhere there are as well the marks of the active hands and laboring or patient bodies for which these things composed the daily circuits, the fascinating presence of absences whose traces were everywhere. At least this village full of abandoned and salvaged objects drew one's attention, through them, to the ordered murmurs of a hundred past or possible villages, and by means of these imbricated traces one began to dream of countless combinations of existences. (PEL1: 21)

Here the necessarily repressive operation of cultural management (museology) becomes a 'royal road' to an overflowing everyday. In the presence of such absence, speculation and dreaming are the necessary responses.

If it is true, as I would argue, that psychoanalysis is something like a deep structure that runs throughout Michel de Certeau's work, then we might want to show this not by going to the most obviously psychoanalytically amenable texts (on mystics, for instance), but to those more concerned with contemporary political clarification. The notion of voice is something that connects the very divergent writing of de Certeau: it is there in the religious history; it is there in the contemporary anthropology; it is there in the cultural-policy work. And it will be voices that will dominate the account he gives of that 'rupture' of social business-as-usual known as the events of May '68: a Parisian spring . . .

OCEANIC RUMBLES: MAY 1968

In May 1968, in Paris and elsewhere in France, students and workers took to the streets. Initially sparked by events at the University of Nanterre on 22 March, a 'movement' gained momentum and roughly half-a-million demonstrators could be found on the streets of Paris in mid-May. By the end of May there was an 'unlimited strike' across France of about nine million workers, including everyone from factory workers (Renault and Sud-Aviation being the first to strike) to school teachers, shop workers, those involved in the film industry (the Cannes Film Festival was closed), as well as government departments.[48] One of the most characteristic aspects of the events was a sloganeering that mixed poetry, utopian desire and a tradition of anarchistic thinking, and found its medium on hastily composed posters, in ad hoc meetings, in street graffiti, in banners and in the conversations taking place in newly convened neighbourhood associations. By the end of June, though, a general election had returned de Gaulle to power with a large majority. The 'events' appeared to be over.

Initially writing about the Paris spring for himself, de Certeau began to publish his commentaries on the 'events' in the Jesuit cultural magazine *Études* in the months June to September 1968. These commentaries were collected, supplemented with annotated bibliographies of other publications about May (what de Certeau refers to as 'the publishers' harvest'), and published as *La prise de parole: Pour une nouvelle culture* (*The Capture of Speech: For a New Culture*) before the year was out.[49] For de Certeau the 'event' was fundamentally and profoundly concerned with speech: its actuality and its potential. In this he was not alone. For Roland Barthes, writing months after the 'events': 'the students' speech so completely overflowed, pouring out everywhere, written everywhere, that one might define, superficially – but also, perhaps, essentially – the university revolt as a *Taking of Speech* (as we say *Taking of the Bastille*).'[50] There is then a close affinity between the two writers on this, and de Certeau's purposeful title – the capture of speech – is designed to suggest both an initial capture by the protesters (speech inhabited, redirected), as

---

48 Out of the vast literature on May '68 the most authoritative account is now, in my opinion, Kristin Ross, *May '68 and its Afterlives* (Chicago and London: University of Chicago Press, 2002). For a short synoptic account of the events see Sylvia Harvey, *May '68 and Film Culture* (London: BFI, 1978).

49 This is now part 1 of *The Capture of Speech* (CS). For some reason, though, a substantial chapter that was originally in *La prise de parole* has been included in *Culture in the Plural* (CP) as Chapter 7: 'The Social Architecture of Knowledge'.

50 Roland Barthes, 'Writing the Event' (1968) in *The Rustle of Language*, translated by Richard Howard (Oxford: Blackwell, 1986), p. 150.

well as a recapture by the social force that institutes the social in the name of order:

> From the beginning to the end, speech is what has played the decisive role, from that of Daniel Cohn-Bendit to that of Charles de Gaulle. I have lingered on this strange fact (it is a way of approaching it) by believing that it was fundamental and that it engaged the entire structuring of our culture (it is an option). (CS: 6)

The entire work of commentary on May '68 is not aimed at discussion of political gains and losses, or social progressiveness, or regressiveness. Rather the entire project is aimed at locating another way of communicating that might possibly alter the culture from within (from the ground up):

> Today [May 1968], it is imprisoned speech that was freed. Thus is affirmed a wild, irrepressible, new right, a right that has become identical with the right of being a human, and no longer a client destined for consumer culture or instruments useful for the anonymous organization of a society. This right commanded, for example, the reactions of assemblies that were always prepared to defend it whenever it appeared to be threatened in the heat of debate: 'Everybody here has the right to speak.' But this right was only given to those who spoke in their own name. The assembly refused to hear whoever was identified with a function or intervened in the name of a group hidden behind the statements of one of its members: to speak is not to be the 'speaker' in the name of a lobby, of a 'neutral' and objective truth, or for convictions held elsewhere. (CS: 11)

Language is in this sense not reflective or representational, it is not the expression of something already in operation (it does not speak on behalf of), rather speech is performative and a form of poesis – it allows to come into being something new that is driven by desire. It is this that (potentially at least) has the power to fundamentally alter forms of social being:

> Something happened to us. Something began to stir in us. Emerging from who knows where, suddenly filling the streets and the factories, circulating amongst us, becoming ours but no longer being the muffled noise of our solitude, voices that had never been heard began to change us. At least that was what we felt. From this something unheard of was produced: we began to speak. It seemed as if it were for the first time. From everywhere emerged the treasures, either aslumber or tacit, of forever unspoken experiences. (CS: 11–12)

What de Certeau is suggesting is that 'the oceanic rumble of the ordinary' breaks the surface of culture and emerges as the very substance of culture.

The 'oceanic rumble' that constitutes the heterogeneity of popular culture, which is always being pacified by cultural managers, is the power that speaks in May. In this there is a faint echo to the opening of Freud's *Civilization and its Discontents*, where an oceanic feeling is the description that Freud's interlocutor ascribes to the source of correct religious sentiment and which Freud describes as 'a feeling of indissoluble connection, of belonging inseparably to the external world as a whole'.[51] There is a sense in which de Certeau's writings attempt a secular (and often non-secular) theology of the oceanic that is to be found in the quotidian. This is a form of liberation theology, and has (here at least) little truck with social reform: it is a revolution, pure and simple, that is being imagined, one that takes place at the level of speech:

> From time to time, a volcanic rift opens up a submerged violence with an abrupt explosion of language. A verbal lava, already metamorphosed in its irruption into daylight, attests to what repression has done to the repressed . . . A revolution would be simmering beneath the feet of every society, as witnessed by the very repetition of its failures. Every piece of speech would signify the violence of an irrepressible *desire*, but in the social language that represses and 'betrays' it (in the double sense of the term: to deceive and to reveal) with *needs* to satisfy or that are satisfied. (CP: 92)

May 1968 reverberates for de Certeau, not as a social revolution to be won or lost, but as an inkling of a way of communicating that is utopian. This utopianism has forerunners, but these aren't limited to moments of social revolution (the Paris Commune of 1871, for instance) – they can also be found within the analytic session (potentially). The utopianism that is presented by psychoanalysis is the idea of 'free association' becoming cultural – an example of which might be Paris in May 1968. This is not to say that May '68 can be reduced to psychoanalysis. For de Certeau, what was revolutionary about May is what is (potentially) revolutionary about psychoanalysis – namely the potential for the fundamental alteration of communication. Here psychoanalysis doesn't herald 'the return of the repressed'; rather it suggests a start to the job of unbinding the pacified heterogeneity of culture.

There is a problem, though, with de Certeau's account of May '68, a problem that I may be compounding by discussing his account of it in a chapter on culture and psychoanalysis. As Kristin Ross has shown in her highly detailed and

[51] Sigmund Freud, *Civilization and its Discontents*, translated by Joan Riviere (London: Hogarth Press, 1957), p. 9 – originally published in German in 1930.

substantive account of the events (which is also an account of how the events were accounted for in the years following 1968 right through to the present), the 'failure' of the May 'revolution' might not just be down to the recuperative power or the state or the reformist ambitions of those willing to compromise on a revolutionary agenda. For Ross the question that May '68 poses is:

> How did a mass movement that sought above all, in my view, to contest the domain of the expert, to disrupt the system of naturalized spheres of competence (especially the sphere of specialized politics), become translated in the years that followed into little more that a 'knowledge' of '68, on the basis of which a whole generation of self-proclaimed experts and authorities could then assert their expertise?[52]

In her view it is 'sociology', in the months and years subsequent to May, that did much to transform May from a practice to a pathology; from the operations of equality to an empty rhetoric of freedom; from communitarianism to individualism. In various anniversaries of May, intellectuals are trotted out to add another layer of mystification. With hindsight, according to Régis Debray, there was little that was revolutionary about the Paris spring, rather it now appears as a 'cradle for a new bourgeois society'.[53] For Ross, de Certeau stands on the side of those who are complicit in the betrayal of May.

We might not, then, want to (or need to) read de Certeau for an ultimate political assessment of May '68, or to gain an insider's sense of what it meant to participate in such an upheaval. What, however, remains both interesting and urgent is the way that a language that bears affinities with psychoanalysis is used in a way that sidesteps the pitfalls of psychopathological social diagnosis (a social neurosis, for instance). The reason why May '68 becomes a topic for de Certeau and the reason why it strikes him as so important is not because it points to either the potential or the impossibility of social change, but because it offers a glimpse of a different mode of social communication, one that is closer to a 'psychoanalytic tuning' (the adjustments that Freud suggests should accompany and constitute any turning towards the other). Like Kristin Ross, de Certeau recognizes May's productivity as practical and operative, yet unlike Ross he sees it in terms of communicative production. Ross, though, is convincing on this, and the loss of a sense of the very real practices of equality being fashioned in the wake of '68 is a political and cultural loss. Yet in certain ways the practice of equality and the psychoanalytic 'tuning-in' that de Certeau is enamoured by might not be as far apart as Ross would want to suggest.

[52] Ross, *May '68*, pp. 6–7.
[53] Debray cited in Ross, *May '68*, p. 185.

Towards the end of his essay on history and psychoanalysis de Certeau enthusiastically flags the importance of the experimental and 'anti-psychiatric' clinic, La Borde, where the political activist and psychoanalyst Félix Guattari worked:

> The experiences of the La Borde clinic open up a new chapter in psychoanalytic history. It is no longer a question of 'applying' psychoanalysis, but of bringing to light a 'revolutionary subjectivity', of 'grasping the point of *rupture* where political economy and libidinal economy *are finally one and the same*. (H: 14–15)

La Borde was an experimental clinic run by analysts who all shared a background in social and political activism; they concentrated only on the treatment of psychotics and focused analytic sessions on group analysis.[54] For Guattari, as for de Certeau, May was an articulation of desire that was then thwarted:

> Our starting point was to consider how during these crucial periods [May 1968], something along the order of desire was manifested throughout the society as a whole, and then was repressed, liquidated, as much by the government and police as by the parties and so-called workers' unions and, to a certain extent, the leftist organizations as well.[55]

The possibility of imagining another form of sociality in the 1960s and 1970s could combine psychoanalysis, communications theory, new technologies and so on. In this it is interesting that both Guattari and de Certeau were keen to increase free independent radio. The airwaves could be a medium not for a collective unconscious but for a swarm of singularities, all tuning and re-tuning to the sound of their swarming. Such anarcho-utopianism is, as we will see (in Chapter 6 below), the basis for a form of cultural policy that for all its uncompromising desire is filled with simple and operationally straightforward practical suggestions (like increasing the availability of radio transmitters).

But now, in the following two chapters, I want to ask what a psychoanalytically altered historical attention to culture means in practical terms, what its historical work looks like, what its cultural work is capable of conjuring up. We should, I hope, not expect to see a field of interpretation based on

---

[54] An account of La Borde can be found in Gary Genosko, *Félix Guattari: An Aberrant Introduction* (London and New York: Continuum, 2002).

[55] Félix Guattari in Gilles Deleuze, *Desert Islands and Other Texts 1953–1974*, translated by Michael Taormina (Los Angeles and New York: Semiotext(e), 2002), p. 216.

psychoanalytic theory. Michel de Certeau's relationship to psychoanalysis is oblique and formal: it provides a way of thinking about the topography of culture; it encourages sensitivity to what is 'hidden in plain view'. Psychoanalysis in de Certeau is psychoanalysis fundamentally altered, re-directed to the business of cultural analysis.

CHAPTER 4

Zones of Silence: Orality, Archives and Resistance

In a society gifted at generalization, endowed with powerful centralizing strategies, the historian moves in the direction of the frontiers of great regions already exploited. He or she 'deviates' by going back to sorcery, madness, festival, popular literature, the forgotten world of the peasant, Occitania, etc., all these zones of silence. (WH: 79)

Historical scholarship has developed, through recursive practice, a tradition that tends to ignore the small drama and fine detail of social existence, especially at its lower depths. A critical historiography can make up for this lacuna by bending closer to the ground in order to pick up the traces of a subaltern life in its passage through time.[1]

UNBINDING MODERNITY

What overflows and comes to the surface in the loose edifice of de Certeau's writing is a different, alternative modernity: a modernity uncoupled from the progressivism that can accompany even the bleakest and most critical accounts of industrial, imperial and secular modernization. In recovering the contemporary social forces to be found in religious ecstasy or the complex modes that make up everyday life, de Certeau recognizes the presence and persistence of different temporalities (different *durabilities*) in the present. His concern with local communities and neighbourhoods (rural, semi-urban), his involvement with the peasant struggles in Latin America, his interest in a 'wild' spirituality re-emerging in the modern institution of religion, all point to a notion of temporal moments crisscrossed by a plurality of times. As such the past is always a component of the present that troubles the self-identity of modernity. This is to foreground the multiple temporalities that characterize

[1] Ranajit Guha, 'Chandra's Death' in *Subaltern Studies V: Writings on South Asian History and Society*, edited by Ranajit Guha (Delhi: Oxford University Press, 1987), p. 138.

the present: it is to designate any moment by what Michel Serres calls 'poly-chronic time'.[2]

The significance of this for an understanding of 'modernity' is colossal. If a certain conventional periodization has taught us to see the hurried uncertainty of modern life and the growth of secular rationality as central to modernity, then we necessarily have to designate other phenomena that cannot fit this characterization (for instance, an increase in religious fundamentalism, to take the most obvious case) as pre- or post-modern, or anti-modern, and so on. The difficulty here is that the term 'modernity', as an identikit, is always going to be inadequate for the job of describing actuality: it is always going to be hedged around by policing actions that work to buttress the concept (modernity) rather than facilitate an understanding of the polychronic moments of the modern. For de Certeau (although modernity is not a privileged term) what emerges is a complex modernity that is fashioned through contradiction, through the saturation of the present with the past. Thus modernity is not a project that is incomplete, or unfinished:[3] instead modernity is the name for contemporary life fashioned out of shards that are simultaneously striving for the future and looking back, over their shoulder, to the past. Modernity is the dynamic suturing of past and present, as well as the failure of this suturing. And this is why psychoanalysis provides something of a model for understanding historicity: a historicity that can accommodate the present-ness of the past, and the past-ness of the present. And this is why often the most vivid examples of modernity come from colonial contexts (two pasts and two presents colliding), where the imbrication of pasts and presents are at their most intense.

With historical interests that stretch from the sixteenth century to the twentieth, Michel de Certeau conceives of modernity as part of a long take that privileges certain operational logics while outlawing others. Yet what makes de Certeau worth pursuing in this over-described arena is his refusal of the absolutism that can often characterize attempts to discuss modernity. As he shows in *The Possession at Loudun*, in seventeenth-century Europe, scientific knowledge becomes more and more dominant as an explanatory form, but it doesn't simply win out; it doesn't eviscerate religious belief, for instance. Religious practices, religious beliefs, become more and more marginalized in certain societies, at certain times, and in this way they become altered, pushed underground, but not fully liquidated. The same would be true, as we will see, for the overenthusiastic accounts of the quickening of daily life: for de Certeau such an abstracted

---

[2] Michel Serres with Bruno Latour, *Conversations on Science, Culture, and Time*, translated by Roxanne Lapidus (Ann Arbor: University of Michigan Press, 1995).

[3] See Jürgen Habermas, 'Modernity – An Incomplete Project', in Hal Foster, ed., *Postmodern Culture* (London and Sydney: Pluto Press, 1985), pp. 3–15.

mono-dimensional approach will never capture the full orchestration of varied paces that will be found in any singular moment.

Yet while de Certeau's work might be a useful antidote to zealous accounts of modernity as progress or perdition (which might actually constitute one and the same operation) it would be in danger of wilful naivety if it didn't also recognize and account for the forms of epistemological domination (epistemological violence, in certain accounts) that push cultural forms underground, or work to pacify or brutally erase the culture of the dominated. As we have already seen, de Certeau's work is precisely attuned to the epistemological conditions (which are always, in the end, also practical material conditions) that operate in disciplinary practices such as historiography. Why de Certeau's work is so crucial and so urgent is precisely because he steadfastly negotiates a position that is aimed at refusing the lure of both epistemological naivety and the chronic epistemological pessimism that can be found in certain accounts of historiographic practice (though we may find that in certain circumstances epistemological pessimism is the only response that accurately describes the situation). So alongside his sustained investigation of epistemological domination (by the church, by ethnologists, by educationalists and so on) de Certeau always and insistently poses an ethical obligation: a critique of epistemological pacification and violence must be accompanied by the invention of new, of other, epistemological conditions, ones that struggle against the process of erasing what they describe. Coupled, then, with the mapping of ethnology's epistemological domination of a vernacular culture (say Jean de Léry's account of the Tupis in the previous chapter) is the demand to listen to the voices of the Tupis – voices that are barely audible and might not really be heard at all in the texts of the West (not in any full sense of the term). Such work is aimed at the recovery of what the archive works to hide: it is dedicated to unbinding the force of what de Certeau calls the 'scriptural economy'.

But this ethical demand isn't simply dedicated to the past: it is crucially aimed at generating different ways of operating (both textually and non-textually) in the present. This is to attempt to fashion a practice of writing that while not being able to place itself entirely outside the scriptural economy is actively making space for voices, for the everyday, within it. It is for this reason that de Certeau's work is both urgent and unfinished. In this chapter, and in subsequent chapters, I am aiming to get a much better sense of how de Certeau's project (or a form of cultural studies that wanted to engage with and pursue de Certeau's project) might go about finding different forms for writing culture. To do this it is important to signal work that has already (knowingly and unknowingly) engaged with these issues: after all, the recognition of the epistemological damage meted out by forms of colonialism, for instance, isn't specific to de Certeau, nor, thankfully, is the ethical demand to fashion new *forms* of knowledge. In many practical ways it will become obvious that others have gone further than de Certeau was able to. His project was always modest enough to recognize the debts it owed to others: 'the poem, as always, precedes our progress' (MF: 293). I will then (and once again) purposefully stray from a concentrated focus on de Certeau's work so as to get a firmer grasp on some of the issues that his work raises but doesn't resolve. And because an ethical demand is always future-orientated, I will move from historiography to more contemporary work (which will take us back to de Certeau). What an engagement with de Certeau's work offers is an optic that brings a certain degree of clarity to a host of projects that are aiming not simply to change the content of culture, but to change the possible forms that it could take, forms that will allow the silences to be heard and to open up a space for new voices to speak.

In this chapter I want to look at how de Certeau's work can be used to think about the practices of analysing cultural materials. One way of holding together and linking the varied approaches that characterize both de Certeau and cultural studies (historiography, contemporary ethnology, cultural commentary and so on) is to recognize that all these practices are reliant on the production of archives. For historiography this is perhaps obvious, but it is no less true for more contemporary work that might be based on an archive that has been collected specifically for a piece of research (a group of novels and films, for instance, or a series of interviews). Thus by looking at the production of archives in the past, and by thinking about how new archives can be produced, we can get a sense of how de Certeau's methodological imagination links the historical to the contemporary. What we do with archives is, of course, as crucial as how they are produced: to this end I want to compare de Certeau's approach with the postcolonial historiography being produced by the Subaltern Studies group, since it is the colonial context that most vividly highlights the problematics of the archive for attending to subjugated standpoints. Lastly I want to show how the contemporary ethnology of everyday life suggests new forms of archives that edge towards another archival economy based on a very different understanding of modernity, one much more hospitable to the voices of the everyday.

ARCHIVAL ABSENCES: VOICES-OFF

One of the most pervasive social and cultural technologies of modernity is the archive. In various contexts, most notably the colonial context, it constituted and disseminated the forceful vocabulary of the modern. In V.Y. Mudimbe's words Africa, as an idea and as an identifying mirror (for Europe), was imagined and invented via a 'colonial library':

It was, I think, fifteenth- and sixteenth-century Europe that invented the savages as a representation of its own negated double. Exploiting travellers' and explorers' writings, at the end of the nineteenth century a 'colonial library' begins to take shape. It represents a body of knowledge constructed with the explicit purpose of faithfully translating and deciphering the African object. Indeed, it fulfilled a political project in which, supposedly, the object unveils its being, its secret, and its potential to a master who could, finally, domesticate it.[4]

In a formulation that is now a central tenet in the cultural sciences, the West's sense of its own modernity is founded by an act (continually reenacted, even today) of *imagining* an 'other' (a 'savage', colonial subject) who becomes the guarantor of the West's 'natural' ascendancy, and in turn legitimates the West's pacifying, catastrophic treatment of the non-West. Unbeknownst to it, the non-West is made to sign its own death warrant. The archive is the marshalling of knowledge to provide the architectonics that performs such sleights-of-hand.

Thus the archive is fundamentally an instrument of government and an instrument of governance. The classic description of its form belongs to Michel Foucault in his 1969 book *The Archaeology of Knowledge*:

The archive is first the law of what can be said, the system that governs the appearance of statements as unique events. But the archive is also that which determines that all these things that were said do not accumulate endlessly in an amorphous mass, nor are they inscribed in an unbroken linearity, nor do they disappear at the mercy of chance accidents; but they are grouped together in distinct figures, composed together in accordance with multiple relations, maintained or blurred in accordance with specific regularities; that which determines that they do not withdraw at the same pace in time, but shine, as it were, like stars, some that seem close to us shining brightly from afar off, while others that are in fact close to us are already growing pale.[5]

Never simply an act of homogenization, 'the archive' constantly, but not consistently, works to differentiate, to categorize and catalogue, to include and exclude.

But this archive, described so vividly by Foucault, is an abstraction – albeit an abstraction that has concrete effects. It is the abstraction that de Certeau names as the 'scriptural economy'. This is 'The Archive', the one that encompasses, but is never reducible to, all those archival actualities – libraries, collections of papers,

[4] V.Y. Mudimbe, *The Idea of Africa* (London: James Currey, 1994), p. xii.
[5] Michel Foucault, *The Archaeology of Knowledge*, translated by A.M. Sheridan Smith (London: Tavistock, 1972), p. 129 – first published in France in 1969.

letters, documents of legislation – all that enormous wealth of relics that historians desire. On the one hand, then, we have 'The Archive' – an impulse that has
fashioned 'the west and the rest', the epistemological violence that has yoked the
diverse, dynamic actuality of life to a chain of signification from which there is
no escape. On the other hand we have 'archives' – messy or ordered collections,
wild or streamlined depositories – that can be read variously: for the official line,
or for anecdotes of 'native' insurgency, for instance. These two archives, which
of course are one and the same material phenomena, point to various epistemological possibilities – most drastically to epistemological pessimism and
epistemological naturalism (or naive realism). No doubt to portray it like this is
to exaggerate excessively, and it is true that historians who mine archives to tell
histories-from-below are rarely the naive empiricists that some forms of cultural
theory might enjoy taking them for. Nor is it often true that those sceptical about
the transparency of archival materials are thereby doomed to a life where the
only thing that can be known is the ruthless restrictions placed on knowing. Yet
inasmuch as these exaggerations point to tendencies that are in operation (and
not just in discussions of cultural theory) I will stay with them for a while. Soon,
of course, they will be jettisoned in favour of a more nuanced approach – available via de Certeau and others. As usual, theoretical clarification may find that
it is simply making explicit what is already operating in practice.[6]

In a review of different approaches to archives, and archival knowledge, written from an anthropological perspective and orientated to examining colonialism, Ann Laura Stoler claims that:

> If one were to characterize what has informed a critical approach to the colo-
> nial archives over the last fifteen years, it would be a commitment to the
> notion of reading colonial archives 'against the grain'. Students of colonial-
> ism, inspired by political economy, were schooled to write popular histories
> 'from the bottom up', histories of resistance that might locate human agency
> in small gestures of refusal and silence amongst the colonized. As such,
> engagement with the colonial archives was devoted to a reading of 'upper
> class sources upside down' in order to reveal the language of rule and the
> biases inherent in statist perceptions.[7]

For Stoler an approach to the archive that mines them for information, which
can then be read against the interests of the archival order (for instance, a court

---

[6] Rather than this discrediting theoretical clarification (making it redundant) it makes the task
more concrete and relevant to practice.
[7] Ann Laura Stoler, 'Colonial Archives and the Arts of Governance', *Archival Science* 2,
2002, p. 99.

ledger which recounts the activities of a 'criminal', which can be read 'against the grain' as the activities of an insurgent) is in danger of ignoring the way that archival forms shape knowledge. For Stoler, cherry picking your way through an archive, gathering up what seems like fragments that could form a counter-narrative of resistance, remains within the logic of the archive and remains blind (potentially) to the patterning effects of archives.

Stoler suggests that the logic of 'archives-as-source' needs to be replaced by the logic of 'archives-as-subject'. This would ask 'historical questions about accredited knowledge and power – what forces, social cues and moral virtues produce qualified knowledges that, in turn, disqualified other ways of knowing, other knowledges'.[8] In many ways she is simply reminding us not to forget Foucault's lessons in general epistemology[9] and urging us to employ these lessons in relation to the colonial archive by reading 'for its [the archive's] regularities, for its logic of recall, for its densities and distributions, for its consistencies of misinformation, omission, and mistake – along the archival grain'.[10] Her point is that unless archival framing is recognized and fully understood (reading along the archival grain) then there is no possibility of reading against the archival grain. Instead the result will entail the collecting of fragments already fully imbricated with the grain of the archive.[11]

The opposition of 'archive-as-source' versus 'archive-as-subject' doesn't, of course, discount the possibility of an approach that manages to negotiate across this duality. And this is where we would need to place de Certeau's approach inasmuch as he has fully ingested the lessons of Foucault at the same time as his project is aimed at straining to hear voices within an archival form working to muffle and subdue them. In *The Practice of Everyday Life* de

---

[8] Stoler, 'Colonial Archives', p. 95. See also Ann Laura Stoler, *Race and the Education of Desire: Foucault's History of Sexuality and the Colonial Order of Things* (Durham and London: Duke University Press, 1995).

[9] See Foucault, *The Archaeology of Knowledge* as well as his crucial essay 'The Order of Discourse' (1970) in Robert Young, ed., *Untying the Text: A Post-Structuralist Reader* (Boston and London: Routledge & Kegan Paul, 1981), pp. 48–78.

[10] Stoler, 'Colonial Archives', p. 100.

[11] The material relevant to this discussion is enormous. For a vivid account of archives that pursues Foucault's approach see Allan Sekula, 'The Body and the Archive', *October* 39 (1986), pp. 3–64. The journal *History of the Human Sciences* has dedicated two special issues to the question of the archive (November 1998 and May 1999) and these offer an excellent range of approaches to the problematic of the archives. Jacques Derrida's *Archive Fever: A Freudian Impression*, translated by Eric Prenowitz (Chicago: University of Chicago Press, 1996) can't be ignored, but nor can Carolyn Steedman's *Dust* (Manchester: Manchester University Press, 2002), which is, in part, a response to Derrida. For an account that relates the archival impulse to colonialism see Thomas Richards, *The Imperial Archive: Knowledge and the Fantasy of Empire* (London: Verso, 1993).

Certeau describes his work 'as a quest for lost and ghostly voices in our "scriptural" societies':

> I am trying to hear these fragile ways in which the body makes itself heard in the language, the multiple voices set aside by the triumphal *conquista* of the economy that has, since the beginning of the 'modern age' (i.e., since the seventeenth or eighteenth century), given itself the name of writing. My subject is orality, but an orality that has been changed by three or four centuries of Western fashioning. (PEL1: 131)

The question that this quest poses is whether something other (orality, voice) is recoverable from this 'Western fashioning'. And I think the answer to this (for de Certeau) is both yes and no. But even this 'yes' and 'no' needs to be doubled; to be grasped both abstractly and concretely, both theoretically and practically.

On an abstract theoretical and on a concrete theoretical level it seems clear that 'The Archive' has so thoroughly operated on 'its' materials, installing in their place its own desire, that there is no access to an unblemished account of, for example, 'the native informant'. On an immediately practical level there is often little substantial historical evidence that exists outside of archives, which means that there is little material that hasn't been mediated by the practices and interests of 'archivists':

> How to know what were these millions of 'little people', not only in the Middle Ages, but more recently, if not through what scholars and lawyers have filtered and retained? A massive unawareness consigns the 'masses' to oblivion, probably because of the privilege enjoyed by written culture, because of its repression of oral culture and of *different* expressions that then became types of 'folklore' along the borderlines of an empire. (CP: 87)

Thus, for instance, the lives of eighteenth-century British 'commoners' – many of whom had limited literacy – are only accessible through probate ledgers and the records of the law courts. If you had nothing to leave to future generations, and didn't go to court, you are, most likely, not available to historiography. Experiences of workers, like those related in the telling of the cat massacre mentioned in Chapter 2, are recorded because of the nature of the labour (high levels of literacy were of course necessary if you were in the printing trade). Vast territories, of course, lay mostly vacant – for instance, a complete and detailed history of the experience of slavery.

Yet de Certeau is not simply suggesting that 'inclusion' and 'exclusion' will work in this way. The archival process is one that over-codes the materials that enter it – the archive is a form of alteration, of mediation, of production.

In recording the lives of others, of those non-elite lives that come up for scrutiny (and de Certeau is particularly interested in the way that the speech of 'possessed women' is incorporated in archives), the archival operation inserts discursive 'knowledge' in place of a specific 'voice':

> Speaking more broadly . . . problems appear in the relation maintained by the ethnographic tale with the 'other society' that it recounts and claims to make heard. With respect to the possessed woman, the primitive, and the patient, demonological discourse, ethnographic discourse, and medical discourse effectively assume identical positions: 'I know what you are saying better than you'; in other words, 'My knowledge can position itself in the place whence you speak.' (WH: 250)

Thus even when lives are given account, even when (and perhaps especially when) those lives are the object of a form of archival scrutiny (theological, anthropological, medical and so on), the archival operation excises as it inscribes – the voice is inflected, fundamentally altered through inscription.

One of the most pertinent examples of the relationship between voice and archive is evidenced in the collaborative project that de Certeau conducted with Dominique Julia and Jacques Revel. And the reason for its pertinence is that it concerns an archive that is driven by the desire to collect and collate speech practices, with the aim 'of annihilating patois and of universalising the use of the French language'. In the wake of the French Revolution Abbé Grégoire, at the behest of other members of the Constituent Assembly, was given the 'revolutionary' task of establishing unified language practices in France. He compiled a dossier (which de Certeau refers to as 'the Gregorian corpus') based on a questionnaire that he sends to contacts in French provincial towns and cities. In this he is studying the diversity of speech (as opposed to written language) and is making an archive of speech (albeit written). But this archive is established as part of a plan to eradicate local differences in language use in order to bind the nation to a common language. From this point of view the material that forms the archive is that which must be expelled from living culture: the archive is the mausoleum that is built for what is fascinating but dangerous:

> This is how patois appears in the Gregorian corpus: it is the vocal subversion of scriptural norms, but also the warmth of origins, the richness of affections . . . An ambivalent aura envelops patois, which is thought of as feminine, like the voice and the vowel. It is both witch and the siren.[12]

---

[12] Michel de Certeau, 'The Word of the Vowel' in Michel de Certeau, Dominique Julia and Jacques Revel, *Une politique de la langue. La Révolution française et les patois: l'enquête de*

The Archival impulse is designed to contain (in the dual sense of 'to hold' and 'to suppress a threat') the disruption of patois. In this the scriptural economy ('the writing laboratory') is the practice of exorcising heterogeneity:

> The writing laboratory has a 'strategic' function: either an item of information received from tradition or from the outside is collected, classified, inserted into a system and thereby transformed, or the rules and models developed in this place (which is not governed by them) allow one to act on the environment and to transform it. The island of the page is a transitional place in which an industrial inversion is made: what comes in is something 'received', what comes out is a 'product'. The things that go in are the indexes of a certain 'passivity' of the subject with respect to a tradition; those that come out, the marks of his power of fabricating objects. (PEL1: 135)

Inserting something (an example of popular speech, for instance) into The Archive fundamentally transforms it, rendering it a product of the Archival impulse.

We can see then how de Certeau edges towards a categorical 'no' to the question of whether the voices of the possessed and the dispossessed can be heard in the archive. It seems, though, that asserting this negative (the voices of the people have been erased in the process of recording) is also what allows him to imagine the possibility of hearing those voices. However, now they are recovered as a vast, undifferentiated expanse of silence: a vast chorus whose deafening silence is heard from within the archive. This is the sound of the presence of an absence. Writing about this again in relation to 'The Sorcerer's Speech' de Certeau will use a dramaturgical analogy to suggest the form that this 'presence of absence' would take:

> Fundamentally, the type of manifestation is always identical, insofar as it is reducible to the relation that an altering passage keeps with a semantic order, or to the relation that an enunciation keeps with a system of statements. This relation can appear in mystical or in diabolical ways, or in terms of madness. It can be seen in ethnological discourse, when the issue is how the Indian is going to speak the language of Occidental knowledge. Or else, it can be asked how the 'madman' or 'madwoman' is going to speak within the discourse of psychiatry or psychoanalytical knowledge. In various ways, the same interrogation insinuates itself as a text-*off*, about which one must ask how it combines with the known body of writing. (WH: 249)

Grégoire (Paris: Gallimard, 1975), reprinted and translated by Jeremy Ahearne in *The Certeau Reader*, edited by Graham Ward (Oxford: Blackwell, 2000), p. 177.

On one level this 'presence of absences' is a terminally limited figure of the archive. If hearing it fundamentally destabilizes the authority of the archive (with the wild silence of both those that it ignored and those it scrutinized), the 'presence of absence' seems to offer little else. Because it consists of an expulsion of voices (albeit differently expelled) the archive homogenizes everything and everyone into a mass remainder.

Pitched like this, de Certeau's epistemological pessimism is unable to recover 'lost voices' as content, except at this most homogenized and general level (voices-off). There is, however, another aspect to this which has already been suggested by the previous quotation. The voices that are expelled have the potential to alter the expeller (even if momentarily) and to unbind the archival impulse, and it is through this alteration, which is evident in the archival text, that the lost voices can be heard. This is what de Certeau means when he claims that: 'orality insinuates itself, like one of the threads of which it is composed, into the network – an endless tapestry – of a scriptural economy' (PEL1: 132). Insinuation is the voice of the other both doubled and altered in the writing of the archive. The most vivid example de Certeau offers is the sixteenth-century account that Jean de Léry gives of the Tupinambous people (already mentioned in Chapters 1 and 3). When de Léry hears the songs of the Tupis he describes himself as being 'ravished', and when he remembers the sonority of their voices his 'heart throbs'. For de Certeau the voice of the Tupis, even though it is absented from the account, tears through the ethnological text of de Léry by its power to alter and affect de Léry: it is 'there' in the ravished body, in the heart that throbs, of the writer who comes undone every time he remembers the Tupis' song. Like the song of the Tupinambous, the speech of patois is always there to (potentially) undo and unbind the particular systems of knowledge that find its fundamental architectonics in The Archive:

> This unceasing phonetic movement threatens the urban order of writing; it proliferates around this order like a virgin forest; it insinuates its way into the forum through the word as it is actually spoken, with the 'imperceptible variations' which alter, 'disfigure', and 'undo' a language unaware of what is happening to it.[13]

So while the archive is established to effect the disappearance of patois, it is implicitly besotted with this sonorous world, and it holds endless examples of popular speech (phrases, intonations and so on) which in the end it can't contain.

There is a variety of ways that the voices of others are included in the actual archival text while also being occluded. Citation, for instance, is a double alteration: first the voice is rendered into a manageable scriptural form, cleaned of

---

[13] de Certeau, 'The Word of the Vowel', p. 179.

'noise', sampled for the desired words; second this amputated sample is inserted into an architecture that accords it a 'proper' place, hedged in on all sides by authoritative commentary and expert interpretation – saturated by context. Yet for all that, a degree of uncanniness potentially unbinds the citation from its scholarly (and necessarily oppressive) moorings:

> Something different returns in this discourse, however, along with the citation of the other; it remains ambivalent; it upholds the danger of an uncanniness which alters the translator's or commentator's knowledge. For discourse, cita-tion is the menace and suspense of the lapsus. Alterity dominated – or pos-sessed – through discourse maintains the power of being a fantastic ghost, or indeed a possessor in a latent state . . . Clearly the citation is not a whole in the ethnographical text through which another landscape or another discourse might be revealed; what is cited is fragmented, used over again and patched together in a text. Therein it is altered. Yet in this position where it keeps noth-ing of its own, it remains capable, as in a dream, of bringing forth something uncanny: the surreptitious and altering power of the repressed. (WH: 251)

For de Certeau culture in its plural, heterogeneous state, despite concerted efforts to shape it and tame it, is never ultimately manageable. One way of read-ing de Certeau's historical work is as an attempt to release that unmanageabil-ity; to purposefully refuse the lure of the explanatory thesis that would order the subterraneous heterogeneity that the archive contains.

Historical and ethnographic work (cultural analysis in general) can't help but cause a 'stir' in the archival waters, bringing to the surface potentially disruptive forces, even if the aim of the work is the management and containment of these materials. Marshalling the archive, then, is always to court the recalcitrance of the material it harbours:

> A half century after Michelet, Freud observes that the dead are in fact 'beginning to speak'. But they are not speaking through the 'medium' of the historian-wizard, as Michelet believed: *it is speaking* [*ça parle*] in the work and in the silences of the historian, but without his knowledge. Their voices – whose disappearance every historian posits, which he replaces with his writ-ing – 're-bite' [*re-mordent*] the space from which they were excluded; they continue to speak in the text/tomb that erudition erects in their place. (H: 8)

Again, such a position is indebted to psychoanalysis: 'ça' (it) is the equivalent of the German 'Es', which for Freud is the unruly terrain of instincts and drives, which is rendered in English as 'id'. Historians, perhaps when they least intend, can't help but release something of the subterranean passions that exist in culture. It is here, also, that we get another sense of the archive. If the archive is a form of governance, of cultural management, then there is also something anarchic in its very form. Logically the successful deployment of classificatory regimes, for instance, is dependent on the structural clarity of the classifications and on the manageability of the materials being classified. At the very basis of archival practice is the desire to collect materials. Exponential expansion of an archive clogs its ability to process data: the heterogeneity of materials short-circuits classificatory regimes. There is then a structural tension between the desire to collect and the will to order: the former ultimately acts against the interests of the latter. The archive is an entropic system that fundamentally encourages its own dissolution. The order of the archive is a much more fragile affair than it would at first seem, and while it exerts orchestrating forces its fissures begin to show when it is 'worked on'.

The epistemological 'no' which claimed that the speech of the dispossessed couldn't be un-problematically recovered is transformed into a guarded 'yes' (or a potential 'yes') through a schema which suggests that the archive is fashioned out of what it attempts to tame. Here forms of discursive repression are never total, even if all that you can recover is a momentary frailty in that force of repression that allows us to hear the echo of something else. This guarded 'yes' also recognizes the more disordered actuality of the archive (which is never the complete concretization of the Archival impulse of the scriptural economy) and the disruptive power of what archives 'receive', that remains relatively un-produced. This epistemological position of the 'scriptural economy' is designed, I think, to solicit two attitudes. One is a recognition of the unavoidable complicity that is attendant on all forms of scholarly work. This shouldn't be internalized as self-flagellating guilt, but as an epistemological reminder, one designed to bring humility into the business of scholarly work and to increase an epistemological commitment to the real. The other attitude is an epistemological optimism that is not only aimed at the past and the ethical obligation to hear lost voices, but is also aimed at the future and the possibility of a different architectonics of the archive that might allow a multitude of voices to be much more than a chorus of roaring silence: to make culture hospitable to the voices that inhabit it. Bringing these two responses together is crucial: merely to encourage epistemological optimism would be to ignore the fact that archives (and forms of cultural analyses are in themselves micro-archives, or synecdoches of archives) are founded on their ability to exclude. No ethical approach to cultural work would be possible unless it were aware of its own involvement in exclusion and were prepared to be accountable for this:

Finally, beyond the question of methods and contents, beyond what it says, the measure of a work is what it keeps silent. And we must say that the scientific studies – and undoubtedly the works they highlight – include vast and strange expanses of silence. These blank spots outline a geography of the *forgotten*. They trace the negative silhouette of the problematics displayed black on white in scholarly books. (H: 131 with Julia and Revel)

But alongside this, and always imbricated with the question of epistemology, is the more practical territory of archival work (which includes the production of 'archives' in ethnological work). Here the abstractions that result in theoretical formulations (which always tend towards the condition of absolutism) give way to the singularity of the example. This is a world of gradients, fine distinctions and specific constellations of forces. In this territory we might learn a thing or two (for instance that the longer the citation the more chance of it loosening the collar of its proprietorial context) but we can't 'bank' this knowledge by turning it into a rule. De Certeau's epistemological questions prepare us for situations that are always singular, that always require ingenuity and a willingness to bend in response to the other. And ultimately it is this looseness, this dogmatic demand to rescind dogma, that is the lesson Michel de Certeau insists on.

'BENDING CLOSER TO THE GROUND': SUBALTERN STUDIES

In this context it is useful to explore the enterprise of Subaltern Studies – a collective of historians concentrating (mainly) on South Asian history and society (often with a Bengali focus), as seen from the perspective of subordinate groups. Like de Certeau, Subaltern Studies historians are interested in the excluded, the absent voice in the archive; they often focus on the singularity of an event and its textual traces; and, as in de Certeau, religion plays a much more central and active role in the shaping of modern culture than it does for many other social and cultural historians. To privilege voice and orality is to favour the subaltern over the elite – it is to side with those whose 'voice' fails to become inscribed in official documents and accounts of Indian history. You get a sense of the way Subaltern Studies historians favour oral culture from the titles of their work. For instance, the contents of *Subaltern Studies IX* included Ranajit Guha's 'The Small Voice of History'; Ajay Skaria's 'Writing, Orality and Power in the Dangs, Western India, 1800s–1920s'; Kamala Vishweswaran's 'Small Speeches, Subaltern Gender: Nationalist Ideology and Its Historiography'; and Shail Mayaram's 'Speech, Silence and the Making of Partition Violence in Mewat'.[14]

---

[14] *Subaltern Studies IX: Writings on South Asian History and Society*, edited by Shahid Amin and Dipesh Chakrabarty (Delhi: Oxford University Press, 1996).

In 'The Small Voice of History', Ranajit Guha, the editor of the first six volumes of *Subaltern Studies* that the collective produced and the driving force behind its initial formation, reasserts the aims of Subaltern Studies as being:

> . . . to try and relate to the past by listening to and conversing with the myriad voices in civil society. These are small voices which are drowned in the noise of statist commands. That is why we don't hear them. That is also why it is up to us to make the extra effort, develop the special skills and above all cultivate the disposition to hear these stories and interact with them. For they have many stories to tell – stories which for their complexity are unequalled by statist discourse and indeed opposed to its abstract and over-simplifying modes.[15]

These are the voices that have been ignored, not simply by those historians whose interests might be close to the administrative centres of the British colonial government, but also those emerging from Indian post-partition nationalism. It is against these two historiographies, both of which want to write accounts of Indian history that privilege the actions of elite agents (of colonial administration or anti-colonial liberation), that Subaltern historiography is pitted.

Thus Guha would write in the very first edition of the collective, in the short programmatic essay 'On Some Aspects of the Historiography of Colonial India':

> What, however, historical writing of this kind [the historiography of colonialist elitism and bourgeois-nationalist elitism] cannot do is to explain Indian nationalism for us. For it fails to acknowledge, far less interpret, the contribution made by the people *on their own*, that is, *independently of the elite* to the making and development of this nationalism. In this particular respect the poverty of this historiography is demonstrated beyond doubt by its failure to understand and assess the mass articulation of this nationalism except, negatively, as a law and order problem, and positively, if at all, either as a response to the charisma of certain elite leaders or in the currently more fashionable terms of vertical mobilization by the manipulations of factions.[16]

---

[15] Ranajit Guha, 'The Small Voice of History' in *Subaltern Studies IX*, p. 3.

[16] Ranajit Guha, 'On Some Aspects of the Historiography of Colonial India' in *Subaltern Studies I: Writings on South Asian History and Society*, edited by Ranajit Guha (Delhi: Oxford University Press, 1982), p. 3.

So as a dialogic project Subaltern Studies clearly marks out its terrain: it sets out to tell the histories of 'the people', and to do this as a counter-narrative to the two dominant positions in regard to the historiography of India:

> Both these varieties of elitism share the prejudice that the making of the Indian nation and the development of the consciousness – nationalism – which informed this process, were exclusively or predominantly elite achievements. In the colonialist and neo-colonialist historiographies these achievements are credited to British colonial rulers, administrators, policies, institutions and culture; in the nationalist and neo-nationalist writings – to Indian elite personalities, institutions, activities and ideas.[17]

Inasmuch as Subaltern Studies wants to tell the story of people who have been left out of the historical account, it can be seen to follow what E.P. Thompson, in the 1960s, called 'history from below'.[18] But in this context Subaltern Studies can be seen as wanting to go below Thompson's below:

> Historical scholarship has developed, through recursive practice, a tradition that tends to ignore the small drama and fine detail of social existence, especially at its lower depths. A critical historiography can make up for this lacuna by bending closer to the ground in order to pick up the traces of a subaltern life in its passage through time.[19]

It would be wrong, though, to write as though Subaltern Studies constituted a settled approach to the practice of historiography. It would be more productive to see Subaltern Studies as a conversation or dialogue; where a group of engaged historians are responding to a range of shared problematics. It is these problematics and the responses to them that most closely relate to Michel de Certeau. Thus in a critical account of Subaltern Studies, which points to the lack of any direct access to the subaltern's perspective, Priyamvada Gopal can suggest that, 'the fact that the subaltern does not speak in any unmediated or immediately accessible ways, far from foreclosing the possibility of knowledge, invests the search for better understanding with

---

[17] Guha, 'On Some Aspects of the Historiography of Colonial India', p. 1.

[18] See E.P. Thompson, 'History from Below', *The Times Literary Supplement*, 7 April 1966, pp. 279–80. The classic formulation of history from below is given in E.P. Thompson, *The Making of the English Working Class* (London: Gollancz, 1963), p. 12: 'I am seeking to rescue the poor stockinger, the luddite cropper, the "obsolete" hand-loom weaver, the "utopian" artisan, and even the deluded follower of Joanna Southcott, from the enormous condescension of posterity.'

[19] Guha, 'Chandra's Death', *Subaltern Studies V*, p. 138.

greater urgency'.[20] Such a position is shared by de Certeau's ethical epistemology: critical epistemology provides the drive, opportunity, and often the resources, to develop more intensive contact with the real.

Subaltern Studies has had such an enormous impact on the global intellectual scene that the study of early twentieth-century Bengali culture, for instance, rather than appearing as an obscure specialism in the Anglophone academy (as it would have done ten years ago), is recognized as working towards what Dipesh Chakrabarty terms 'provincializing Europe'. Chakrabarty's historiography (most vividly seen in his books *Provincializing Europe: Postcolonial Thought and Historical Difference* and *Habitations of Modernity: Essays in the Wake of Subaltern Studies*[21]) echoes with formulations that can be found within de Certeau's work: for one thing, the very activity of 'provincializing' is not to simply reverse the positions of margin and centre, to replace Europe with India, for instance. It requires a double dismantling of the terms of this relationship:

The project of provincializing Europe has to include certain . . . moves: first, the recognition that Europe's acquisition of the adjective 'modern' for itself is an integral part of the story of European imperialism within global history; and second, the understanding that this equating of a certain version of Europe with 'modernity' is not the work of Europeans alone; third-world nationalisms, as modernizing ideologies par excellence, have been equal partners in the process. . . In unravelling the necessary entanglement of history – a disciplined and institutionally regulated form of collective memory – with the grand narratives of rights, citizenship, the nation state, and public and private spheres, one cannot but problematise 'India' at the same time as one dismantles 'Europe'.[22]

Chakrabarty's historiography is directed at the entanglements of 'Europe' and 'India', not so as to un-entangle them, but so as to figure their imbrications. Thus, a subaltern 'Indian' historiography, for Chakrabarty, doesn't seek to free itself from 'Europe', but to recognize the problems and possibilities of their imbrication:

What historically enables a project such as that of 'provincializing Europe' is the experience of political modernity in a country like India. European

[20] Priyamvada Gopal, 'Reading Subaltern History' in Neil Lazarus, ed., *Postcolonial Literary Studies* (Cambridge: Cambridge University Press, 2004), p. 151.
[21] Dipesh Chakrabarty, *Provincializing Europe: Postcolonial Thought and Historical Difference* (Princeton and Oxford: Princeton University Press, 2000); Dipesh Chakrabarty, *Habitations of Modernity: Essays in the Wake of Subaltern Studies* (Delhi: Permanent Black, 2002).
[22] Chakrabarty, *Provincializing Europe*, p. 43.

thought has a contradictory relationship to such an instance of political modernity. It is both indispensable and inadequate in helping us to think through the various life practices that constitute the political and the historical in India. Exploring – on both theoretical and factual registers – this simultaneous indispensability and inadequacy of social science thought is the task that this book has set itself.[23]

Such a project as Chakrabarty's works in spite of, and because of, the contradictions that constitute it.

Like de Certeau's historiography, Chakrabarty's work accepts the impossibility of its project, and finds in that impossibility the force to articulate a writing of culture that is aware of its relationship with death:

> I ask for a history that deliberately makes visible, within the very structures of its narrative forms, its own repressive strategies and practices, the part it plays in collusion with the narratives of citizenship in assimilating to the projects of the modern state all other possibilities of human solidarity. . . This is a history that will attempt the impossible: to look toward its own death by tracing that which resists and escapes the best human effort at translation across cultural and other semiotic systems, so that the world may once again be imagined as radically heterogeneous.[24]

Thus Dipesh Chakrabarty might be fulfilling the ethical and epistemological challenge that Michel de Certeau demands, responding to it by articulating a practice whose fragility can bear to flirt with its own demise.

In this discussion of Subaltern Studies we might be able to taste a certain historical sensitivity that is aligned with deconstruction. This, no doubt, is partly attributable to the intervention within the Subaltern Studies group of Gayatri Chakravorty Spivak. In many ways Spivak is oddly placed within Subaltern Studies – for instance, her historical work is, as we will see, not orientated towards subaltern perspectives (her main historical project is related to minor royalty) – yet her intervention via deconstruction and feminism is profound and can be registered across the work of the Subaltern Studies group (rarely as a position to wholeheartedly adopt; but certainly as a position to be in dialogue with). Spivak's position as a 'theorist' (and one aligned with Jacques Derrida) may suggest that her involvement with Subaltern Studies would be highly abstract and philosophical, yet it might actually be her professional role as a professor of literature that really characterizes her contribution. As a reader of texts, Spivak

[23] Chakrabarty, *Provincializing Europe*, p. 6.
[24] Chakrabarty, *Provincializing Europe*, pp. 45–6.

asked different kinds of questions within the archive, ones that, like de Certeau, took epistemological doubt as constitutive of practice. In this she wanted the group to recognize that their project would entail reflections on the semiotic nature of Indian history:

> The Subaltern Studies group seem to me to be . . . proposing at least two things: first, that the moment(s) of change be pluralized and plotted as confrontations rather than transitions (they would thus be seen in relation to histories of domination and exploitation rather than within the great modes-of-production narrative) and, secondly, that such changes are signalled or marked by a functional change in sign-systems. The most important functional change is from the religious to the militant. There are, however, many other functional changes in sign-systems indicated in these collections: from crime to insurgency, from bondsman to worker, and so on.[25]

Inasmuch as she was suggesting to the group that deconstruction might be a productive orientation for them, she wasn't encouraging abstract thought, but a practical epistemology that seems to me to be close to de Certeau's: 'this is the great gift of deconstruction: to question the authority of the investigating subject without paralyzing him, persistently transforming conditions of impossibility into possibility'.[26]

In her historical research, which concerned the 'Rani of Sirmur',[27] a minor royal in the Himalayan hill states in the early nineteenth century who was thought by the colonial administration to be about to be a *sati* (a widow sacrifice), Spivak aimed to pursue this approach by proposing a reading practice orientated to what the imperial archive didn't contain – the voice of the female 'native': 'as we approach [the Rani of] Sirmur, we move from the discourse of class, and race, into gender – and we are in the shadows of shadows'.[28]

[25] Gayatri Chakravorty Spivak, 'Subaltern Studies: Deconstructing Historiography' in *In Other Worlds: Essays in Cultural Politics* (New York and London: Routledge, 1988), p. 197. Spivak's essay first appeared in *Subaltern Studies IV* (1986).

[26] Spivak, 'Subaltern Studies', p. 201 – the use of the masculine pronoun is intentional.

[27] Gayatri Chakravorty Spivak, 'The Rani of Sirmur' in Francis Barker, Peter Hulme, Margaret Iversen, Diana Loxley, eds, *Europe and Its Others: Volume One* (Colchester: University of Essex, 1985), pp. 128–51. That same year a very similar version of the essay was published in *History and Theory* 24 – there the title was 'The Rani of Sirmur: An Essay in Reading the Archives' – pp. 247–72. This essay is also rewritten and included in Gayatri Chakravorty Spivak, *A Critique of Postcolonial Reason: Toward a History of the Vanishing Present* (Cambridge and London: Harvard University Press, 1999). There is then the possibility of analysing all the small and large alterations that take place in the many representations of this essay. To do so partly evidences the growing momentum of postcolonial studies in the 1980s and 1990s.

[28] Spivak, 'The Rani of Sirmur', p. 142.

In relation to what this book has been investigating so far, it is worth noting that the Rani doesn't exist in the archives (these are, of course, the colonial archives, dominated by those of the East India Company), or in the eyes of the colonialists who can only see her as a problem, as someone who might respond to her husband's death in a way that the colonialists want to stop:

> One never encounters the testimony of the women's voice consciousness. Such a testimony would not be ideology-transcendent or 'fully' subjective, of course, but it would constitute the ingredients for producing a counter-sentence. As one goes down the grotesquely mistranscribed names of these women, the sacrificed widows, in the police reports included in the records of the East India Company, one cannot put together a 'voice'.[29]

In searching for a voice that doesn't exist, Spivak establishes a reading practice aimed at uncovering the epistemological violence at the heart of the colonial culture. As far as this goes she wants to distance herself from the positions she sees emerging in critical historiography that would entail a straightforward reversal of classical historiography's aversion to the literary:

> Perhaps my intent is to displace (not transcend) the mere reversal of the literary and the archival implicit in much of LaCapra's work. To me, literature and the archives seem complicit in that they are both a crosshatching of condensations, a traffic in telescoped symbols, that can only too easily be read as each other's repetition-with-a-displacement.[30]

What this means in practice is a close reading of administrative correspondence that pays close attention to the tropic aspects of colonial rule. In this way the poetics of colonialism are revealed as the very opposite of rhetorical froth: they are seen as the determining material substance of colonial domination (forms of worlding and othering).

There is I think an epistemological absolutism in Spivak's work that you don't quite encounter in de Certeau. Towards the end of her first version of the account, she imagines travelling to Jaipur to search for traces of the Rani:

> I have never been to those hills. My own class provenance was not such as to allow summer vacations in so fashionable a resort area. This first trip will be an act of *private* piety. I want to touch the Rani's picture, some remote substance of her, if it can be unearthed. But the account of her representation is

---

[29] Spivak, *A Critique of Postcolonial Reason*, p. 287.
[30] Spivak, 'The Rani of Sirmur', p. 130.

enough for the book. To retrieve her as information will be no disciplinary triumph. Caught in the cracks between the production of the archives and indigenous patriarchy, today distanced by the waves of hegemonic 'feminism', there is no 'real Rani' to be found.[31]

The book that Spivak writes of won't be published for another 15 years. In the meantime she has the chance to travel to 'those hills' (she makes 15 visits) and see if she can find more material on the Rani. She sleeps in the palace; she discovers that Rani Gulari died much later than this time of 'threatened sati'. These facts do not alter the epistemological status of the Rani, but they do suggest to Spivak that she might well look elsewhere. In this she, like de Certeau, looks towards the everyday – the ordinary life of the Rani – as a source for different epistemological possibilities:

> I want to dwell on this very ordinariness. I want to ask what is not considered important enough by the hidden parts of the discipline, hidden only because they are too well known in their typicality to be of interest to anyone engaged in the retrieval of knowledge. I want to dwell on it because work with deconstructive approaches to the subject and with the ethical concerns of the final Foucault have made me more and more aware of the importance of the neglected details of the everyday.[32]

It is here that Spivak moves towards Subaltern Studies – not as a historiographic enterprise but as practice of the present. In her very first visit to track the Rani she encountered women who:

> . . . gathered leaves and vegetation from the hillside to feed their goats. . . They were the rural subaltern, the real constituency of feminism, accepting their lot as the norm, quite different from the urban female sub-proletarian in crisis and resistance. If I wanted to touch their everyday without the epistemic transcoding of anthropological field work, the effort would be a much greater undoing, indeed, of life's goals, than the effort to catch the Rani, in vain, in history.[33]

Subaltern Studies and other postcolonial projects are, perhaps, uniquely positioned to respond to the dual imperatives of recognizing epistemological complicity ('a training in a literary habit of reading the world can attempt to

---

[31] Spivak, 'The Rani of Sirmur', p. 147.
[32] Spivak, *A Critique of Postcolonial Reason*, p. 238.
[33] Spivak, *A Critique of Postcolonial Reason*, p. 242.

put a curb on ... superpower triumphalism only if it does not perceive acknowledgement of complicity as an inconvenience'[34]) while responding to ethical demands. Of course such practitioners don't 'need' Michel de Certeau for this; yet there are, as I've been suggesting, points of elective affinity that work to enlighten both bodies of work. To imagine the world as 'radically heterogeneous' will require all sorts of work: de Certeau's work presents, I like to think, a labour of clarification that is productive for its 'resources of hope', which are to be found within its form of attention, its metamethodology.

As I have mentioned already: attending to the past is only one aspect of this form of attention – equally important is its orientation to the future. The response to the epistemological and ethical challenge, then, is never finished, and can't be adequately responded to through historiography alone. The ethical challenge to create spaces for speech, for voices to multiply, is evidenced in de Certeau's work in two ways: in his work within cultural policy (Chapter 6) and his project of contemporary ethnography (the work on everyday life). To see the two volumes of *The Practice of Everyday Life* as a different form of archival practice, one that attempts to let 'the other' speak, is, I think, the most productive way of viewing them: it is a way of transforming them from theoretical models into examples of practice – and a practice that is both epistemologically and ethically informed.

OPAQUE, STUBBORN LIFE: ANOTHER LANDSCAPE – EVERYDAY LIFE

If I have been concentrating on the historiographic aspect of de Certeau's work it is because it is here that the epistemological and ethical challenge can be most vividly seen; but as we will see in the rest of the book, such challenges are also orientated to the present and the future. It is necessary then to show how de Certeau can imagine and practise a form of ethnography, that while not outside the 'scriptural economy' can work to find a more hospitable place in it for other voices.[35] If archives and historiography have tended to absent the singularity of that which they purport to describe and to house, then the ethical demand never simply rests on the acknowledgement of this: the responsibility, the obligation that is incurred in such a move requires a counter-operation, a generative move to find ways of including the voice of others, a way of listening that doesn't at the same

---

[34] Spivak, *A Critique of Postcolonial Reason*, p. xii.

[35] A third volume of *The Practice of Everyday Life* was planned – this would have been dedicated to the '"fine art of talk" in the everyday practices of language' (PEL1: ix); it was never completed.

time completely erase what it is that is heard. One of the ways of 'listening' revolves around not just the historiographic work but the work on everyday contemporary life. More specifically it revolves around the nature of these practices that are never accounted for in their singularity, but only with the confines of a sociological vision that often works to bury the texture of specificity, singularity. It is, then, in the work on everyday life that we can best see what another archival practice might look like. Crucially there are a number of prerequisites to this practice that need stating at the outset. One is that it must rely on a notion of modernity that is (as I've said above) inclusive of both the success and failure of suturing the past and the present. Another is that it needs to have a more nuanced account of everyday politics that doesn't simply measure politics from the perspective of oppression or hegemony but can also begin to recognize a vast variety of practices that neither submit to the demands of hegemony, nor confront hegemony head-to-head. And lastly it needs to recognize the partiality of any attempt to inscribe the everyday: this is a field that doesn't admit to exhaustive scrutiny, its subterranean status is an aspect of its epistemological condition – such opacity will not be amenable to the harsh light of 'theoretical application'.

Michel de Certeau's work on everyday life evidences a subtle, nuanced and heterological approach. Commenting on his book *The Practice of Everyday Life*, Meaghan Morris writes: 'one of the pleasures of this text for me is the range of moods that it admits to a field of study which – surprisingly, since 'everyday life' is at issue – often seems to be occupied only by cheerleaders and prophets of doom'.[36] And yet, for the most part, responses to de Certeau's work have opted for a limited focus, considering only those aspects of his work that evoke daily practices of subversive and guerrilla-like opposition, ignoring those practices, perhaps more 'everyday', that connect with memory, stubbornness and inertia. Within that scattered field of cultural studies, 'the range of moods' in de Certeau's work seems to have been massively constrained and contained. Exegesis and employment of his work is often caught between a celebratory account of minor acts of 'transgressive' opposition (ripped jeans, fanzines, skateboarding, graffiti and so on) and the condemnation of such celebration in the name of a more pragmatic politics.[37]

---

[36] Meaghan Morris, 'Banality in Cultural Studies' in Patricia Mellancamp, ed., *Logics of Television: Essays in Cultural Criticism* (Bloomington and Indianapolis: Indiana University Press, 1990), p. 26.

[37] For examples of de Certeau being used to account for transgressions see John Fiske, *Understanding Popular Culture* (London: Routledge, 1989) and Henry Jenkins, *Textual Poachers: Television Fans and Participatory Culture* (London: Routledge, 1992). For counter-arguments see Tony Bennett, *Culture: A Reformer's Science* (London: Sage, 1998) and John Frow, 'Michel de Certeau and the Practices of Representation', *Cultural Studies*, 5:1, 1991, pp. 52–60.

Sketching out a poetics of everyday life in *Culture in the Plural*, de Certeau is clear that everyday culture oscillates across two distinct forms:

> On the one hand, there are slowly developing phenomena, latencies, delays that are piled up in the thick breadth of mentalities, evident things and social ritualizations, an opaque, stubborn life buried in everyday gestures that are at the same time both immediate and millenary. On the other hand, irruptions, deviations, that is, all these margins of an inventiveness from which future generations will successively draw their 'cultivated culture'. (CP: 137–8)

Alongside an inventive creativity, de Certeau describes an unhurried culture, 'thick' with the residues of past practices. In this section I want to privilege this 'opaque, stubborn' everyday life, partly as a corrective to an insistence on minor transgressions, and partly because I believe it offers a better perspective for understanding the nature of de Certeau's project as it is connected with providing counter-narratives and counter-archives of cultural practice.

In this de Certeau and his colleagues' project of writing about the practice of everyday life can be seen as a partial response to the archival practice of the Abbé Grégoire. On the most obvious level it works inversely to the 'Gregorian' practice because it is designed to amplify what it approaches rather than put an end to the unruliness of the everyday. De Certeau's practice also presents a very different archival economy: little epistemological differentiation separates theories and sources, or primary and secondary materials; at the same time the singularity of each voice that enters the 'archive' is insisted upon. This shows itself most forcefully in the second volume of *The Practice of Everyday Life* with the decision to include the transcripts of two interviews (interviews characterized by their informal, conversational tone) unedited.

But what does it mean to characterize everyday practices as obstinate as well as inventive, and how does it affect what is a central claim in de Certeau's work, namely, that everyday life can be seen as an arena of resistance? To focus on stubborn, obstinate and 'sheeplike subversion' (PEL1: 200), rather than the 'irruptions, deviations, that is, all these margins of an inventiveness', is not to leave resistance behind. Instead it is to refuse an equation that would all too easily associate resistance with the oppositional and the progressive. Rather than seeing 'resistance' as the work of a liberatory force, we need, if we are going to understand de Certeau's use of the word, to give it a less heroic connotation. Here 'resistance' is more productively associated with its use by engineers and electricians (and psychoanalysts): it limits flows and dissipates energies. If everyday life is resistant it is because it is never fully assimilated to the rhythms that want to govern and orchestrate modern life: perpetual modernization, market economics and discursive regimes. As Mark Poster argues:

The theory of the everyday is surely no outline of revolution, no grand strategy of upheaval. Instead, de Certeau's position serves to confirm the unsutured nature of the social, the impossibility of the full colonization of daily life by the system, the continued fact of resistance to the temporal logic of democratic capitalism, and the ubiquitous eruption of the heterogeneous.[38]

If, as Poster suggests, the everyday evidences a resistance to the 'temporal logic of democratic capitalism', then de Certeau's work might usefully be read in relation to critical accounts of this temporal logic. Those theorists who have tried to describe the logics and experiences of capitalist modernity (Georg Simmel and Walter Benjamin, for instance) should, therefore, provide a productive context for discussing de Certeau's work. It might also work to situate de Certeau within a dialectical tradition of accounting for modern everyday life rather than within the more dominant theoretical framework (Foucault and poststructuralism in general) that is usually reserved for discussing de Certeau. Discussions of modernity might also provide a context for grasping the deeply ambivalent character of 'resistance' in everyday life. But before we can test this claim we need to fill in some details about the nature of de Certeau's project on everyday life.[39]

First published in Paris in 1980, the two volumes that make up *The Practice of Everyday Life* were the result of a research project (1974–78) directed by de Certeau under the auspices of the prestigious *Délégation Générale à la Recherche Scientifique et Technique* (General Office for Science and Technology Research). While the first volume (*Arts de faire*) is authored by de Certeau alone, the majority of the second volume is written by de Certeau's colleagues on the project (Luce Giard and Pierre Mayol) and offers a more empirical attempt to attend to everyday practices of cooking (*cuisiner*) and dwelling (*habiter*). As a prelude to any discussion of the project it is worth emphasizing the preliminary nature of de Certeau's investigation of everyday life. As he states in the introduction to *The Practice of Everyday Life*: 'The point is not so much to discuss this elusive yet fundamental subject as to make such a discussion possible; that is by means of inquiries and hypothesis, to indicate pathways for further research' (PEL1: xi). Rather than revealing the findings of established methodological research, de Certeau's work seeks to locate some of the ground from which it might be possible to register the everyday in the first place. In attending to everyday life de Certeau is not addressing an already constituted theoretical

---

[38] Mark Poster, *Cultural History and Postmodernity: Disciplinary Readings and Challenges* (New York: Columbia University Press, 1997), p. 125.

[39] For a more detailed account of the everyday-life aspect of de Certeau's work see my *Everyday Life and Cultural Theory: An Introduction* (London and New York: Routledge, 2002), Chapter 8.

object, but responding to a long history of silences and erasures. Even after the publication of both volumes of *The Practice of Everyday Life*, de Certeau and Luce Giard can write:

> We know poorly the types of operations at stake in ordinary practices, their registers and their combinations, because our instruments of analysis, modeling and formalization were constructed for other objects and with other aims. The essential analytic work, which remains to be done, will have to revolve around the subtle combinatory set of types of operations and registers, that stages and activates a making-do [*avec-faire* – also 'making-with'], right here and now, which is a singular action linked to one situation, certain circumstances, particular actors. (PEL2: 256 with Giard)[40]

If 'essential analytic work' 'remains to be done' then de Certeau's work needs to be seen as a starting point, rather than as a fully worked-out account. De Certeau seeks to generate 'a body of theoretical questions, methods, categories, and perspectives' that would allow 'ways of operating' to be articulated. Such a science would attend to 'microbe-like' operations and practices, rather than the 'incoherent (and often contradictory) plurality' (PEL1: xi) that is the locus of the individual. The point is worth stressing. As Ian Buchanan argues, de Certeau offers 'a means of analysing culture without recourse to such a blunt and inflexible instrument as identity'.[41] De Certeau's approach to everyday life is concerned with singular operations seen in relation to particular circumstances and it is here that resistance lies, rather than in the valorization of specific identities.

If, as de Certeau and Giard suggest, the usual 'instruments of analysis, modeling and formalization' are inadequate to the everyday, then what instruments will a science of singularity employ? Here de Certeau's work is concerned with inventively adapting analytical approaches for articulating the everyday. But he is also interested in registering reflective understandings from within the everyday. In speculating that the everyday articulates a logic that is peculiar to it, it should seem reasonable that the everyday will also provide the tools for understanding this logic (theory *in* everyday life rather than simply *of* everyday life). Here de Certeau finds theoretical resources in everyday stories and games and the cultural forms associated with them. De Certeau's project needs to be understood as a poetics of the everyday, that is, an attempt to speculatively map the formal logics of an ordinary and daily production (*poesis*). It is the productivity

---

[40] This is from the essay 'La culture comme on la pratique' and although now included in PEL2, it was not originally part of the French publication of Volume 2 that came out in 1980. Originally it was published in *Le français dans le monde* 181, November–December 1983, pp. 19–24.

[41] Ian Buchanan, 'De Certeau and Cultural Studies', *new formations* 31, 1996, p. 182.

of the everyday (its inventive and generative activities and meanings) that remains opaque to analysis. It is this productivity that a poetics of everyday life seeks to register. And while no theoretical resource is simply going to be adequate to the task, de Certeau will use (and alter) a whole variety of theoretical practices to help foreground the dynamics of everyday life. As discussed in the previous chapter, psychoanalysis provides a model that is adapted and transformed in an attempt to chart the forms of practice that operate within the shadowy realm of daily life. Psychoanalysis provides the form not the content for a theory of everyday life. But what general form do these everyday practices take? What figures does a poetics of daily life find in the *poesis* of the everyday? Here it is useful to look very briefly at the way that de Certeau uses the architecture of speech-act theory.

The 'characteristics of the speech act', de Certeau tells us, 'can be found in many . . . practices (walking, cooking, etc.)' (PEL1: xiii). In his account of 'walking in the city', de Certeau suggests that: 'the act of walking is to the urban system what the speech act is to language or to the statements uttered' (PEL1: 97). Unlike urban semioticians who treat the city as a text that is both written and read,[42] de Certeau insists on the analogy of speech as an *act*: 'surveys of routes miss what was: the act of passing by' (PEL1: 97). For de Certeau, walking (or cooking, reading, shopping, dwelling and so on) operates as a practice of enunciation. In the same way that the speech act actualizes language, walking actualizes the urban: the walker makes the urban 'exist as well as emerge' (PEL1: 98). Just as the speech act appropriates and reappropriates language, so the walker selects and uses urban space: the walker 'condemns certain places to inertia or disappearance and composes with others spatial "turns of phrase" that are "rare", "accidental" or "illegitimate" ' (PEL1: 99). And while the speech act connects and communicates with others ('hi', 'OK?', and so on), this phatic aspect is also shared by walking: walking 'with a light or heavy step' operates 'like a series of "hellos" in an echoing labyrinth' (PEL1: 99). Speech-act theory allows de Certeau to insist on an attention to the concrete particularity of activities seen as both constrained by a culture already in place *and* dynamically productive: 'the speech act is at the same time a use *of* language and an operation performed *on* it' (PEL1: 33). Walking both uses the city and operates on it.

De Certeau's poetics of the everyday is built around acts of appropriation and reappropriation that actualize culture and can't be confined by its dominant meanings. The everyday constitutes the singularity of actualized moments (*poesis*) while a poetics of everyday life generalizes about the forms that such actualization take. Here the *way* cultural material is appropriated and reappropriated

---

[42] For instance, Roland Barthes, 'Semiology and Urbanism' (1967) in *The Semiotic Challenge*, translated by Richard Howard (New York: Hill and Wang, 1988).

is crucial. The cunning, stubborn and hidden forms of such appropriation characterize everyday ways of operating.

The impulse behind de Certeau's project is unequivocal: 'If it is true that the grid of "discipline" is everywhere becoming clearer and more extensive, it is all the more urgent to discover how an entire society resists being reduced to it' (PEL1: xiv). Everyday resistance is not seen as the confrontation or contestation of 'discipline', but simply as that which isn't reducible to it. The everyday is both remainder and excess to such a 'grid'. But while de Certeau tends to describe the forces that shape society in terms of scientific rationality and disciplinarity it is worth remembering that modern society is driven (pell-mell) by forces of disruption as much as by regulatory forces. If de Certeau's descriptions of cunning tactics make sense in relation to the regulatory impetus of discipline, his descriptions of stubborn practices make more sense in relation to the revolutionary transformations of modernization.

The language de Certeau uses to describe practices of everyday life fall unevenly into roughly four (overlapping) categories. First, these practices are 'hidden' ('dark', 'opaque', 'obscure', 'silent', 'invisible', 'surreptitious', 'unreadable', 'elusive'). Second, everyday practices are both heterogeneous ('singular' and 'plural')[43] and extensive ('multiform', 'dispersed', 'scattered', 'swarming'). Third, they are 'devious' ('guileful', 'tricky', 'tactical', 'clandestine', 'insinuating', 'rueful', 'disguised', 'clever', 'cunning'). Fourth, they are 'stubborn' ('tenacious', 'obstinate', 'inert', 'persistent', 'ancient'). Although this hardly exhausts the plethora of descriptive terms in the books, it does allow us to sketch out the most prominent tropes. And while de Certeau is famous for designating the everyday as 'devious' and 'tricky', the weight of description (especially when the empirical work of Mayol and Giard in Volume 2 is taken into account) often falls on the 'hidden' and the 'stubborn'. But what are the practices of everyday life hidden from? In regard to what can they be seen as stubborn and tenacious?

Modernity is, of course, a nebulous term, but it does allow us to recognize a frantic speeding up of social life. For the sociologist Georg Simmel, writing in 1903, modern urban life is characterized by 'the intensification of emotional life due to the swift and continuous shift of external and internal stimuli'.[44] These stimuli are especially apparent in modern (industrial) urban environments 'with every crossing of the street, with the tempo and multiplicity of economic, occupational and social life'. For Simmel, 'the consequence of those rapidly shifting stimulations of the nerves which are thrown together in all their contrasts' is

---

[43] This seeming contradiction can best be explained with the example of walking. The city evidences a 'chorus of idle footsteps'. These footsteps constitute a heterogeneity that is both singular and plural: 'Their swarming mass is an innumerable collection of singularities' (PEL1: 97).

[44] Georg Simmel, 'The Metropolis and Mental Life' in *On Individuality and Social Forms* (Chicago and London: University of Chicago Press, 1971), p. 325.

either the blasé attitude of the metropolitan type or the shattered nerves of the neurasthenic.[45] The blasé attitude is 'an indifference toward the distinction between things', it is the assimilation by the individual of the characteristics of a money economy: 'it has been money economy which has thus filled the life of so many people with weighing, calculating, enumerating and the reduction of qualitative values to quantitative terms'.[46] For Simmel the helter-skelter of urban modernity is to be found in increases in traffic, in the extensiveness of financial exchange, and in the spectacular displays of the commodity. The blasé attitude is a defensive and adaptive response to the rhythms of modernization. It is the assimilation of the disruptions of modernity into the psychological fabric of everyday life. De Certeau, as we will see, suggests another response, one less passively adaptive (more 'resistant') to the onslaughts of modernity.

Writing in the wake of Simmel, Walter Benjamin also wrote of the intensification of nervous life in the modern city. To make the rhythm of modernity even more vivid he describes outmoded practices of walking (*flânerie*) to counterpoise against the modern pedestrian surrendering to the tempo of social life:

Around 1840 it was briefly fashionable to take turtles for a walk in the arcades. The *flâneurs* liked to have the turtles set the pace for them. If they had had their way, progress would have been obliged to accommodate itself to this pace. But this attitude did not prevail; Taylor, who popularized the watchword 'Down with dawdling!' carried the day.[47]

The incessantly speeding-up assembly line of modern life wins out against the art of dawdling. Benjamin narrates a tale in which modernity witnesses the invasion of everyday life by the dynamics of capitalism. Against this de Certeau offers, not a counter-narrative, but a para-narrative (and a para-archive) where everyday life can be seen to move at multiple speeds with varied rhythms, where the daily articulates moments of cunning and stubborn resistance. In contemporary everyday life, dawdling might not win the day, but it is never fully obliterated either.

Seen from this perspective, modernity is a revolutionary force disrupting all areas of social life and is only managed by the regulatory drive of modernity's institutional regimes. But if the choice is on the one hand shattered nerves and on the other a willingness to surrender to discipline and the tempo of modern

[45] Simmel, 'The Metropolis and Mental Life', p. 329.
[46] Simmel, 'The Metropolis and Mental Life', p. 328.
[47] Walter Benjamin, 'The Paris of the Second Empire in Baudelaire' (1938) in *Charles Baudelaire: A Lyric Poet in the Era of High Capitalism*, translated by Harry Zohn (London: Verso, 1983), p. 54.

life, de Certeau sees the everyday as the arena for a third choice. Here the activities of everyday life stubbornly evade capture by discipline and tenaciously hold on to aspects of life that are in many ways residual and excessive to the revolutionary force of modernization. The persistence of memory, affable dawdling, rituals of conviviality and genial communication stubbornly persist in the face of what Luce Giard calls 'overmodernization'.

Writing about the Croix-Rousse neighbourhood of Lyons, France, Pierre Mayol (in Volume two of *The Practice of Everyday Life*) finds a conviviality that is resistant to modernization through the stubborn persistence of everyday ways of operating. In his ethnographic study of this urban area, Mayol, who grew up here, pays particular attention to the small shops that serve the neighbourhood. 'Robert's' store is especially significant for Mayol's informants and it is clear that Robert is much more than a 'grocer' or a provider of essential materials. As Madame Marie (an 83-year-old inhabitant of the neighbourhood) explains: 'he's nice with everyone, everyone likes him a lot, he's the *universal Robert* of the neighborhood' (PEL2: 72 Mayol). This 'universal' status is due to his knowledge and memory: 'he forgets nothing, records everything, knows the preferences of each and every person, calls almost all his customers by their first name, is still on intimate terms with all those he knew in childhood and knows all their children' (PEL2: 74 Mayol). Prior to Mayol's research, the significance of Robert's store was threatened by a seemingly inevitable modernization. The shop changed from being a small shop with counter service to being a self-service 'store' that was part of a much larger chain. While this transformation was done in the name of efficiency and profit and might have put an end to the convivial dawdling (reminiscing, 'gossiping', etc.) that was so central to the standing of the shop, Robert's maintained its neighbourhood significance. Under circumstances that might not have been conducive to conviviality (increased through-put orchestrated by self-service), 'Robert continues, under a redesigned format, to make use of an ancient practice of consumption, in other words, a speaking practice: discussions, information, help in choosing, credit, and so on' (PEL2: 75 Mayol). Within this modernized environment Robert stubbornly continues his everyday practices: 'he comes and goes, discusses with this person and that, scolds one child, gives another some candy, serves a customer, and asks how things are going' (PEL2: 74 Mayol).

Within the terms of de Certeau's theorizing about everyday life, the example of Robert's store evidences a number of features. Significantly, it shows a tenacious ability to continue certain practices in the face of disruption. This can be understood both as a stubbornness in regard to modernization, as well as a 'tricky' adaptation of a modern form to ancient ends: the newly designed shop is made to fit the persistent practices of easy conviviality. The modern shopping environment (self-service, payment check-out, etc.) has been appropriated and actualized in accordance with the everyday practices of a neighbourhood. For de Certeau this is not a generalized practice; its singularity must be insisted upon – this shop, these practices, here and now.

Luce Giard's portrayal of cooking is similarly marked by 'invention' on the one hand and persistence on the other. For Giard the everyday art of cooking evidences 'a subtle intelligence full of nuances and strokes of genius, a light and lively intelligence that can be perceived without exhibiting itself, in short, a very ordinary intelligence' (PEL2: 158 Giard). Giard situates an 'art of cooking' in a space that neither succumbs to the seductions of capitalist modernity, nor simply mourns a romanticized past:

> Between the symmetrical errors of archaistic nostalgia and frenetic over-modernization, room remains for microinventions, for the practice of reasoned differences, to resist with a sweet obstinance the contagion of conformism, to reinforce the network of exchanges and relations, to learn how to make one's own choice amongst the tools and commodities produced by the industrial era. (PEL2: 213 Giard)

For Giard the resistant nature of everyday life is revealed as (partly) a 'conservative' response, precisely because industrial modernity is figured as revolutionary ('frenetic overmodernization'). But as Giard insists, to resist a modernizing impulse doesn't throw us back into the realm of nostalgia. This is not to desire a past that is gone, but to continue practices that have, so to speak, gone to ground. While Giard is clearly attempting to celebrate inventive work that has been denigrated precisely because it has been deemed 'women's work', her account of cooking is located in a sensual realm that, as Certeau reminds us, 'cannot be captured in a picture, nor . . . circumscribed in a text' (PEL1: 102).

Each gesture, each smell, each culinary trick is thick with the condensation of memories. 'Doing Cooking' is never simply the more or less inventive response to the limitations of circumstance; it always smells and tastes of the past. Cooking, like psychoanalysis, 'recognizes the past in the present' (H: 4). Cooking and eating articulate the tenacity of memory: 'These are memories stubbornly faithful to the marvelous treasure of childhood flavors' (PEL2: 188 Giard). Quoting from Gaston Bachelard, Giard's sensual realm of 'cooking' evidences the density of cultural memory: 'This glass of pale, cool, dry wine marshals my entire life in the Champagne. People may think I am drinking: I am remembering . . .' (PEL2: 188 Giard).

These practices are hidden, scattered, tricky and obstinate. They fall below the horizon of visibility. Rarely do they make it into the archive. Their assumed triviality condemns them to the realm of the insignificant and registers a gendering of everyday life. But they also remain opaque because they constitute the world of day-dreaming and corporeal memory. Such a world resists empirical recording and only gets registered through the speculative approaches of theory and literature. De Certeau and Giard situate the everyday as both a practical world of singular actions and an interior landscape of fantasy, imagination and remembrance. In the practical world of ethnographic fieldwork, de Certeau, Giard and Mayol offer an example of a deceptively simple practice. Their 'native informants' are friends and associates (not scientific samples); in collecting their voices these informants aren't interrogated. Instead it is the art of conversation that is used to solicit practices of daily life. The authors take the side of native informants; there is little epistemological distinction to be made between materials that emerge out of self-reflection and those that are garnered from novels or friends. One aspect of this work that might be easily missed is the tone: there is little here that speaks in an authoritative way – interpretations aren't made in the light of evidence, rather descriptions are stitched together and accumulate in an archive of plurality, undirected by a theoretical argument.

The everyday world echoes with a clatter of footsteps: footsteps that are out of step with the rhythms of urban modernity. Everydayness is the movement that drags, that takes detours or 'constantly leaps, or skips like a child, hopping on one foot' (PEL1: 101). This doesn't mean that 'capitalist modernity' (or 'discourse', or 'discipline', etc.) hasn't colonized the everyday in substantial and terminal ways, just that something else is there too, something that resists total assimilation. It is this that holds out some kind of promise. It would, however, be hard to get too optimistic from de Certeau's account of everyday life; to do so would require a very partial reading of his work. Yet his work does serve as an antidote to those kinds of accounts that would reduce experience to the machinations of power and discipline.

Questions remain. Why has the reading of de Certeau so clearly insisted on privileging moments of visible cunning over 'obscure, stubborn life'? Why has the inventive tactics of *la perruque* ('the worker's own work disguised as work for his employer' [PEL1: 25]), been favoured over all those stubborn instances of cultural inertia? Perhaps it is because this aspect of de Certeau's work is the easiest to hitch to an already established form of cultural politics. Perhaps to focus on 'tactics' rather than the persistence of memory, registers a gendered perspective, privileging the street over the home, the machismo of the 'cultural guerrilla' over the sensuality of the ordinary. Perhaps, also, over-achieving academics find it difficult to enthuse about slow and obstinate practices (the 'right to laziness' is, after all, not a slogan common to the academy). Perhaps though, 'obscure, stubborn life' is recognized as harbouring the seeds of something much more dangerous than the playful subversions of subcultural rituals. Doesn't the obstinate and stubborn also articulate those practices of cultural conservatism that resist, not just overmodernization, but all the liberal changes that have been made against social inequality? Doesn't the everyday host another resistance that obstinately clings to xenophobic and racist 'ways of operating' in the face of multiculturalism? Isn't the everyday home to a range of phobic fantasies that articulate a dominant heterosexism and misogyny? Resistance to capitalist globalization doesn't always come in an emancipatory form: nationalism and religious intolerance are also the stubborn and daily practices of a resistance to modernization. While these oppressive resistances are not limited to 'obstinate' forms (racist, homophobic, nationalistic, sexist, etc., ways of operating can also have a cunning tactical character) it is, perhaps, opaque and stubborn life that offers the most vivid examples of oppressive resistance. This is due to the way that such oppressive everyday resistance is often camouflaged by the patina of 'tradition'.

Writing in 1940, only months prior to his suicide, Benjamin gives the singularly most haunting critique of modernization as progress. He writes of an 'angel of history' caught in the storm of modernity:

> His eyes are staring, his mouth is open, his wings are spread. This is how one pictures the angel of history. His face is turned toward the past. Where we perceive a chain of events, he sees one single catastrophe which keeps piling wreckage upon wreckage and hurls it in front of his feet. . . . This storm irresistibly propels him into the future to which his back is turned, while the pile of debris before him grows skyward. This storm is what we call progress.[48]

Facing immanent capture by Fascist forces, Benjamin's characterization of capitalist modernity is understandably bleak. While this well-known passage is clearly allegorical, it also deserves a more literal reading. From the perspective of an everyday urban modernity, Benjamin's description of 'progress' as the piling-up of wreckage might seem resolutely non-figurative. Urban modernization orchestrated by the machinations of global capital creates debris: it wrecks, pulls-down and re-locates as part of its 'enterprise'. In city spaces (often the poorest, the cheapest, the most profitable) the feeding frenzy of capitalist expansion decimates not just buildings but whole neighbourhood communities. Resistance can take many different forms, but one notable tendency has been the surfacing of an incipient racism expressed as the maintenance of *traditional* community. Faced with the juggernaut of trans-national capitalism, elements within threatened neighbourhoods (neighbourhoods that evidence a richly diverse multiculturalism) have sometimes opted for the tactic of claiming a neighbourhood as *belonging* to them. Mobilizing the language of propriety,

---

[48] Walter Benjamin, 'Theses on the Philosophy of History' (1940) in *Illuminations*, translated by Harry Zohn (London: Fontana, 1982), p. 259–60.

self-declared representatives of a white working-class culture (for instance) can attempt to resist the wreckage of modernity by conjuring up images of 'traditional' neighbourhood communities, specifically excluding newer, immigrant communities. The surfacing of oppressive resistance in such moments of crisis may register a more everyday 'opaque and stubborn' way of operating that is used to stop certain groups from ever achieving a sense of belonging to a neighbourhood in the first place. From this perspective we might need to revisit 'Robert's' shop in the Croix-Rousse neighbourhood. What kind of 'ancient' 'speaking practice' is possible in the corner shop in Croix-Rousse? What gets said about the gay couple that moves in down the road, or the pregnant woman who lives alone, or the Muslim family in the next street?[49] The speaking practices that de Certeau sees as central to everyday life must be seen as flagrantly ambivalent: the same *mode* of operating can be both expansively inclusive and oppressively exclusive. This is why de Certeau insists on the *singularity* of operations within the everyday. But the *potential* of everyday practices to be both convivially inclusive and resistant to the rhythms of capitalist modernity needs to be insisted upon. It is this that makes de Certeau's work more than just a description of the everyday. The everyday, for de Certeau, is where both practical critiques and utopian practices must be found.

De Certeau's work is not a nostalgia for something that has passed, but a willingness to listen to different temporalities that exist together in the present. In refusing to ascribe a single rhythm to the social he opens up the way to thinking and recording 'culture in the plural'. The everyday becomes a performative field of operations (for example, speech acts) that bring to the surface (often in obscure ways) repressed and sometimes repressive activities. Seen in this light the resistance in the everyday can't have an unambiguous political value. Resistance would need to be recognized as a formal ingredient in an everyday that can't simply be mined for instances of ethically progressive practice. If, as de Certeau and Giard insist, analytic work 'remains to be done' then one direction that it will need to pursue is the dialectical reading of 'obscure, stubborn life'. Here the everyday will evidence bitter hatreds alongside 'sweet obstinance', and phobic pathologies will run parallel with amiable conviviality.

The production of archival singularities in the present (the everyday-life project) needs to be seen in relation to the same epistemological and ethical problems that exist in attempting to read the past. This is an archive that includes the ordinary, not in an attempt to provide unmediated access to the

---

[49] For an account of one specific oral 'event' that promoted anti-Semitism see Edgar Morin (in collaboration with Bernard Paillard, Evelyn Burguière, Claude Capulier, Suzanne de Lusignan, Julia Vérone), *Rumour in Orleans,* translated by Peter Green (London: Anthony Blond, 1971) – published in France in 1969.

real, but so as to access a dense and obscure actuality that unbinds a sense of progressive modernization and archival control. The everyday-life project is an attempt to write the archive differently, to fill it with what exceeds capture. In the last two substantive chapters I want to pursue the methodological and practical aspects of this. First, in the next chapter, by looking at what the epistemological and ethical demand of de Certeau, when orientated to the present and the future, might mean for the practice of writing and the practice of literature (including new forms of literary historiography). And in the chapter following that, by looking at how these epistemological and ethical considerations might inform cultural policy.

CHAPTER 5

The Zoo of Everyday Practices: Literature, Narratives, Voices

Is it not then time to recognize the theoretical legitimacy of narrative, which is then to be looked upon not as some ineradicable remnant (or a remnant still to be eradicated) but rather as a necessary form for a theory of practices? In this hypothesis, *a narrative theory would be indissociable from any theory of practices*, for it would be its precondition as well as its production. (H: 192)

To do that would be to recognize the theoretical value of the novel, which becomes the zoo of everyday practices since the establishment of modern science. (PEL: 78)

INTRA-DISCIPLINARITY AND EXTRA-DISCIPLINARITY

At the start of *The Mystic Fable* de Certeau describes an orientation composed of four trajectories:

> Here are the areas of inquiry on the basis of which the advancing line of four approaches, like four sides of a frame, will gradually appear: the link between this 'modern' *mystics* and a new eroticism, a psychoanalytic theory, historiography itself, and the 'fable' (which relates simultaneously to orality and fiction). These four discursive practices establish a framework. The organization of a space, though necessary, will be seen to be unable to 'stop' the subject matter. (MF: 3)[1]

This four-cornered or four-starred cosmology might seem to function as a general sign of de Certeau's interdisciplinary approach to the study of culture – it is composed of known and identifiable disciplines or arenas of knowing: epistemology (positioned in relation to desire and sexuality); psychoanalysis; historiography; and literary studies (where the emphasis is on oral culture and fables). It should be clear by now that de Certeau's approach to the analysis of

---

[1] On the meaning of 'mystics' for de Certeau see note 50 in Chapter 2.

culture wanders across disciplinary boundaries, and that, in doing so, he reveals something of the contingency of those boundaries. Is he, then, to be thought of as offering an interdisciplinary approach to the analysis of culture? Is he simply a prime example of erudition navigating, with consummate ease, across the various borderlands of discourse? Something more, I think, is at stake here. Interdisciplinarity follows the logic of accumulation and application: apply a little bit of this (semiotics, say), and then a little of that (political economy, say), followed by a liberal helping of this (cultural history, for instance) and then, hey presto, you have a complete picture. What this notion of interdisciplinarity leaves intact are the disciplinary fields themselves.

Throughout this book I have been arguing that the best approach to the work of Michel de Certeau is to understand it as a methodologically driven project – one that is driven, through epistemological critique, to search out better ways of making contact with the actual, the real. There is, I think, coherence to this method, but it isn't to be found by looking for a consistent set of tools. The coherence lies in the consistency by which epistemological and ethical challenges root and uproot the analysis of culture: the result is work that is at once intensely critical (and fundamentally self-critical) at the same time as being socially and culturally directed to the production of more hospitable, more liberating, more inclusive circumstances. At the centre of this (and as a model for more extensive change) is the transformation of the very means most readily available to de Certeau – the academic disciplines and their cognate methodologies. In transforming the means of cultural analysis, de Certeau privileges the unmanageability of the cultural material under scrutiny. This means that the object (the cultural world 'under investigation') exceeds or escapes the grip of analysis – but not before it has marked and altered the form of attention that attempts to grasp it. A contradiction opens up a space whereby the object and the form of analysis are altered as part of the process of analysing. A contradiction exists because this 'object' is both a product of the investigation (to a degree the performativity of analysis calls it forth) *and* an obdurate object that resists this performative productivity. What emerges as the productivity of analysis is neither the 'object', nor the application of a tool-kit; the analysis is the performance of a form of attention that has been fashioned as the result of meeting the concrete social and ultimately ungraspable cultural world. Cultural analysis, for de Certeau, is both partial and dynamic – it is analysis bitten by the cultural world.

In this chapter I am going to focus on aspects of narrative and literature to show more precisely how de Certeau's ethical and epistemological challenge can result in writing practices that are attuned to the heterogeneity of the daily and how this can produce very fruitful forms of analytic cultural writing. Here, novels become a rich resource for such heterogeneity, and in what follows I show how the work of Mikhail Bakhtin compares to de Certeau in this regard. I will go on to look at how, for de Certeau, narrative becomes a resource in everyday life, both for practical performances, and also for conveying social memory. To do this I will look specifically at the work of Marguerite Duras, a novelist ever-present in de Certeau's work. While Duras' work doesn't offer itself up as a model of historical and cultural writing that can be developed (it is too stylist-ically specific for that), it should sensitize us to the possibilities of experimental narrative forms for the telling of culture. To make this more vivid and practical I show how two writers interested in giving accounts of gay (and, for the most part, male) culture, use experimental narrative forms to provide fuller, thicker tellings of cultural life. But first I need to show how 'literature', in de Certeau's hands, is transformed into something like a scientific enquiry into culture.

My argument is that de Certeau transforms the very ground of cultural analy-sis and that he does this by refusing a logic-of-application (for the study of cul-ture), replacing it with a logic-of-alteration. What this means in practice is that there is no application of psychoanalysis, for instance (no new objects to be thrown in psychoanalysis' way, to be devoured by it); instead psychoanalysis and cultural objects meet when each bend towards their other, when each alter in response, and in so doing become fundamentally transformed. Under these cir-cumstances it would seem unlikely that 'interdisciplinarity' is going to be the best description of de Certeau's 'logics-of-alteration'; interdisciplinarity won't be an adequate descriptor for the reformatting of cultural analysis.

Across de Certeau's oeuvre, historiography, literary studies, epistemology and psychoanalysis congregate (always in response to the cultural world), and as they congregate each one of them undergoes an alteration that reveals fundamentally shared elements: but these are secret similarities that set these discourses off in new directions, under 'new management', so to speak. Thus, for de Certeau, to recognize psychoanalysis you first need to recognize it as a form of literature:

> My first thesis is: Lacan is first of all an exercise of literature (a literature which would know what it is). Maybe it is a scandal within the discipline, but why will literature always be labeled 'not serious'? If we follow Lacan where he leads, toward a 'speaking' [*dire*] whose nature is revealed by its ana-lytical experience, he points toward the 'truth' of literary practice. (H: 51)

Recognizing the literariness of psychoanalysis requires both intra-disciplinary and extra-disciplinary work: it means looking to see what is essential to the dis-cipline as a cultural operation; and it means looking outside it to see its relation to culture at large (in this sense literature is the name of the extra-disciplinary field). By bending psychoanalysis into a form of literature, two operations are per-formed: literature is given a theoretical and analytic status – a serious, 'scientific' position, one from where it can conduct analyses; psychoanalysis is resituated (and resuscitated), not as a form of interpretation or explanation, but as a vocal-izing practice, a production of speech. In this way the literary text is not an object that desires interpretation, nor is psychoanalysis something designed to perform this operation. Both coalesce (to some degree) through the transformation of the terms of their meeting. In this, 'literature' isn't the needle that would puncture the epistemological dreams used to secure the science of psychoanalysis; rather, literature is used to liberate the essential element in psychoanalysis, which turns out to be its literary (therefore 'scientific') characteristic – its ability to deal in fables, to produce speech, etc. In this process the dominant epistemological cur-rency (science *versus* literature) is converted to a general economy based on the imbrication of the terms (literary science and scientific literariness) which also results in the transformation of these terms.

But if psychoanalysis is a form of literature (' "literary" is that language which makes something else heard than that which it says; conversely, psychoanalysis is a literary practice of language' [H: 53]), literature, crucially, turns out to be a form of historiography:

> I will state my argument without delay: literature is the theoretical discourse of the historical process. It creates the non-topos where the effective oper-ations of a society attain a formalization. Far from envisioning literature as the expression of a referential, it would be necessary to recognize here the analogue of that which for a long time mathematics has been for the exact sciences: a 'logical' discourse of history, the 'fiction' which allows it to be thought. (H: 18)

Rather than the meeting of literature and history being used to reveal the rhetor-ical foundation of historiography (history, the argument might go, is a form of literature if only it could admit it and shrug off its pretensions towards objec-tive truth) here literature becomes a form of meta-history. Literature is where commentaries on historicity are produced, where a grammar of historical action is revealed, and where remembering and forgetting are figured as essential social and cultural elements. There are few novels, for instance, that don't deal in the past (try to imagine one!): seen in this way the arena that most insistently deals in the relationships between the past, the present and the future is actually liter-ature rather than historiography.

Inasmuch as there will be a 'literary' aspect to all discourse (the moments when a discourse 'catches itself in the mirror', for instance), then the job of alter-ing disciplines, for de Certeau, is partly going to be realized when that literary element is brought into the foreground. But, as I have been insisting, this does not result in an epistemological pessimism (that all that can be known are 'fictions', for instance). We need to remember that what is being privileged is literature's involvement with the world, its refusal of disciplinary specialism: in this way literature is the name of what is possible (and what has been achieved) when disciplinarity specialisms are overcome (it is the extra-disciplinary). This, then, should leave little comfort for the literary analyst who might imagine that a traditional form of 'literary criticism' is thereby epistemologically or ethically more justified than other disciplinary approaches:

> It is a function of the historian to flush the literary analysts out of their alleged position as pure spectators by showing them that social mechanisms of selec-tions, critique, and repression are everywhere present, by reminding them that it is violence that invariably founds a system of knowledge. (H: 136)

History interrupts the business of literary analysis, just as literature (the liter-ary) derails and re-rails the business of historiography and psychoanalysis. As Gayatri Chakravorty Spivak has written, and in a way that chimes with de Certeau's position: 'the performance of these tasks, of the historian and the teacher of literature, must critically "interrupt" each other, bring each other to crisis, in order to serve their constituencies; especially when each seems to claim all for its own'.[2]

We could, without too much of an ill-fit, situate de Certeau within a broad tradition of 'criticism-becoming-literary'; a form of 'literary theory' or 'literary analysis' that Jane Gallop qualifies by insisting that 'by this phrase we under-stand not a theory of literature, but a theory that was itself truly literary'.[3] This is also what Tom Conley points to when he titles his introduction to de Certeau's *The Writing of History*: 'For a *Literary* Historiography' – italicizing something that is not an object of study but a form of study (WH: vii Conley). In the early 1980s the art critic Rosalind Krauss described the work of Roland Barthes and Jacques Derrida as 'paraliterary', and the term might also be extended to include de Certeau. Referring to the late work of Barthes, Krauss writes that it 'simply cannot be called criticism, but it cannot for that matter be called non-criticism either. Rather, criticism finds itself caught in a dramatic web of many voices, citations, asides, divagations. And what is created, as in the case of so much of Derrida, is a kind of paraliterature.'[4] This sense of writing moving by digression and drift as much as by seamless argument fits well with de Certeau; but more important for understanding de Certeau is this sense of a 'dramatic web of many

---

[2] Gayatri Chakravorty Spivak, 'A Literary Representation of The Subaltern: A Woman's Text from the Third World' in *In Other Worlds: Essays in Cultural Politics* (New York and London: Routledge, 1988), p. 241.

[3] Jane Gallop, *Anecdotal Theory* (Durham and London: Duke University Press, 2002), p. 2.

[4] Rosalind Krauss, 'Poststructuralism and the Paraliterary' in *The Originality of the Avant-Garde and Other Modernist Myths* (Cambridge: MIT Press, 1985), p. 292.

voices' that writing is thrown into. And it is here that it is useful to point to some parallels between the Russian theorist Mikhail Bakhtin and Michel de Certeau.

For Bakhtin, as for de Certeau, the historical emergence of the novel opens up a space for the figuring of social and cultural forces in ways that allow the novel to be, potentially, a 'realist utopia' (it shows the full range of life – including the social management of life) as well as a critical counter-discourse at odds with the dominant social discourses (the discourses of governance, the scriptural economy). Writing about the pre-history of the novel, and the range of literary genres that were available in Roman times, Bakhtin offers a utopian image of what the novel could be:

> I imagine this whole [the variety of Roman genres] to be something like an immense novel, multi-generic, multi-styled, mercilessly critical, soberly mocking, reflecting in all its fullness the heteroglossia and multiple voices of a given culture, people and epoch. In this huge novel – in this mirror of constantly evolving heteroglossia – any direct word and especially that of the dominant discourse is reflected as something more or less bounded, typical and characteristic of a particular era, aging, dying, ripe for change and renewal.[5]

The bringing together of competing and contrasting genres allows something of the messy social world to come through; and it also points out that the conditions for change are inscribed in the foundations of culture – in its messy actuality, in the constant contestation that is aimed at any single account of social and cultural life.

One fundamental aspect of their work that links Bakhtin and de Certeau might best be summed up in de Certeau's words: 'I shall assume that plurality is originary' (PEL1: 133). For Bakhtin social life in its actuality is always the messy hodge-podge of competing, conflicting voices. As the above quotation shows, the word he uses to describe this basic situation is heteroglossia – the multitude of voices that represents the dynamic and constantly changing social world, voices that spiral out, undercutting attempts to unify culture. Heteroglossia is the centrifugal force that exists as a basic fact of social life and means that any attempt to organize social life 'monologically' (culture ordered in a unified direction) is faced with the task of countering heteroglossia with a centripetal force capable of subduing its immense, disruptive influence. Gary Saul Morson and Caryl Emerson, in their book *Mikhail Bakhtin: Creation of a Prosaics*, give the following account of heteroglossia:

---

[5] Mikhail Bakhtin, 'From the Pre-history of Novelistic Discourse' in *The Dialogic Imagination: Four Essays*, translated by Caryl Emerson and Michael Holquist (Austin: Texas University Press, 1981), p. 60.

Centrifugal forces register and respond to the most diverse events of daily life, to the prosaic facts that never quite fit any official or unofficial definition. They are an essential part of our moment-to-moment lives, and our responses to them record their effect on all our cultural institutions, on language, and on ourselves. Heteroglossia – Bakhtin's term for linguistic centrifugal forces and their products – continually translates the minute alterations and re-evaluations of everyday life into new meanings and tones, which, in sum and over time, always threatens the wholeness of any language.[6]

Emerson and Morson explain that heteroglossia doesn't describe a situation where the subversive centrifugal forces of the multitude are pitted against the ruthless will-to-order of official discourse as a head-to-head conflict. In Bakhtin's understanding of the world, centrifugal forces are *by definition* disparate, conflicting and disorganized: they are not a unified or even 'collective' response to social governance. The various elements of heteroglossia are as resolutely antagonistic to one another as they are towards a central organizing and dominating discourse. In this sense the chorus of the multitude is fundamentally discordant. But these voices are not endlessly individuated voices – they are social voices, or, as Bakhtin will go on to say, 'speech genres'.[7]

There is much here that the world of de Certeau connects to, but also much that is different. While Bakhtin emphasizes the always unfinished and partial unity of culture, which is always facing (and being partly undone by) the ineradicable presence of heteroglossia,[8] de Certeau's epistemologically more sceptical understanding posits something akin to heteroglossia as an invisible but insistent substrate of a culture that seems on the face of it more regulated. This is a heteroglossia that you occasionally get a glimpse of within the much more successful orderings of the scriptural economy. De Certeau recognizes the same rich, creative, polyphonic world of heteroglossia that Bakhtin describes, but it is not an easily accessible realm for de Certeau. While it constitutes everyday life for de Certeau there is always the problem that when this aspect of everyday life becomes a topic of disciplinary scrutiny, it is cut, managed – its radical and unsettling plurality is controlled. Yet what Bakhtin and de Certeau would both agree on would be the importance of speech for describing a world where

[6] Gary Saul Morson and Caryl Emerson, *Mikhail Bakhtin: Creation of a Prosaics* (Stanford: Stanford University Press, 1990), p. 30.

[7] See the essay 'The Problem of Speech Genres' in Mikhail Bakhtin, *Speech Genres and Other Late Essays*, translated by Vern W. McGee (Austin: University of Texas Press, 1986), pp. 60–102.

[8] Given that Bakhtin is theorizing heteroglossia at a time and a place that saw one of the most successful, ruthless and tragic implementations of monologic culture (Stalin's Russia), and that he was sentenced to exile in Kazakhstan during the early 1930s, Bakhtin's theory must count as one of the great acts of intellectual optimism.

polyphony is the unbound aspect of a scriptural economy. And they would also agree that the novel offers one of the most compelling accounts of this: its form is the most plastic and accommodating to the descant of heteroglossia.

For Bakhtin the historical emergence of the novel creates a cultural form that is peculiarly suited to orchestrating the competing language forms that circulate in the world at large:

> The novel orchestrates all its themes, the totality of the world of objects and ideas depicted and expressed in it, by means of the social diversity of speech types and by the differing individual voices that flourish under such conditions. Authorial speech, the speeches of narrators, inserted genres, the speech of characters are merely those fundamental compositional unities with whose help heteroglossia can enter the novel; each of them permits a multiplicity of social voices and a wide variety of their links and interrelationships (always more or less dialogized).[9]

The novel, for Bakhtin, offers a condensed slice of heteroglossia, a synecdoche of heteroglossia, because it always contains a multiplicity of voices or speech genres. Bakhtin itemizes the various genres (speech and written) that are usually found in novels, as follows: 'direct authorial literary artistic narration'; 'various forms of oral everyday narration'; 'semiliterary (written) everyday narration (the letter, the diary, etc.)'; 'various forms of literary but extra-artistic authorial speech (moral, philosophical or scientific statements, oratory, ethnographic descriptions, memoranda and so forth)'; and 'stylistically individualized speech of characters'.[10] The cavalcade of voices that Bakhtin finds in the novel is partly due to the authors that interest him – François Rabelais and Fyodor Dostoevsky, for instance – but also relates to the novel in its early and classic form.[11]

This attention to literature, and its evaluation as a form of extra-disciplinary description of the social world, is very similar to de Certeau's assessment of the novel in its classic, nineteenth-century version:

> As indexes of particulars – the poetic or tragic murmurings of the everyday – ways of operating enter massively into the novel or the short story, most notably into the nineteenth-century realistic novel. They find there a new

---

[9] Bakhtin, 'Discourse in the Novel' (1934–5) in *The Dialogic Imagination*, p. 263.

[10] Bakhtin, 'Discourse in the Novel', p. 262.

[11] See Mikhail Bakhtin, *Rabelais and his World*, translated by Hélène Iswolsky (Bloomington: Indiana University Press, 1984), first published in 1965, and Mikhail Bakhtin, *Problems of Dostoevsky's Poetics*, translated by Caryl Emerson (Manchester: Manchester University Press, 1984) – a version of this book first appeared in Russia in 1929, a much-expanded second edition (which is the one translated into English) first appeared in 1963.

representational space, that of fiction, populated by everyday virtuosities that science doesn't know what to do with and which become the signatures, easily recognized by readers, of everyone's micro-stories. *Literature* is transformed into a repertory of these practices that have no technological copyright. They soon occupy a privileged place in the stories that patients tell in the wards of psychiatric institutions or in psychoanalysts' offices. (PEL1: 70)

For de Certeau the classic realist novel comes to preeminence at a peculiarly precipitative moment: as scholarly disciplines harden and take on the mantle of professionalism, dividing up the world into discrete units of attention, it is the world 'at large', in its everyday sense, that falls between the borders of disciplinary knowledge. As such it is the extra-disciplinary tendencies of the novel that are available to sweep up the undisciplined scraps of everyday life and make them into a vivid archive of the day-to-day.

What becomes crucial here, though, is to recognize that the novel doesn't emerge as an object requiring a discipline to unbind the significance of heteroglossia or the everyday within it. It is, rather, the extra-disciplinary form of the novel that makes it a discursive form adequate for attending to the unbinding effects of heteroglossia and the daily.

There is then, in de Certeau's understanding of literature, a seismic shift away from the professionalism of '*lit crit*'. It is precisely by moving in the opposite direction to the stress that has been placed on the irreducible *representationality* of the text (and all the intricacies that this entails) that de Certeau's work is pitched. It is as 'counter-archive', as living resource for actions, as extra-disciplinarity, and as meta-critical theory, that novels and stories are privileged in de Certeau's work:

> The folktale provides scientific discourse with a model, and not merely with textual objects to be dealt with. It no longer has the status of a document that does not know what it says, cited (summoned and quoted) before and by the analysis that knows it. On the contrary, it is a know-how-to-say ('*savoir-dire*') exactly adjusted to its object, and, as such, no longer the Other of knowledge; rather it is a variant of the discourse that knows and an authority in what concerns theory. One can then understand the alterations and complicities, the procedural homologies and social imbrications that link the 'arts of speaking' to the 'arts of operating': the same practices appear now in a verbal field, now in a field of non-linguistic actions; they move from one field to the other, being equally tactical and subtle in both; they keep the ball moving between them – from the workday to evening, from cooking to legends and gossip, from the devices of lived history to those of history retold. (PEL1: 78)

The 'science of literature' is not going to be found in the technical accounts of narrative (narratology), for instance. If literature is a science it is a 'life science' – an intricate and theoretical account of the actualities and possibilities of life. In many respects this returns us to an earlier phase of literary criticism associated with people like F.R. Leavis, who want to value a novel because of the way it recognizes and addresses 'experience'.[12] Yet, and here's the rub, we now turn to the novel (or the animated cartoon for that matter) as a vast repertoire for acting in the world, and as a synechdoche for an epistemologically 'lost' world of the ordinary.

NARRATIVE PRACTICES AND PRACTICAL LIFE

For de Certeau the importance of the novel is tied to its social relevance and this is guaranteed through the centrality of narrative to its form. Stories are crucial for de Certeau mainly because they are ubiquitous. But there is, in his privileging of narrative, a contradiction, a conflict. Narrative is both good object and bad; it is both a resource for invention and a source for domination. This should come as no surprise – stories, after all, constitute the most extensive field of culture. How we narrate our lives, for instance, is a deep cultural structure ('one important way of characterizing a culture is by the narrative models it makes available for describing the course of a life'[13]) and one that sets limits to how we can think of our lives as well as providing opportunities for the course of a life. For Barthes narrative is almost coterminous with social actuality: 'narrative begins with the very history of humanity; there is not, there has never been, any people anywhere without narrative . . . narrative is *there*, like life'.[14] One thing that many theorists of narrative agree on is that the ubiquity of narrative is its most salient feature. Thus, J. Hillis Miller writes:

> From our earliest childhood we hear stories and learn to repeat them. . . As adults, we hear, read, see and tell stories all day long – for example, in the newspaper, on television, in encounters with co-workers or family members. In a continuous silent internal activity, we tell stories to ourselves all day long. Jokes are one form of narration. Advertising is another: 'Use this product, and then you will feel much better.' At night we sleep, and our unconscious minds

[12] See for instance, F.R. Leavis, *The Common Pursuit* (Harmondsworth: Penguin, 1976). For a useful discussion of Leavis in this regard, see Michael Pickering, *History, Experience and Cultural Studies* (Houndmills: Macmillan, 1997).

[13] Jerome Bruner, 'Life as Narrative', *Social Research*, vol. 54, no. 1, 1987, p. 15.

[14] Roland Barthes, 'Introduction to the Structural Analysis of Narratives' (1966) in *The Semiotic Challenge*, translated by Richard Howard (New York: Hill and Wang, 1988), p. 95.

tell us more stories in our dreams, often exceedingly strange ones. Even within
'literature proper' the range of narrative is wide and diverse. It includes not
only short stories and novels but also dramas, epics, Platonic dialogues, narrative poems, and so on.[15]

The plethora of narratives, often in a densely truncated form (buy this,
become more attractive), suggest a massive arena of ideas, persuasively framed
as stories.

For de Certeau this ubiquity of stories can be recognized as a passive culture
of persuasion: the great archive of ideological positions:

> From morning to night, narrations constantly haunt streets and buildings. . . .
> Captured by the radio (the voice is the law) as soon as he awakens, the listener
> walks all day long through the forest of narrativities from journalism, adver-
> tising, and television, narrativities that still find time, as he is getting ready for
> bed, to slip a few final messages under the portals of sleep. Even more than the
> God told about by the theologians of earlier days, these stories have a provi-
> dential and predestining function: they organize in advance our work, our
> celebrations, and even our dreams. (PEL1: 186)

Stories here saturate the social field and 'organize' it 'in advance'. But this store
of persuasion, that solicits our passive acceptance, is only ever a partial account
of the narrative activity that is at work in culture (in its fullest and most general
sense).

Narrative's most vital relationship with everyday life, for de Certeau, is not
as an ideological persuader, but more hopefully as a space for recording forms
of action and for the rehearsal of potential activities. In this, narrative is a practical resource for performances and actions: it supplies a repertoire for different
responses to different situations. This isn't to say that some narratives are ideological and ask for our acquiescence while other narratives offer suggestions for
different ways of acting: rather, the same narrative might be used in distinct,
even antagonistic, ways. And it is because de Certeau's work is always, in the
end, concerned with practices (material operations very broadly conceived) that
it can bear the contradiction of narrative as simultaneous good object and bad.
For instance, the fable of 'Little Red Riding Hood', in its many different versions, might ideologically tell the story of a young female's encounter with a
predatory male, suggesting in some versions that rape is caused by, and is the

---

[15] J. Hillis Miller, 'Narrative' in Frank Lentricchia and Thomas McLaughlin, eds, *Critical
Terms for Literary Study*, second edition (Chicago and London: University of Chicago Press,
1995), p. 66.

fault of, female naivety.[16] Yet as a story of performativity the ideological 'moral' is less important, or less determining than might be imagined: instead what is offered is a repertoire of subterfuges, feints and deceits that can be used in a variety of ways (there isn't any guaranteed correspondence between wolf and predatory male, for instance – the tale can be read literally, for instance, and used in any number of ways).

Narrative, for de Certeau, covers a wide range of different practices: from oral traditions of storytelling to the playing and recounting of games; from the micronarratives of proverbs and other forms of popular wisdom to the more elaborated telling of folktales; from condensed advertising narrative to the sprawling and expansive novel. These resources, while in many ways very different, share a common denominator in that they are resources that often, if not always, describe and comment on the performance of everyday practices. And they do this outside of the pressures of life. Thus games, and the accounts of games, as well as many fables and legends, describe practices:

> Tales and legends seem to have the same role [as games]. They are deployed, like games, in a space outside of and isolated from daily competition, that of the past, the marvelous, the original. In that space can thus be revealed, dressed as gods or heroes, the models of good or bad ruses that can be used everyday. Moves, not truths, are recounted. (PEL: 23)

What is crucial here is the meta-everyday aspect of stories: they address the everyday as a practice, yet are safely outside of that immediate practical and urgent world. They provide a space for 'trial runs', for the practice of practice, so to speak.

Games, and play more generally, cement a link between narrative and everyday life by conceiving of the field of culture as simultaneously rule-governed as well as endlessly mutable. It also conceives of the social subject as a 'player'; someone who, potentially at least, is skilled in the arts of the everyday, who is experienced in the various moves that work best in a given situation. The social field is then itself like a game (of hopscotch, for instance, or chess) not because it is fun, or inconsequential, but because it is simultaneously limited (by available resources, by the conditions of the game) and limitless (each game enacts the conditions of the game in different ways).[17] So while chess can be explained

[16] For a brief account of this story and its various versions see Jack Zipes, *Creative Storytelling: Building Community, Changing Lives* (New York and London: Routledge, 1995), pp. 23–9. For a more detailed analysis see Jack Zipes, *The Trials and Tribulations of Little Red Riding Hood* (New York and London: Routledge, 1993).

[17] Two useful accounts of games are Roger Caillois, *Man, Play and Games*, translated by Meyer Barash (Urbana and Chicago: University of Illinois Press, 2001) – first published in France in

in relation to the board, the pieces and the possible moves that the pieces can make, there are limitless possibilities for a game of chess. The actuality of chess is the singular game played using the rules of the game: the rules of chess on their own do not circumscribe this endlessly inventive (and potential) actuality:

> If, in every society, games make clear the formality of its practices for the reason that, outside of the conflicts of everyday life, it no longer has to be concealed, then the old game of hopscotch becomes a kind of map in which, on a series of places and according to a sum of rules, a social art unfolds a field of play in order to create itineraries, and to make use of the surprises that lie ahead. It is a scale model, a theoretical fiction. In effect, culture can be compared to this art, conditioned by places, rules, and givens; it is a pro-liferation of inventions in limited spaces. (CP: viii)

For de Certeau the human subject is essentially a subject who invents, who can invent – and it is this 'species being' that means that while it may be difficult to imagine forms of sociality outside of social rules, it is also impossible to see social life as reducible to these rules.

In seeing narratives as offering the equivalent of 'moves in the game', de Certeau draws an analogy between actual games and stories, and suggests that both offer examples of practical means for a tactical response to forms of power. Examples of this might be taken from the game of poker, where bluffing is an integral part of the game, and where bluffing can be seen as an 'available' form to be extended and re-employed in bluffing the boss or teacher about lateness or unfinished work. What the game of poker makes available (as do more obvi-ous narrative forms like legends) is a site outside the everyday that can be used in the everyday: here a space is opened up to try out the bluff while practising your 'poker face' (the necessary blankness that alone can guarantee believability of the bluff, or at least render the face inscrutable for tells – signs that 'give the game away'). Indeed, phrases related to card games pepper everyday talk, par-ticularly in describing negotiations with authority: 'keeping your cards close to your chest' is an everyday piece of advice that suggests continual vigilance and an understanding that it might not be in your best interest to 'show your hand'.

Like games, stories contain useful resources, practical 'know-how'. Ancient tales and legends like Homer's *Odyssey* or Virgil's *Iliad* provide a rich source for 'playing and foiling the other's game', where cunning and wit are valued over brute strength, or numerical superiority. But while examples of cunning (out-foxing an army by using guile and subterfuge) mirror the more minor practices

---

1958; and Brian Sutton-Smith, *The Ambiguity of Play* (Cambridge: Harvard University Press, 2001).

of subterfuge in everyday life, de Certeau is just as interested in the imaginative space that narrative produces and the way that this can articulate hope when all the evidence might suggest a more pessimistic account of the situation would be more accurate. And it is this imaginative space that suggests narrative forms that can carry contradictory materials.

Narratives that offer magical and miraculous solutions to the inequalities of daily life can be seen to offer another social consciousness, one that exists alongside the ordinary and often pessimistic analysis of social situations. De Certeau examines this use of stories by exploring the relationship between a social group's knowledge of the actuality of daily life and the lack of legitimacy that is given to this knowledge. A group may know, after years of exploitation and struggle, that the 'strong always win and words always deceive', yet this is not the only epistemological space that the group inhabits. De Certeau points to the existence of other utopian spaces that circulate alongside this socio-economic one. In the peasant struggles of the Pernambuco Indians of Brazil such knowledge of everyday life is set against the continual recounting of miraculous stories of 'the celestial punishments' that Frei Damião (a priest who was the popular hero of the area) 'visited upon his enemies'. For de Certeau the actuality of the Pernambuco was comprised of a combination of two discursive worlds:

> The discourse parted space in such a way as to stratify it on two levels. On the one hand, a socio-economic space, organized by an immemorial struggle between 'the powerful' and 'the poor', presented itself as the field of constant victories by the rich and the police . . . On the other hand, distinct from this . . . was also a *utopian* space in which a possibility, by definition miraculous in nature, was affirmed by religious stories. Frei Damião was the almost immobile centre of this space, constantly qualified by the successive accounts of the celestial punishments visited upon his enemies. (PEL1: 16)

The former 'realist discourse' seems at first to be the only epistemologically justified account: experience shows that the powerful win – popular analysis reveals a society structured for the benefit of an elite. Yet, in what might be considered a deeply unrealistic version, the Pernambuco 'believe' that right will defeat might. The epistemology for this is based not on experience, but on the potential for the world to be reconceived by a form of justice presently missing:

> It recognized in that injustice an order of things that seemed immutable: it is always so; people see it every day. But no legitimacy whatever was accorded this state of affairs. On the contrary, just because it was a constantly repeated fact, this relationship of forces did not become any more acceptable. The *fact* was not accepted as a *law*, even if it remained inescapably a fact. (PEL1: 16)

For de Certeau and for us what needs commenting on here is the simultaneity of the two accounts, of the two narrative forms. This also points to two or more worlds that might be inhabited simultaneously: one a practical world, urgent, demanding immediate responses; the others not limited to practicalities, animated by desires, anxieties, love, shame and hatred.

This is what makes it possible for de Certeau to continue to assert the importance of religion in a historical moment where religious belief is 'impossible'. It is not as a truth but as a possibility that religion as a narrative potential is employed, and it is often employed in opposition to the deployment that was initially imagined:[18]

> Religious practices and representations constitute another, symbolic, space in which hope can be evinced. This second discourse utters a *nonetheless*. It avails itself of a poetics that for the most part was imported by the European colonizer. But the native *exploits it* in order to construct the objective picture of misery on the poem (that is still atopical and without grounding) of a different, egalitarian society in which the poor finally make good and the bodies of the sick are cured. Here what *cannot be observed* is stated as *possible*, extraordinary, and miraculous. This religious language, inhabited by the experience of sorrow, increases as the effectiveness of democratic institutions decreases; the former is weakened when the latter is strengthened. It is the figure of what cannot yet be articulated in any sociopolitical form. (CS: 84–5)

The narrative forms that are closest to Bakhtin's account of the novel, by their multiple generic forms, are able to stitch together the practical worlds and the affective worlds and point to areas of conflict and contradiction between the two. While de Certeau tends mainly to offer examples of fables, he is also interested in more complex narrative forms. I need to shift the focus now to these more complex examples. I want to get back to the practical question animating this book, the one that concerns the question of method, of how *to do* cultural analysis in the wake of the critiques emerging out of poststructuralist epistemology, for instance. Just to remind you: one of the critiques that emerge in the study of historiography is the idea that the realist form of most conventional history writing is borrowed from the nineteenth-century realist novel. A number of critical theorists of history have suggested that we trade in this version of historiography and 'modernize' it by employing some of the new forms available from literature.

---

[18] For a rich empirical example of the way cultural materials like religion are re-used, often against the grain of their active deployment, see Stuart Hall, 'Negotiating Caribbean Identities', *New Left Review* 209, 1995, pp. 3–14.

One reason for doing this is that it will force a recognition of classic realism as a genre amongst genres; it doesn't have any *a priori* epistemological claims in the business of depicting and analysing actuality (though nor would any other genre). Epistemology has to be proved in the field, in relation to other depictions, according to ethical values that aren't absolute but are themselves open to critical appraisal (and as far as this goes we might expect certain forms of complex realism to do quite well). The other related reason (one that would need to be demonstrated) involves the claim that the dominant forms of realism simply can't cope with too much complexity and that they don't easily sustain inquiry into contradiction, for instance (this is to claim that they are epistemologically 'light' and less adequate than other forms). The argument then is that realist, linear narrative forms determine what can be known of the past: genre is a shaper of knowledge, and inasmuch as it shapes a false coherency (monologizes the heteroglossia) it is often a violent exclusion of the disparate actuality of the past. Thus critiques of narrative have consistently argued that it is an essential ideological tool: 'it is now possible . . . to say of narrative what Marx said of religion, that it is an "opiate" which mystifies our understanding by providing a false coherence, an "illusion of sequence".'[19]

For a certain branch of critical historiography (which would also include de Certeau) it is not a question of embracing or avoiding the literary aspect of writing history but of deciding what kind of literary historiography you are going to produce. For Jacques Rancière: 'the problem is therefore not to know if the historian does or doesn't have to produce literature, but what literature he [*sic*] produces.'[20] The choice is most often posed as between a nineteenth-century realist literature and a vague sense of modernism – with the favoured example being the work of James Joyce (though Rancière usefully opts for Virginia Woolf). The problem here is that this position is itself prone to a very unhelpful generalization that seems to suggest that as long as a narrative form isn't held in check by the linear conventions of realism then all other forms are more or less equal. What is needed, if more new literary models of historiography are to become available, is a much more nuanced approach that could establish some of the productivity of a historiography informed by Woolf as opposed to one informed by Joyce, for instance. This is not the place to conduct a large-scale audit of narrative forms for historiography (which anyway would have to be a multiple-volume project), but there is room to begin a very limited attempt to consider one or two relevant forms.

[19] W.J.T. Mitchell, 'Foreword' in W.J.T. Mitchell, ed., *On Narrative* (Chicago and London: University of Chicago Press, 1981), p. viii.
[20] Jacques Rancière, *The Names of History: On the Poetics of Knowledge*, translated by Hassan Melehy (Minneapolis: University of Minnesota Press, 1994), p. 101.

I want to look at the novels of Marguerite Duras, for reasons that I hope will become clear, and then to go on to look at historical and autobiographical forms that might be seen as evidencing some of the productivity that also animates Duras' work. Attending to this work will bring us back to earlier discussions of orality, to questions of subalterns and others, and to the possibilities of history writing. This discussion of Duras' work runs the risk of turning Duras into another 'modernist exemplar' (instead of Joyce or Woolf). What would be needed to get a full sense of the specific productivity of Duras' potential for historiography would be a careful differentiation that would establish the difference not just between Joyce and Duras, and Woolf and Duras, but between Duras and her closest peers such as Nathalie Sarrute, Alain Robbe-Grillet, Georges Perec, etc., as well as in relation to a wider tradition of experimental narrativity represented by the likes of Gabriel García Márquez, Clarice Lispector and others. For now though we will need to make do with a more limited perspective.

MARGUERITE DURAS: VOICES AND LISTENING

In the work of Michel de Certeau, no novelist, filmmaker or dramatist is mentioned as often or as insistently as Marguerite Duras.[21] It is testament to his involvement with this body of writing that her novels and films are a constant resource of examples across the range of his investigations; and it indicates something of the ambience of Duras' work that it can bear being used for exemplifying mystic speech as much as the hidden resonances of everyday life. In this, Duras' literary production is capable of a varied range of moods and atmospheres that relate to both practical life and to various affective states, including, importantly, various responses to trauma (shame and rage, for instance). It is perhaps no surprise that Duras is referenced in the work of de Certeau: her work, especially in the 1970s and 1980s, had a prominence in France unmatched by other French authors. She was also a novelist who had been celebrated by various prominent voices of poststructuralist theory, most famously in the work of Jacques Lacan.[22] But there is a particularity to Duras' novels and films that would, I think, have made them irresistible to de Certeau: Duras presents narratives that are woven out of speech, and form histories that are never

[21] Luce Giard, in a public lecture at the Victoria and Albert Museum (15 April 2003), remembered that de Certeau, herself, and others involved with his research into everyday life were constantly reading contemporary novelists, and that foremost amongst them were the novels of Marguerite Duras.

[22] Jacques Lacan, 'Homage to Marguerite Duras, on *Le ravissement de Lol V. Stein*' in Marguerite Duras, *Marguerite Duras*, translated by Edith Cohen and Peter Connor (San Francisco: City Lights Books, 1987), pp. 122–9 – first published in France in 1976.

sure of themselves.[23] Her film *India Song* visualizes listening in a way that is perhaps unique in the history of cinema[24] – and would, I believe, have related productively with de Certeau's understanding of listening as an active and altering
condition of communication.

The work of Duras from 1964 to about 1976, starting with the publication
of *Le Ravissement de Lol V. Stein* (*The Ravishing of Lol Stein*), is marked by loop-
ing narrative repetitions and cyclical returns. The body of work that includes
the novels *The Ravishing of Lol Stein* (1964) and *The Vice-Consul* (1966), and
the films *India Song* (1975) and *Son Nom de Venise dans Calcutta desert* (1976)
(amongst others), is often referred to as her 'Indian Cycle'.[25] At the heart of it
lies the traumatic event (though readers, listeners and viewers are never really
sure what has 'happened') of Lol Stein being abandoned by her fiancé at a ball,
where he falls (immediately and with abandon) for the endlessly glamorous and
tragic Anne-Marie Stretter. This event, though it lies outside the narrative time
of the novels and films (it is remembered, not enacted), gives rise to other
occurrences as it is displaced and re-enacted in various new settings across the
cycle. For the Duras scholar Susan Cohen this production of characters and
'events' produces a cultural form that is best described as the production of 'legends', in that they constitute a collection of mythologized events that are transmitted from the past, and have uncertain provenance. The power of the cycle is
based on its 'legend'-like form:

> Duras' narrative configurations effect a framing conducive to mythologiz-
> ing. . . . Over and over speakers retell or re-invent multiple reconstructions
> of inaccessible, absent stories. Repetition, distance, unverifiability charac-
> terize the textual matter of legends, while reverence and/or fascination char-
> acterize their telling.[26]

---

[23] As already mentioned, the first chapter of de Certeau's *The Possession at Loudun* is titled 'History
is Never Sure'.

[24] This is not, of course, the place to enter into a digression about visualizing listening in film,
but if one were to follow such a digression, I think it should include works such as Francis Ford
Coppola's 1974 film *The Conversation*, and Humphrey Jennings' 1942 film *Listen to Britain*,
alongside Duras' *India Song*.

[25] Marguerite Duras, *The Ravishing of Lol Stein*, translated by Richard Seaver (New York:
Grove Press, 1966); Marguerite Duras, *The Vice-Consul*, translated by Eileen Ellenbogen
(London: Hamish Hamilton, 1968). The film of *India Song* was originally published as a
theatrical script, Marguerite Duras, *India Song*, translated by Barbara Bray (New York: Grove
Press, 1976) and was first published in France in 1973. Changes between the theatrical script
and the film are noted in Marguerite Duras, *Marguerite Duras*, translated by Cohen and
Connor.

[26] Susan D. Cohen, *Women and Discourse in the Fiction of Marguerite Duras* (Houndmills:
Macmillan, 1993), p. 178.

It should be immediately clear from this that the 'reconstructions of inaccessible, absent stories' relate directly to the work of the historian, and that it is precisely for this reason that de Certeau can claim that 'literature is the theoretical discourse of the historical process' (H: 18). The stories in Duras' work – and for all her experimentation with narrative sequence and with the position of the narrator, narrative is the material she works with – take on the mantle of fables. And they are fables that figure both the impossibility of historiography ever fully recovering the past, of being sure in its knowledge of the past, while also articulating the urgent and insistent pull that the past exerts on the present. Rather than evidencing the swarming heteroglossia that Bakhtin sees as key to novelness, Duras' writing offers a more contained narrative form, but one whose power is partly secured by its legendary quality.

Since the end of the Second World War, Duras had been a relatively well-known novelist in France; however, it was in the 1960s and 1970s that she really came to prominence and the Indian Cycle was the body of work that she became most closely associated with. This work was bound up with urgent cultural debates at the time; but it isn't Lacan's opaque and self-aggrandizing championing of her (Lacan suggests that Duras' is in fact a teacher of Lacanian psychoanalysis) that should be most remembered. The most vivid figuring of Duras at this time is as the central exemplification of what Hélène Cixous termed *écriture féminine* (feminine writing) – though in case this should be mistaken for writing that only women produce Cixous suggests that the practitioners would include Marguerite Duras, Jean Genet, as well as writers that she would focus on in the 1980s like Clarice Lispector.[27] What this writing performed was an interruption in the logic of the phallus, the logic of identity and self-presence; it would disrupt a binary economy that split culture into male and female, masculine and feminine, and so on. *Écriture féminine*, then, is a polemical term for a form of cultural production that looks to a future that has superseded the structural divisions of power which guarantee patriarchal dominance in culture. One such division is that which divides writing and speaking. For Cixous *écriture féminine* is the overturning of the dichotomy writing-versus-speech, replacing it with a form that imbricates voice and inscription:

First I sense femininity in writing by: a privilege of *voice: writing and voice* are entwined and interwoven and writing's continuity/voice's rhythm take each other's breath away through interchanging, make the text gasp or form

---

[27] A useful introduction to Cixous and *écriture féminine* can be found in Toril Moi, *Sexual/Textual Politics: Feminist Literary Theory* (London: Methuen, 1985). For Cixous' response to Lispector see Hélène Cixous, *Reading with Clarice Lispector*, translated by Verna Andermatt Conley (Minneapolis: University of Minnesota Press, 1990).

it out of suspense and silences, make it lose its voice or rend it with cries. . . Listen to woman speak in a gathering (if she is not painfully out of breath): she doesn't 'speak', she throws her trembling body into the air, she lets herself go, she flies, she goes completely into her voice, she vitally defends the 'logic' of her discourse with her body; her flesh speaks true.[28]

As in de Certeau's work, voices, and orality more generally, become a privileged form for culture that is either actively suppressed or finds little to hold on to in a dominantly scriptural economy – though here, and, as we shall see, in the work of Duras, it is specifically women's voices that are privileged emitters of an other culture:

> Voice! That, too, is launching forth and effusion without return. Exclamation, cry, breathlessness, yell, cough, vomit, music. Voice leaves. Voice loses. She leaves. She loses. And that is how she writes, as one throws a voice – forward, into the void. She goes away, she goes forward, doesn't turn back to look at her tracks.[29]

It should be clear from this quotation (and the one above) that Cixous herself practises a poetics that is meant to dislodge the sure-footedness and seeming transparency of philosophical critical writing. In adopting a 'poetic' (allusive, impressionistic) style she is freer to exploit contradictions: for instance the contradiction between recognizing that 'feminine' and 'masculine' are culturally produced imaginaries, while employing terms like 'feminine' and 'woman' to engage polemically with the potential and actuality of women's lives. This strategic essentialism (a use of 'feminine nature' to overcome the naturalness of femininity) is deployed to unbind femininity from the logic of the logos (the Word) and the phallus, propelling culture into a future space where a new sex–gender economy operates.

In Duras' oeuvre voices and speech are not something buried in the text that requires a critical reading to unpick. Orality is the privileged materiality of her work. Thus she can write that: 'the film *India Song* will be *built* with *sound* and then with *light*'.[30] But of course Duras is primarily a writer not an oral storyteller: her medium is writing, although often relayed via soundtracks and theatrical forms. There is then no straightforward separation of oral culture and scriptural culture in Duras' work, and this is, I think, crucial for de Certeau.

---

[28] Hélène Cixous and Catherine Clément, *The Newly Born Woman*, translated by Betsy Wing (Manchester: Manchester University Press, 1986), p. 92 – first published in France in 1975.
[29] Cixous and Clément, *The Newly Born Woman*, p. 94.
[30] Duras, *Marguerite Duras*, p. 31.

Voices penetrate the text, rip up any all-seeing vision that a disembodied narrative voice (or a textual authority without any sonorous specificity) could bring. Her voices always have bodies (even if we only discover whose bodies they are late in the day); these voices inject writing with an unruly subjectivity that make it epistemologically tentative in a way writing rarely achieves.

The blurring of the boundaries between writing and voice, that de Certeau sees as securing the power of the scriptural economy, has been theorized by critics involved in re-evaluating unofficial and vernacular cultures:

> Performance studies complicates the familiar dichotomy between speech and writing with what Kenyan novelist and director Ngũgĩ wa Thiong'o calls 'orature'. Orature comprises a range of forms, which, though they may invest themselves variously in gesture, song, dance, processions, storytelling, proverbs, gossip, customs, rites, and rituals, are nevertheless produced alongside or within mediated literacies of various kinds and degrees. In other words, orature goes beyond a schematized opposition of literacy and orality as transcendent categories; rather, it acknowledges that these modes of communication have produced one another interactively over time and that their historic operations may be usefully examined under the rubric of performance.[31]

It is not incidental that 'orature' has been used to explore and celebrate the cultural world of 'marginalized' groups: African-American culture in the United States for instance. The re-assessment of 'orature' culture will become a central tenet in the bringing into the foreground of the cultures of the dominated.

For Duras, her film-work of the late '60s and early '70s allowed her to give a prominence to orature in way that, though implicit in her earlier novels, enabled her to make a breakthrough in terms of the way narrative worked in relation to the spoken:

> This discovery [using 'voices external to the narrative' as a '*means* of exploration'] made it possible to let the narrative be forgotten and put at the disposal of memories other than that of the author: memories which might remember, in the same way, any other love story. Memories that distort. That create.[32]

---

[31] Joseph Roach, *Cities of the Dead: Circum-Atlantic Performance* (New York: Columbia University Press, 1996), pp. 11–12. The reference to Ngũgĩ wa Thiong'o comes from an interview included in G.D. Killam, ed., *Critical Perspective on Ngũgĩ wa Thiong'o* (Washington: Three Continents, 1984).

[32] Marguerite Duras, *India Song*, p. 6.

For Duras, then, the separation of the soundtrack from the image-track and from its reliance on 'telling the story' – something that is most vividly performed with the film *India Song* – doesn't gesture towards internalizing the voice as an expression of the author; rather it allows the act of remembering to take on a more communicative and social function (what do we remember?). The voices that speak don't simply speak from the body, they also speak to the body on the screen (and potentially to the bodies in the audience). Duras produces a cinema of listening bodies: bodies that walk, sit, turn and lie while listening to their 'own' voices:

> While directing the film, she recorded the actors reading the entire text of *India Song* which was then played back during the filming of each scene. Thus, throughout the film, the actors do not speak but instead listen to their own recorded voices, as they perform the prescribed movements and gestures. In this way, *India Song* generates a radical fracture between the voice-off and the body on-screen, making the actors appear like spectres or shadows rather than realistic incarnations of the protagonists.[33]

Fundamentally then this is not an expressive cinema but one where the separation of communicative functions opens up a space – a space, potentially, that will allow the historicity of the social to find a different sort of a foothold.

While the trauma that animates *India Song* and *The Ravishing of Lol Stein* (and her work more generally) seems to be conceived in relation to intensely personal circumstances (and it would be hard to use the word 'trauma' to categorize material that didn't affect someone personally), the context of trauma relating to Duras and her generation was catastrophically social and political. Duras came from a generation who had direct experience of war: she fought in the resistance alongside François Mitterrand, she narrowly escaped from the Gestapo, while her husband was taken to a concentration camp.[34] Trauma, in this work, is not a narrative device; it is the material circumstances of the historicity of a life: 'There is Auschwitz, all my life, yes, I carry it with me. There's nothing I can do. It's there all the time.'[35] It would, I think, be hard to overestimate the importance of war for many French intellectuals of Duras' generation – but the Second World War and the wars that came after it were also deeply traumatizing for a slightly younger generation of French intellectuals, the peers of Michel de Certeau. Thus the cultural philosopher Michel Serres can speak of the general context of trauma for an entire generation:

---

[33] Renate Günther, *Marguerite Duras* (Manchester: Manchester University Press, 2002), p. 30.
[34] For information on Duras' life see Laure Adler, *Marguerite Duras: A Life*, translated by Anne-Marie Glasheen (London: Phoenix, 2001).
[35] Duras cited in Günther, *Marguerite Duras*, p. 9.

My contemporaries will recognize themselves in what I have to say first. Here is the vital environment of those who were born, like me, around 1930 [de Certeau was born slightly earlier in 1925]: at age six, the war of 1936 in Spain; at age nine, the blitzkrieg of 1939, defeat and debacle; at age twelve, the split between the Resistance and the collaborators, the tragedy of the concentration camps and deportations; at age fourteen, Liberation and the settling of scores it brought with it in France; at age fifteen, Hiroshima. In short, from age nine to seventeen, when the body and sensitivity are being formed, it was the reign of hunger and rationing, death and bombings, a thousand crimes. We continued immediately with the colonial wars, in Indochina and then in Algeria. Between birth and age twenty-five . . . around me, for me – for us, around us – there was nothing but battles. War, always war.[36]

For Serres, de Certeau and Duras – in different ways and under different circumstances – the formative years of their life were fashioned out of trauma. The history of the twentieth century is, of course, a history of such trauma.

For Duras, though, the trauma of war connected to a larger history of trauma that related to colonial domination. The daughter of French school teachers, who went to find financial comfort and career success in the colonies of French Indochina (now Cambodia, Vietnam and Laos) but who ended up drastically impoverished (the father died; the mother was persuaded to invest in financially disastrous projects) and living on the edges of Western colonial society, Duras' upbringing was not the privileged one that she portrays for her colonial characters.[37] In this respect her positioning of trauma – not as material in the present but as 'ur-trauma', or as a foundational trauma that is constitutive of the sociality being conceived – relates to a larger critical understanding of history and its relation to colonialism. So while 'the films displace the trauma from the immediacy of the present', and 'make it an event which never takes place',[38] we are catapulted into the realm facing the historian of 'zones of silence': how to make the traumatic absence of the archive speak? In *India Song* and in other productions the foundational history of trauma is presented, not as subject matter, but as material landscape. Thus the film, which is supposedly

[36] Michel Serres with Bruno Latour, *Conversations on Science, Culture, and Time*, translated by Roxanne Lapidus (Ann Arbor: University of Michigan Press, 1995), p. 2.
[37] For two very different accounts of Duras' position within postcolonialism see: Jane Bradley Winston, *Postcolonial Duras: Cultural Memory in Postwar France* (New York and Houndmills: Palgrave, 2001); and Marie-Paule Ha, *Figuring the East: Segalen, Malraux, Duras, and Barthes* (Albany: State University of New York Press, 2000).
[38] Joan Copjec, '*India Song/Son nom de Venise dans Calcutta désert*: The Compulsion to Repeat' in Constance Penley, ed., *Feminism and Film Theory* (New York and London: Routledge and BFI Publishing, 1988), p. 236.

about events taking place in buildings related to the colonial administration in Calcutta (the embassy, a hotel) are actually filmed in a mansion in Paris:

> . . . by setting *India Song* in the Rothschild Palace [a Jewish residence confiscated by the Nazis in the Second World War and used as Goering's residence during occupation], she established the 'place' of Nazism and the 'place' of colonialism as rigorously the same. By choosing the Rothschild Palace, she refused to 'other' either Nazism or colonialism by 'placing' them outside of French geographical, cultural, or psychic bounds. Quite the contrary: identifying the 'place' of Nazism and colonialism as an actual material, social, cultural, and historical site of oppression and decay in the very heart of post-Empire France, she established *India Song* as the swan song of the French colonial 'solution'.[39]

In locating trauma as the abysmal centre of narrative structures, and as the abysmal centre of Western culture, Duras inoculates her narrative experiments from the danger of subjectivism. In *India Song* she presents a dying colonialism: 'the embassy is a leaking ship. Leprosy enters everywhere with the song of the beggar woman.'[40] In this way she establishes a sense of the everyday as shot through with the deep impact of historical circumstances: historical circumstances (such as Auschwitz and colonialism) that don't simply scar – but whose nightmarish qualities it is not a question of awakening from, rather of clutching on to as the only precaution against their repetition.

This excursion into the literary world of Duras is not meant to reveal a 'good' postcolonial critic, or a 'bad' colonially saturated Frenchwoman. What I have been concerned with is the question of rethinking writing in relation to the various challenges that de Certeau has implicitly laid down. One of these challenges is to rethink the writing of history, not as an epistemologically impossible job that should be jettisoned but as a job that has much to take from the experimentation and scientific investigations of literature. Thus the question that concerns me is what sort of a historiography might be possible if we took as a model the work of Marguerite Duras (as a novelist privileged within the oeuvre of de Certeau)? As a model of a literary history Duras does not offer a form that can simply be re-used for historiography. Rather Duras' work presents historiography with various issues and forms that would need to be adapted, transformed, if they were to circulate in historiography. One of these might be ideas

---

[39] Winston, *Postcolonial Duras*, p. 65.

[40] Duras, cited in Christine Anne Holmund, 'Displacing Limits of Difference: Gender, Race, and Colonialism in Edward Said and Homi Bhabha's Theoretical Models and Marguerite Duras's Experimental Films' in Hamid Naficy and Teshome H. Gabriel, eds, *Otherness and the Media: Ethnography of the Imagined and the Imaged* (Chur: Harwood, 1993), p. 11.

of repetition or ways of figuring a constitutive trauma as a continual presence (text-off) in the work. The examples that follow, while not Durasian, explore to some extent these possibilities.

ANOTHER WAY OF TELLING: TOWARDS A LITERARY HISTORIOGRAPHY

Historiography, though, hasn't remained completely inert while theorists champion the emergence of a yet-to-be-achieved literary historiography. Indeed de Certeau's own historiographical work can be seen to fashion itself in ways that are distinctly different from the usual conventions of historiographic production (if such a form exists as something more than a theoretical fiction). Yet the form of historiography has tended to remain the same despite the expansion of what gets included as worth historicizing. Thus in a recent collection of more experimental historiography one editor can write:

> While the discipline [history] has in the past century undergone an enormous expansion in methodologies of research and areas of focus, opening up fields and topics little dreamed of by earlier generations (e.g. quantitative, social, gender, ethnic, cultural, subaltern, postcolonial, feminist, queer, and leisure histories, to name but a few), the means of presenting the findings of historical research has altered little. The monograph and synthetic works that historians produce continue, for the most part, to tell the past as stories narrated in the third person, linear stories with a clear sense of cause and effect, and a beginning, a middle, and an end.[41]

One response to this tendency to formal inertia is to find examples of historiography that doesn't accord to 'the most part': examples like de Certeau, but also the experimental history that he points towards. One historian whom de Certeau singles out is Martin Duberman, who is probably best known for his explorations of the 'gay past'.[42] Duberman is a useful example for developing a notion of 'literary historiography' for a number of reasons, and what I'm going to do in this section is look fleetingly at some of Duberman's work and, in more detail, but still briefly, at the work of the novelist and critic Samuel Delany, who connects to the same historical issues (recovering a gay past, for instance) but

---

[41] Robert A. Ronsenstone, 'Introduction: Practice and Theory' in Alun Munslow and Robert A. Ronsenstone, eds, *Experiments in Rethinking History* (London and New York: Routledge, 2004), p. 1.

[42] For instance, Martin Bauml Duberman, *About Time: Exploring the Gay Past* (New York: Gay Presses of New York, 1986).

also develops a form that emphasizes epistemological issues, at the same time as producing (through epistemological critique, rather than in spite of) new ways of telling the past.

The historiographies of sexualities, especially sexualities that have been seen as pathological and deviant, provide an especially vivid example of the epistemological challenge that faces historiography more generally. How do you write the history of a sexuality that has, in the past, 'dared not speak its name', that in the written archive has dominantly been written about as a pathology within medical records, or more generally within a literature of confession, or in coded form, between the lines, so to speak? The epistemological issue is different in degree from that suggested by Spivak in her account of the subaltern: whereas the female subaltern may be entirely absent from the archival record, the Western gay male (for instance) may either be present as medical, psychoanalytic example (but absent as a subject in the full sense of the term), or else emphatically present as artist or politician – general agent of history – yet shorn of their sexuality. As the historian of visual culture Gavin Butt has recently shown – in his fascinating account of artists like Jasper Johns and Andy Warhol, an account which uses 'orature' like gossip as historiographic material (opening up a new epistemological space for sexual 'evidence') – for an artist as obviously queer as Warhol to be allowed into the archive of canonical artists he had to be 'inned', re-closeted and de-sexualized as part of the process of legitimation.[43] To reclaim a fuller subject-hood for such an artist (which might be plural and contradictory, for instance), a subject-hood that would recognize sexuality as a material element in the production of cultural objects, it is not enough to simply 'mine' the archive.

For Martin Duberman the job of a historian concerned with the recovery of dissident sexualities has meant performing a number of tasks, of which one important strand has been the production of new archives and new historical accounts of the sexual past.[44] But it has also meant the production of new forms of history: for instance the book *Stonewall*, which orchestrates a cast of six voices to produce an oral history of the emergence of the Stonewall gay liberation movement that is vivid, overlapping, contradictory, polyphonic and so on.[45] It is history edging closer to the condition of heteroglossia, employing a 'discordant chorus' as the teller of history. In an earlier book on the history of Black Mountain (an experimental community for artists, like John Cage,

---

[43] Gavin Butt, *Between You and Me: Queer Disclosures in the New York Art World, 1948–1963* (Durham and London: Duke University Press, 2005) – see Chapter 4: 'Dishing on the Swish, or, the "Inning" of Andy Warhol'.

[44] Duberman, *About Time*, and the collection, Martin Bauml Duberman, Martha Vicinus and George Chauncey, Jr., eds, *Hidden from History: Reclaiming the Gay and Lesbian Past* (Harmondsworth: Penguin, 1991).

[45] Martin Duberman, *Stonewall* (New York: Plume, 1994).

Charles Olson, etc. operative between 1933–56 in North Carolina) – his first
self-conscious experiment with the form of historical telling – the form refuses
the usual 'objectivity' of the third person account and replaces it with a first
person singular voice who is immersed in the telling. Thus, at the end of *Black
Mountain*, Duberman can write:

> I completed the book a few minutes ago. I'm strangely, idiotically, near tears.
> So many completions are involved, my own and Black Mountain's, that they
> blend into some indistinguishable sadness. Is it really over; do I want it to be
> over – the place, my writing about it? I've looked forward for so long to
> having the weight removed, to getting on to other things. Yet I'll miss the
> weight itself; it filled such a space. And all those extraordinary people, their
> foolishness, their valor, their *trying* – yes, above all, their trying.[46]

In this telling the historian is not a distanced, anonymous, god-like narrator,
but is implicated in the telling, in the choice of what gets told, and in the force
of what has been relayed (the attempt to establish a community, and all that that
might mean). In this, *Black Mountain* is always historiography and never simply
history: the threading of archival sources, oral histories, the protocols of professional practices, is visible. The text displays a writing mind that wants to reveal
its desires and fears – that wants to be recognized as writing, as a production.
    For de Certeau it is this refusal of false objectivity (which is on one level
simply a rhetorical device designed to cover the traces of labour – of research-
ing, collecting, collating, writing) that is so important: 'the marvelous liberty
that allows Martin Duberman to become in his discourse the interlocutor of
his absent characters and to tell of himself by telling of them' (WH: 14). But
this isn't simply a permission slip that could allow the historian to write more
'personally', it actually points to new epistemological circumstances:

> Studies of this kind inaugurate a different epistemology from that which
> defined the place of knowledge in terms of a position 'proper' to itself and
> which measured the authority of the 'subject of knowledge' by the elimination
> of everything concerning the speaker. In making this elimination explicit, his-
> toriography returns once again to the particularities of the commonplace, to
> the reciprocal affects which structure representations, and to the multiple pasts
> which determine the use of its techniques from within. (H: 218)

By refusing the propriety of 'proper' history, historiography doesn't end
up with the absolute relativism feared by professional historians (Duberman's

---

[46] Martin Duberman, *Black Mountain: An Exploration in Community* (London: Wildwood
House, 1974), p. 413.

history of *Black Mountain* isn't 'subjective' in the sense that the author may have willed this historiography into being like a planet in a science-fiction novel). The opposite is the case. By becoming a voice, the historian doesn't become the voice of relativism (whatever that would be) but one voice amongst many, and in doing so he or she opens the gates to the polyphonic heteroglossia that threatens propriety in the name of historical fullness; that threatens generic conventions and protocols in the name of truths. The doors are open to the commonplace and to the multitude.

Samuel Delany's glorious autobiography *The Motion of Light in Water: Sex and Science Fiction Writing in the East Village 1960–1965*[47] provides an example of how a form of history writing can be used to make vivid the 'presence of absence' of daily life, while also retrieving 'something' from the occultation performed by a scriptural economy.[48] Delany (known by his nickname 'Chip' throughout much of the book) grew up in Harlem in New York. The form of the book resembles a complex filing system that allows 'entries' to follow various themes while encouraging a more meandering sequence. The entries move backwards and forward in time as Chip attends school in the Bronx, gets married and moves into the East Village in the 1960s, and begins his literary career. An African-American who could pass as white; a gay man who was married; a science-fiction writer and a poet – Chip lives life in the plural. For de Certeau, as I've already mentioned, 'plurality is originary' (PEL1: 133), and although his theorizing of everyday life is not centred on the individual, the radical plurality of an individual can offer a vivid indication of the difficult potential of writing the ordinary by writing 'culture in the plural'.

Delany writes of three particular daily (and for Delany, repetitively ordinary) occurrences. One is a vision disturbance (the foreground receding into the distance) brought on whenever he is tired and occurring once or twice a day. Another is a jolt he gets (like the soles of his feet being struck) just as he is about to go to sleep. The other consists of panic attacks (brought on by the sudden awareness of death) that vary in severity and happen two or three times a day (often leaving him exhausted). After recounting these embodied experiences Delany asks the reader to:

> Consider these three things inscribed again and again, page by page, in a second column of type that doubles the one that makes up this book, a parallel column devoted only to those elements that are repeated and repeated

---

[47] Samuel R. Delany, *The Motion of Light in Water: Sex and Science Fiction Writing in the East Village* (New York: Richard Kasak, 1993).

[48] The historian Joan Scott has also used Delany's book for writing about historiographical issues, see, Joan W. Scott, 'The Evidence of Experience', *Critical Inquiry*, vol. 17, no. 4, 1991, pp. 773–97.

throughout any day, any life, incidents that constitute at once the basal and quotidian – waking up, breakfast, lunch, dinner, washing, elimination, drifting off to sleep – as well as the endlessly repeated risings and fallings of desire.[49]

Of course this is precisely what is most difficult to consider for long. Within a page or two (perhaps sooner) we are swept along by the drift of a narrativity that articulates a different sense (temporality) of an everyday life filled with actions, progressions, aspirations and movements. We 'forget' the author's instructions as we become lost in the writing. This overflow of bodily experience is, it seems, impossible to contain with the narrative conventions of writing, but here at least our attention is drawn to the presence of these absences as they refuse inscription.

Later in the book Chip/Delany tries to recount his first day at Bronx Science high school. Here the unbending economy of the scriptural makes vivid another occultation. Here it is the difficulty of writing the self as plural that is in evidence. In remembering his first day, he writes about the friends he made, about his teacher and about how he was voted on to a student board. But by the end of his account he realizes he has left out a more important friendship:

> Reviewing it, however, what strikes me is how quickly the written narrative closes it out – puts it outside of language. Reading over what I've already written of that first day, searching for a margin in which to inscribe it, within and round what's already written, I suspect it might well be printed in a column parallel with the above . . .[50]

What it closes out is the narrative of another friendship that within the terms of the first narrative can find no place. Delany writes the day again, this time it is the erotic charge that accompanies his friendship with Joey that becomes the centre of the narrative. These two accounts (Delany suggests that there would be others too) are again imagined within a different technology of writing (two simultaneous columns), with 'one resplendent and lucid with the writings of legitimacy, the other dark and hollow with the voices of the illegitimate'.[51] The simultaneity of the plurality is both pointed to and impossible to convey (in this sense Delany's suggestion of two columns of text is necessarily metaphorical). The everyday as overflow (of desire, of the ordinary) is registered here as vivid and theoretically productive trace. Such doubling or pluralizing of accounts rips

---

[49] Delany, *The Motion of Light in Water*, p. 45.
[50] Delany, *The Motion of Light in Water*, p. 64.
[51] Delany, *The Motion of Light in Water*, p. 69.

holes in the linear form of narrative and opens up a space for complex and contradictory desires: it is a form that would bear comparison with the repetitions
that Duras' novels and films put into play, and with the multiple, situated
accounts of the same event that make up the wonderful novel, *Chronicle of a
Death Foretold*, by Gabriel García Márquez.[52]

Delany's book is both ethnographic and literary. Its fragments register an
overflow that disrupts the consistency of self-presentation. It displays the
employment and re-employment of a proliferating narrativity (both 'legitimate'
and 'illegitimate') for a life lived in the plural. Both de Certeau and Delany take
different routes to arrive at a similar place. Both suggest the importance of a
writing that takes place in the margins and interstices of a cultural orthodoxy.
The reason for this is the insistence of culture in the plural. What makes the
everyday (or the individual) excessive, overflowing, is its plurality. It is a plurality that can't find a place within a scriptural economy dedicated to the consistency of the same, instead what is required is writing dedicated to the plurality
of swarming singularities. What is being imagined is a writing that will give
space to an unmanageable remainder (the body, love, 'libidinal saturation', etc.),
and will begin to constitute ethnography in the plural.

In a later piece of writing, more explicitly addressed to the epistemological
issues at stake in recovering the experience and historicity of (dissident) sexualities, Delany writes:

> But 'the gay experience' has always resided largely outside of language –
> because all sexuality, even all experience, in part resides there. Simple aver-
> sion – at whatever social level – is enough to divert our accounts from much
> of what occurs. But even to seek the averse is to divert our accounts from the
> characteristic. And because of this economy, in anything that I can recognize
> as a socially and politically meaningful discussion of sex, the triplicity of aver-
> sion, perversion, and diversion cannot, as far as I know, be avoided.[53]

What Delany is partly insisting on is that the experience of gay sexuality, in a
historical period that has consistently wanted to exclude it from representation,
must also include this non-representationality as part of its constituency. What
Delany also points to, and in a way that can be extended into other domains, is
the centrality of such history from the 'margins'. And this is to push historicity
beyond its obligation to the history of its identifiable constituency:

[52] Gabriel García Márquez, *Chronicle of a Death Foretold* (Harmondsworth: Penguin, 1982).

[53] Samuel R. Delany, 'Aversion/Perversion/Diversion' in Monica Dorenkamp and Richard
Henke, eds, *Negotiating Lesbian and Gay Subjects* (New York and London: Routledge,
1995), p. 27.

It seems to me that when one begins to consider the range of diversities throughout the sexual landscape, then the absolute unquestioned normalcy of the heterosexual male whose sexual fantasies are almost wholly circumscribed by photographs of . . . female movie stars! suddenly looks – well, I will not say, 'less normal'. But I will say that it takes on a mode of sexual and social specificity that marks it in the way every other one of these tales is marked, i.e., as perverse.[54]

The histories of sexual dissidents, to use Jonathan Dollimore's evocative phrase, or the histories of colonized subjects, or the histories of the various 'zones of silence', are not there to fill the historical record – to fill in the gaps. Such history will work to unsettle the notion of centre and margin, of major and minor, in constitutive ways.

Narrative, then, for de Certeau, is both good object and bad object. But for it to be valued for the practice of writing culture it has to be an open form that invites experimentation. Such experiments are not conducted in the name of some vacuous relativism, but in the name of an ethical striving to produce accounts more adequate to the pulsing heteroglossia of daily life. That formal experimentation with narrative form has often been conducted in the name of those left out of the dominant accounts is of crucial importance. The reordering of narrative forms in response to epistemological critique and ethical challenge is not something bounded by scholarly interests. In the next chapter I want to look at how epistemological doubt and ethical responsibility can fashion a form of cultural policy that is attentive to the traumas of the past while dedicated to the hopes of the future.

[54] Delany, 'Aversion/Perversion/Diversion', p. 30.

CHAPTER 6

An Art of Diversion: Cultural Policy and the Counter Public Sphere

Let us try to make a *perruque*[1] in the economic system whose rules and hierarchies are repeated, as always, in scientific institutions. In the area of scientific research (which defines the current order of knowledge), working with its machines and making use of its scraps, we can divert the time owed to the institution; we can make textual objects that signify an art of solidarities; we can play the game of free exchange, even if it is penalized by bosses and colleagues when they are not willing to 'turn a blind eye' on it; we can create networks of connivances and sleights of hand; we can exchange gifts; and in these ways we can subvert the law that, in the scientific factory, puts work at the service of the machine and, by a similar logic, progressively destroys the requirement of creation and the 'obligation to give'. I know of investigators experienced in this art of diversion, which is a return to the ethical, of pleasure and of invention within the scientific institution. (PEL I: 28)

FREE ASSOCIATION

Ethics, pleasure and invention – these are the values that underwrite a practice that tries to open up a space for 'free association'. This phrase – 'free association' – is, of course, saturated with psychoanalytic connotations, many of them circulating through comedy routines (Woody Allen, for instance) or films like *Blade Runner* ('describe in single words, only the good things that come into your mind about your mother'). The phrase, though, is unstoppably edging towards the social: who could want to simply pin down *free association* to a trick with words? Yet in edging towards the social, in edging towards the 'orchestration' of the social, isn't there danger that a practice, when it becomes involved in generating policy, moves inevitably towards prescribing ways of operating? If, as I have been

[1] This is de Certeau's term (though it is also a popular, vernacular term) for 'diversionary' practices, such as using your employer's time and facilities for doing your own 'work' – the most ubiquitous and banal example for office workers probably being conducting personal email correspondence while at work.

arguing, Michel de Certeau's ethical practice tries to guard against the cultural pacification of heterogeneity, then isn't there something contradictory about operating in the field of cultural policy? Wouldn't we imagine that de Certeau's position would side with a critique of cultural policy, a critique that reveals policy as necessarily involving the *management* of cultural activities? Yet, as I want to argue here, it might be that we can only really fully understand de Certeau's contribution to the study of culture when we look at it from the perspective of his involvement with cultural policy. Here in this final substantive chapter I want to show how the methodology of de Certeau is always also social. Explicating his work of cultural policy is a way of making vivid something that is already there in the historiography, in the contemporary ethnology.

I've been attempting throughout this book to suggest that de Certeau's work is a response to a combined challenge that is simultaneously epistemological and ethical. That response faces a history rife with complicity between analysis and domination. While the historical antecedents for this are striking and obvious (the ethnology produced under colonialism was necessarily and existentially linked to colonial forms of domination) it is perhaps harder to see contemporary forms of cultural studies and sociology, for instance, as similarly complicit in forms of domination. Yet the continuation of a relationship between intellectual life and a dominating social order is precisely the ground in which de Certeau's ethical commitments are rooted – any attempt to 'write culture' is necessarily compromised, right from the start. Inasmuch as scholarly work participates in the uneven distribution of knowledge (where the anthropologist or sociologist's career advances while the 'objects' of study fall further into decline) and actively sides with the brokers of knowledge rather than the objects-of-knowledge, then it has to be recognized as muddily imbricated in a system that perpetuates the uneven distribution of resources and the purposeful withholding of cultural power. This is not to condemn, out of hand, the business of academic knowledge production (I wouldn't be writing this if I felt that way), but it is to have a realist sense of complicity, while also striving to find better ways (ways that alter the communicative ground of culture) for undertaking the practice of studying culture. Indeed for de Certeau it is the *recognition* of complicity that drives the undertaking to search out and invent better, more equitable, ways of writing culture – recognition is the condition of epistemological possibility, it is what allows for better (more complete and analytic) knowledge of the world.

A similar point about complicity is made quite differently by Donna Haraway in her essay 'A Cyborg Manifesto: Science, Technology, and Socialist-Feminism in the Late Twentieth Century'. Haraway is recognizing that her 'formation' as someone working in the area of critical science studies and feminism is determined by forces that are both constitutive of, and in conflict with, her declared critical position: 'A PhD in biology for an Irish Catholic girl was made possible by Sputnik's impact on the US national science-education policy. I have a body and mind as much constructed by the post-Second World War arms race and cold war as by the women's movements.'[2]

It is this messy, compromised epistemology that is also the starting point for de Certeau's methodology of cultural analysis. And it is here where we most clearly see the promise of a practical ethics. The gap between the intention (to launch a feminist critique of science knowledge, for instance) and the actuality (science funding is ultimately tied to governmental interests, for instance) is where ethics exists. In this there is also a direct link between epistemology and ethics: both recognize inequalities; and both actively seek out more hospitable circumstances for heterogeneity. Both ethics and epistemology are aimed at the future, and are orientated to practical aims: 'ethics is articulated through effective operations, and it defines a distance between what is and what ought to be. The distance designates a space where there is something to do' (H: 199). And because this work is both necessarily practical and necessarily future orientated, the work of cultural policy needs to be recognized alongside the work of fashioning new ways of writing cultural history. In this, cultural policy shares the same methodological directives as the other work: it is ethically dedicated to subjugated standpoints, while recognizing that there is no direct access to these standpoints. De Certeau's cultural-policy work is practically linked to the more scholarly work of historiography and contemporary ethnology; but it is also the ultimate sphere of practical knowledge – the space where de Certeau's work most insistently aligns epistemological scepticism to ethical invention, in its most social, practicable forum.

In this chapter I want to listen to de Certeau's policy work; but not as an additional element of his work – not as another aspect that needs to be taken into account to get a fully rounded picture of all his different involvements. Rather I want to ask what happens when we see cultural-policy work as the necessary outcome of his theoretical and methodological practices. In this way the work of cultural policy can be seen as the future-orientated response to his ethical and epistemological challenge; directly related to the past-orientated response that is evident in his historiographic writing. In other words, to move into the realms of policy work is not to leave the struggle of epistemology behind, nor is it to quietly jettison the orientation towards a form of cultural psychoanalysis and the communicative practices it could presage; instead, it would be the ultimate opportunity for capitalizing on the social promise of

[2] Donna J. Haraway, 'A Cyborg Manifesto: Science, Technology, and Socialist-Feminism in the Late Twentieth Century', in *Simians, Cyborgs, and Women: The Reinvention of Nature* (London: Free Association Books, 1991), p. 173.

psychoanalysis. In this, de Certeau's cultural-policy work has to be seen as distinct from the cultural-policy remit adopted by Anglophone cultural studies in recent decades.[3]

Perhaps one of the most elaborate discussions, and most stringent defences, of the 'cultural-policy shift' in Anglophone cultural studies is given by Tony Bennett in his book *Culture: A Reformer's Science*.[4] In an earlier, programmatic paper that outlines the main thrust of his later book, he argues that a shift towards cultural policy will require cultural studies to establish a set of imperatives:

> *First*, the need to include policy considerations in the definition of culture in viewing it as a particular field of government; *second*, the need to distinguish different regions of culture within this overall field in terms of the objects, targets, and techniques of government peculiar to them; *third*, the need to identify the political relations specific to different regions of culture so defined and to develop appropriately specific ways of engaging with and within them; and, *fourth*, the need for intellectual work to be conducted in a manner such that, in both its substance and its style, it can be calculated to influence or service the conduct of identifiable agents within the region of culture concerned.[5]

This shift towards cultural policy, for Anglophone cultural studies, necessitated 'giving up on the scorn of bureaucracy and the idealization of the intellectual as remote from the messy, corrupting world'.[6] It has as its most distinctive aim an instrumentality that would suggest it should be judged in terms of its 'calculated' ability 'to influence'. In this, cultural studies (as cultural policy) clearly had to recognize that social effectiveness would only result from some form of complicity with forms of governance: cultural studies had to stop worrying about getting its hands dirty. This messy commerce with the world was the cost that a form of cultural studies had to pay for having some sort of measurable impact on the social world. Yet in de Certeau's critical epistemology, *any* form of intellectual work is already deeply imbedded within 'the messy,

[3] For examples of this work see Justin Lewis and Toby Miller, eds, *Critical Cultural Policy Studies: A Reader* (Oxford: Blackwell, 2003) and the journal *Culture and Policy: Review of the Institute for Cultural Policy Studies* – produced by the policy studies department at Griffith University, Australia. For a recent contribution to policy studies see Jim McGuigan, *Rethinking Cultural Policy* (Maidenhead: Open University Press, 2004).

[4] Tony Bennett, *Culture: A Reformer's Science* (London: Sage, 1998).

[5] Tony Bennett, 'Putting Policy into Cultural Studies' in Lawrence Grossberg, Cary Nelson and Paula Treichler, eds, *Cultural Studies* (London and New York: Routledge, 1992), p. 23.

[6] Simon During, *Cultural Studies: A Critical Introduction* (London and New York: Routledge, 2005), p. 73.

corrupting world'. This is, no doubt, a point that would now be made within Anglophone cultural-policy work;[7] yet the very fact that de Certeau simultaneously conducted what might be considered esoteric studies on demonic and mystic possessions while also undertaking government policy studies suggests that the split between the 'real world politics' of policy work and the purity of intellectual pursuits wasn't an operational one for him.

The simultaneity of de Certeau's various operations should alert us to the possibility of an underlying operational methodology at work here. No doubt the conditions for cultural policy in France (especially in the wake of May 1968) were less instrumentalist than they were in other countries (particularly in the UK and the US) – yet I don't think that it is the relative freedom and prestige of the public intellectual in France that explains the difference between de Certeau and Anglophone cultural-policy work. More crucially, I think, de Certeau's policy work emerges out of the same epistemological and ethical cauldron that informs his entire oeuvre. In this, policy work doesn't involve a tactical withdrawal of critical theorizing or of the more avant-garde tendencies of cultural studies. Policy work, like historiography and the writing of culture, is similarly dedicated to fashioning spaces more hospitable to the voices of others; and, unlike even the most liberal policy positions, it is completely committed to siding with the unmanageability of the ordinary and the radical heterogeneity of the multitude. This, of course, doesn't mean that de Certeau's policy work is exempt from political critique: it might be argued, for instance, that by remaining resolutely utopian in his desire for radical democratic policies, his suggestions consistently fail to be taken up, unadulterated, as policy (which, not surprisingly, might be the main reason for being involved in policy work). This at any rate would be the kind of critique that I could imagine being launched against him. In this chapter, though, I want to look at the potential of his policy work, not simply for understanding the oeuvre in general but for thinking about cultural policy in the future and for thinking about different situations for cultural practice. In this de Certeau offers a distinct approach to cultural policy, one that can be usefully compared to what seems to be a much more reformist, instrumentalist and limited position advocated by Anglophone cultural policy in all its various guises.

---

[7] One of the tenets of cultural-policy work in Anglophone culture is that a university lecturer teaching cultural studies is always already involved (tacitly and implicitly) in forms of governance: cultural-policy studies wants to make that role explicit, reflexive, socially effective and open to argument. Of course there are many different forms of governance, and many other possible roles to pursue under the heading of cultural studies. Nevertheless there is some sense that this argument is unnecessary in France: the nomination 'intellectual' already suggests someone who would be involved in wider social issues and larger social forums than the gated communities of academe.

First the bare facts: 'Michel de Certeau was more or less constantly engaged between 1970 and 1985 in a series of cultural policy and consultative projects centred largely around the research unit of the Ministry of Culture and the National Plan.'[8] Jeremy Ahearne, who has been instrumental in rethinking de Certeau's work from the perspective of cultural policy, itemizes de Certeau's involvement in various government agencies: Commission for Cultural Affairs (1970–71); Council for Cultural Development (1971–73); Ministry of Culture (various); government-funded research (1974–77); and – after returning from the US – two cultural-policy commissions in 1982 and 1983.[9] More crucial, for Ahearne, is the way that de Certeau inflects cultural-policy themes in France – away from a notion of cultural policy as predominantly understood in terms of widening access to elite culture (democratizing access to the established canon) towards a more experimental practice of policy initiatives coupled with a realization of the gulf that often exists between the aspirations of policy makers and the conditions of cultural life existing in French society (standardized working practices, mass consumerism and so on).

In what follows I want to explore two themes of de Certeau's cultural policy – the insistence on ordinary and amateur culture, and the privileging of immigrants as primary producers and consumers of public culture (addressors and addressees) – and suggest various contexts for developing these ideas. These contexts are aesthetic and social. Various examples of 'public' art, particularly art participating in radical democratic forms, will be discussed as spaces for amateur and immigrant production and consumption. Ideas of an oppositional public sphere or a counter public, as discussed by Alexander Kluge, Oskar Negt, Lauren Berlant and Michael Warner, will be used as an alternative to the more consensual and ordered public sphere described by Jürgen Habermas, and will be offered as the kind of possible social formation underwriting the forms of cultural policy advocated by de Certeau.

AMATEURS AND IMMIGRANTS: AN ETHICS OF HOSPITALITY

If 'cultural policy', as an arm of government and governance, has partly worked to reproduce the symbolism of the nation state (its cultural currency), then we

---

[8] Jeremy Ahearne, *Between Cultural Theory and Policy: The Cultural Policy Thinking of Pierre Bourdieu, Michel de Certeau and Régis Debray*, Centre for Cultural Policy Studies, Research Papers, no. 7 (Warwick: University of Warwick, 2004), p. 12. A free digital version of this book is available on the publications page of the centre's website (http://www.warwick.ac.uk/culturalpolicy). I am indebted to Ahearne's work on French cultural policy and de Certeau in much of this chapter.

[9] See Ahearne, *Between Cultural Theory and Policy*, p. 78.

could say that de Certeau's approach to cultural policy has purposefully refused to maintain the conditions under which such reproduction can flourish. Rather than the symbolism of the nation state (which actually might also include a sense of limited 'diversity'), de Certeau's cultural policy is founded on a desire for foreignness: it is profoundly *xenophilic*. But it isn't just the foreigner who arrives from another nation who is the citizen who will be directing policy (albeit remotely); it is also the 'foreigner' to Culture (to museum culture, for instance), who had tended to be treated as the recipient of culture, rather than the practitioner of culture. Thus alongside the 'immigrant' stands the figure of the 'amateur' as the two underlying value-bearers directing cultural policy.

Such a position needs to be seen in context. As Ahearne has shown, the French postwar attitude to cultural policy was shaped most decisively by the beliefs and practices of André Malraux, and the major platform for Malraux's policy was the extension of cultural quality to as wide a public as possible.[10] In today's policy vernacular, the terms underwriting such policy would be 'inclusion' and 'access'. Malraux, the creator of the 'museum without walls', sought to take a diet of great works to the people – to extend the walls of the museum to include as many as possible. Unlike Malraux, de Certeau and others (especially in the years after May 1968) thought that the initial building block of any democratic cultural policy had to be the kinds of cultural practices already being undertaken by people. Thus, any success in widening the scope of cultural policy to include as many people as possible could only work if it was scaffolded on to the abilities, interests and enthusiasms that were already in circulation.

> Whereas the scheme underlying Malraux's cultural action was to project universally valid artistic goods into spaces imagined as cultural deserts, the scheme characterising 'cultural development' was to build on the cultural activity already present in social groups. This activity was conceived in a broad way (reading, amateur artistic activity, cinema, gardening, local associations, etc.), and the objectives were generally to wrest such activity from the alienating and levelling effects of 'mass culture'.[11]

Ahearne situates de Certeau's policy positions within a larger remit of 'cultural development' aimed as a two-pronged policy: to defend culture from

---

[10] See David L. Looseley, *The Politics of Fun: Cultural Policy and Debate in Contemporary France* (Oxford: Berg, 1995) and Jeremy Ahearne, ed., *French Cultural Policy Debates: A Reader* (London and New York: Routledge, 2002).

[11] Ahearne, *Between Cultural Theory and Policy*, p. 82.

the deleterious effects of industrialized culture (especially culture stamped as US import); and to promote a sort of indigenous (but not nation specific), grass-roots culture – a heterogeneous global vernacular.

It is, momentarily, worth recognizing the promotion of amateurism in culture as part of radical democratic and anti-bourgeois practice, even if the association with 'amateurism' (amateur dramatics, amateur painting) can seem, particularly in the context of the UK, decidedly middle-class. Yet you get a sense of its radical potential when you simply recognize the range of things that might be included under the banner of 'amateur' practices and the depth to which these penetrate culture. For de Certeau such cultural practices would include everything from cooking and gardening to making home movies: in this sense it is hard to imagine anyone not being involved in some sort of activity that comes under the banner of amateur culture. In postwar France, amateur cultures become, in the hands of a few writers (including de Certeau), a set of alternatives to the cultural hegemonies of either high French culture or the culture industries being imported from the US. In this sense the Sunday painter or the cacti grower can be valued precisely because they aren't simply mopping up the latest offering of Hollywood-Coca-Cola.[12] Alongside this, amateur culture, which might include camping and walking as well as photography, is seen as being driven by passion in a way that cinema-going or TV-watching isn't. For Henri Lefebvre, while camping and photography, for instance, are not free from commodification, they also establish a relationship with the world that suggests a very different passionate engagement (a searching out of place, an involvement in situation) that can often be missing from more passive involvements in cultural consumption.[13] For Roland Barthes it was precisely because amateurism related to an economy of love rather than to one of expertise that it could be classified as (potentially) anti-bourgeois:

> The Amateur (someone who engages in painting, music, sport, science, without the spirit of mastery or competition), the Amateur renews his pleasure (*amator*: one who loves and loves again); he is anything but a hero (of creation, of performance); he establishes himself *graciously* (for nothing) in the signifier: in the immediately definitive substance of music, of painting; his praxis, usually, involves no *rubato* (that theft of the object for the

---

[12] On what was sometimes called *coca-colonisés*, see Richard Kuisel, *Seducing the French: The Dilemma of Americanization* (Berkeley, Los Angeles and London: University of California Press, 1993).

[13] Henri Lefebvre, *Critique of Everyday Life: Volume 1*, translated by John Moore (London: Verso, 1991). This book was initially published in 1947, but the second edition of 1958 included a substantial new foreword – which is where the passages related to amateur culture can be found: pp. 29–42.

sake of the attribute); he is – he will be perhaps – the counter-bourgeois artist.[14]

In the wake of the Second World War, in response to widespread Americanization, and in relation to experiments in democracy emerging after May 1968, radical forms of cultural policy in France would be based around cultural development, around the notion that culture is what is already taking place, and is what is being threatened by mass-culture on the one hand, and by the snobbery of elite culture on the other.

In one sense, then, de Certeau's study of the practices of everyday life finds its context immediately within the terms of cultural-policy debates: 'everyday culture' is the foundation for a powerful arm of post-1968 cultural-policy work in France. It is a substantial challenge to the cultural values of Malraux, and the culture of the establishment more generally. If Georges Bataille can challenge the passions of art lovers when he writes, 'I challenge any art lover, to love a canvas as much as fetishist loves a shoe',[15] then de Certeau and others can challenge the official values of cultural policy by posing common cooking (for instance) as evidencing levels of skill, facility and invention on a level with the 'great' works of literature. While de Certeau doesn't make the kind of counter-bourgeois claims for the amateur that Barthes does, he sees amateurism (as everyday life culture) as a much more extensive field of practice: a massive subterranean 'oceanic' resource – it is the poetics of practice, and extends from the arts of the body (ways of walking, holding yourself, etc.) to the arts of speaking, inhabiting, cooking and so on. The vastness of this emphatically declares itself as the name of heterogeneity and threads memory into practice:

> As gestural 'idiolects', the practices of inhabitants creates, on the same urban space, a multitude of possible combinations between ancient places (the secrets of which childhoods or which deaths?) and new situations. They turn the city into an immense memory where many poetics proliferate. (PEL2: 141)

The range and ubiquity of this culture make it a truly 'common' and popular culture, not in the sense of a shared, unified culture, but in the sense of a swarming mass of different practices that everyone participates in, but which for the most part fall below the horizon of visibility.

---

[14] Roland Barthes, *Roland Barthes by Roland Barthes*, translated by Richard Howard (New York: Hill and Wang, 1977), p. 52.

[15] Georges Bataille, from *Documents* (1930), cited in Denis Hollier, *Absent Without Leave: French Literature Under the Threat of War*, translated by Catherine Porter (Cambridge: Harvard University Press, 1997), p. 133.

De Certeau's policy work, then, is an articulation of an ethical demand for the heterogeneous. Such an ethics has to be answerable to the other, the alien, the stranger. In this de Certeau's policy work finds its most distinctive formulation by figuring 'the immigrant' as privileged agent of culture: 'Accepting the real presence of immigrants means in truth to open to them a free space of speech and demonstration in which their own culture can be displayed or offered for the knowledge of others' (CS: 134, with Giard). And it is this figure who is the first and last arbiter of policy. As we will see, this connects to a strain of ethical thinking most forcefully represented in the writing of Emmanuel Levinas, but (and this might be contrary to expectation) the privileging of the stranger also works to foreground cultural dynamism and cultural mutability, rather than the fixities of identity:

> A foreigner amongst us, the bearer of the visible stigma of difference, since he or she moves with the marks of an idiom, a tradition, usages, tastes, and behavior that are not familiar and in which we fail to see ourselves, the immigrant teaches us how to circulate in our language and our customs, and adapts to our material and symbolic universe. So different from ourselves, the immigrant is also the figure who already resembles us, whose destiny anticipates our own. He or she is the exemplary figure imposed by modernity, with the abandonment of our familiar points of reference, the adaptation to other codes, the acquisition of new ways of thinking and acting. The immigrant has already faced this test of imposed change, of obligatory displacement, and has faced it successfully, since immigrants are amongst us, the recognizable bearers of their original identity, of their *difference*. (CS: 133, with Giard)

The immigrant is the stranger, who in Georg Simmel's essay from 1908, is the one 'who comes today and stays tomorrow'.[16] In the aftermath of decolonization in North Africa in the 1960s (particularly in the wake of the bloody war in Algeria), and with the rise, in France (and elsewhere), of the far right and ferocious forms of racism, the issue of immigration was highly charged in the 1970s and 1980s (as it still is today). For a number of intellectuals the figure of the foreign and the immigrant has been the touchstone for deriving an ethics that couldn't fail to resonate politically within a new global culture.

The late writings of Derrida (who was one of the first to respond to Levinas' writings) directed deconstruction towards ethics in works like *On Cosmopolitanism and Forgiveness*, *Politics of Friendship*, and *Of Hospitality*.[17] Here the

---

[16] Georg Simmel, 'The Stranger' (1908) in *On Individuality and Social Forms* (Chicago and London: University of Chicago Press, 1971), p. 143.

[17] The initial encounter with Levinas is in Jacques Derrida, 'Violence and Metaphysics: An Essay on the Thought of Emmanuel Levinas' in *Writing and Difference*, translated by Alan Bass

figures of hospitality and friendship become the ground for establishing a response to ethical demands that opens up communication to a meeting with difference that is not resolved by asking the immigrant to 'integrate' (whatever that can mean). The language of 'integration' and 'assimilation' places the onus on the immigrant to adopt and adapt to the new culture:[18] when cultural policy is based on the ethics of hospitality, of opening towards the other (in the name of heterogeneity) then the onus is on the host culture. This form of social ethics is well described by Levinas' English translator, the philosopher Alphonso Lingis, who insists on linking the ethical demand from the other to a form of responsibility:

> I would like to connect responsibility very much to sensitivity. . . . To be sensitive to the other person is to be responsive. Responsibility is connected with the notion of answering to the other, responding to the other's moves and to the other's sensibility. It's too weak to say that the other person is not responsive to my feelings. It is much more than that. It is more to do with a kind of sensibility – the way I perceive things, the way I make sense of the whole environment about me.[19]

To answer to the other (to any other person, but most crucially to the foreigner and the immigrant) is not simply to 'tolerate' differences and forms of otherness: it is to *retune* yourself as a responsive act. Tolerance alone fails to engage with the other and can subject the other to repression.[20]

(London: Routledge and Kegan Paul, 1978), pp. 79–153 – first published in France in 1964. The other volumes mentioned are: Jacques Derrida, *Politics of Friendship*, translated by George Collins (London: Verso, 1997); Jacques Derrida, *Of Hospitality*, translated by Rachel Bowlby (Stanford: Stanford University Press, 2000); and Jacques Derrida, *On Cosmopolitanism and Forgiveness*, translated by Mark Dooley and Michael Hughes (London and New York: Routledge, 2001). A related but different ethics of alterity is pursued by Julia Kristeva, see Julia Kristeva, *Strangers to Ourselves*, translated by Leon S. Roudiez (New York: Columbia University Press, 1991) and Julia Kristeva, *Nations without Nationalism*, translated by Leon S. Roudiez (New York: Columbia University Press, 1993).

[18] It is, of course, impossible to migrate and not adapt – migrating necessarily requires adapting to new forms. While the ideology of integration and assimilation try and seem reasonable they are actually veiled threats: this is not about adapting, but about total and uncritical acceptance of the host culture, for instance. It is epistemological bullying.

[19] Alphonso Lingis (in conversation with Mary Zournazi), 'Murmors of Life' in Mary Zournazi, *Hope: New Philosophies for Change* (London: Lawrence and Wishart, 2002), pp. 34–5.

[20] In the 1960s Herbert Marcuse wrote of a repressive tolerance: tolerance that would 'allow' forms of cultural dissent (offering them a marginal space in a market-driven cultural economy), but would fail to engage with their critiques. For de Certeau's response to Marcuse in the context of May 1968 see *Culture in the Plural*, pp. 91–6.

In the work of Levinas and his interlocutors an ethical demand is primary and forces us to face up to the fact that our 'being' is not something internal to us, it is not based on notions of identity, but is always a form of social being that finds itself only in relation to the other. In this it isn't the immigrant who needs 'us', but 'us' who need immigrants so that we can be. It is the ethical demand of the other who precedes us:

> With Levinas we are . . . introduced into an entirely new conception of the ethical, a conception which engages with, but also departs from, the ethical model developed by Immanuel Kant. . . . Levinas's ethics is also foundation-less, which means that it is not based on any prior principle to which I can refer in order to verify my obligation and morality. But for Levinas it is the Other who is the source of both my reason and my obligation. Obligation thus *happens to me*, it precedes me. This obligation is free of any specific content – Levinas does not therefore give us a list of commandments, he does not tell us how to live and act. It is obligation *as such*, rather than an oblig-ation *to do something* that is the source of ethics.[21]

While it is tempting to draw strong parallels between Levinas and de Certeau, it is enough at the moment to suggest that both (as well as others) were working with a notion of ethics that sees the core element of social life as a rela-tionship with alterity (which in de Certeau is forcefully related to heterogene-ity) – and where both figure the relationship with alterity to be open and constitutive, rather than tolerant or integrative.

For cultural policy, such an ethical basis negates the usual 'flagship' men-tality of policy bureaucrats and introduces a fundamentally revolutionary agenda. To open culture up to the other is to make a policy whereby culture is the hospitality shown to immigrants, not in making minor adjustments so they can be tolerated, but literally making them at home – fundamentally allowing alterations to occur so that a home culture can be *remade* in response to the other. This is to alter the relations of culture (which might include changing laws, for instance) and alter the role of the policy researcher. Here the policy researcher works to find ways of facilitating the transformation of culture in ways that can't be known in advance, that can't be orchestrated. Cultural policy in this light is a wager on the oceanic heterogeneity of daily life in a society animated by international movement. For de Certeau it meant

---

[21] Joanna Zylinska, *The Ethics of Cultural Studies* (London and New York: Continuum Books, 2005), p. 15. Levinas' key work is *Totality and Infinity: An Essay on Exteriority*, translated by Alphonso Lingis (Dordrecht, Boston and London: Kluwer Academic Publishers, 1991) – first published in France in 1961.

allowing spaces and communicative forms where otherness and heterogeneity could proliferate:

> We suggest that places in cities be set aside for speech making, that festivals of orality and writing be created, that questions be opened to competition (for the production of texts or cassette recordings), that the circulation of recordings as a means of social exchange be developed, and so on. Similarly, the collection and archiving of oral patrimony should be stimulated, by associating with it what pertains to gestures and techniques of the body. (CS: 139 with Giard)

In Ahearne's commentary, the opening up of speech situations (particularly the opportunities presented by small and independent radio networks) allows for a form of cultural policy aligned to the facilitation of materials that are essentially uncontrolled and deregulated:

> As speaking subjects take hold of a preexisting linguistic system and bend it to their purposes while simultaneously following its laws, so Certeau's ordinary subjects are not simply moulded by the regulations and symbolic structures of social life. These constitute instead the material on which their creative practices of 'reemployment', 'metaphorization', 'insinuation' and 'utterance' can be put to work, with greater or lesser effect.[22]

When this is given over to others, when such spaces allow the demand of the other to flourish, such cultural practices have the potential to transform society. It is here that we can see the politics involved in the epistemological and ethical challenge that de Certeau presents. If cultural management (in all its forms, from the writing of official histories to the running of TV networks) works (epistemologically) to render others speechless (by acknowledging only its own itineraries of knowledge), then the ethical demand is to find ways for the other to speak: this is both an epistemological and an ethical demand. We can see, I think, how this would form not simply the meta-methodological basis for a historiographic practice, but also a meta-methodological basis for cultural policy research as well. Such a notion of culture is not, I think, compatible with a notion of 'public culture' that might be arrived at through the understanding of the public sphere via Habermas: a more accommodating and heterogeneous idea of public is offered by the notion of counter public spheres.

---

[22] Ahearne, *Between Cultural Theory and Policy*, p. 99.

COUNTER PUBLIC SPHERES

Cultural policies, paid for out of the 'public purse', are inevitably reliant on a notion of the public, as their ultimate, though remote, client. In the last few decades, intellectual discussion of 'the public' has been dominated by a range of theories of the public sphere, most notably by Jürgen Habermas' *The Structural Transformation of the Public Sphere*[23] and Richard Sennett's *The Fall of Public Man*.[24] The term 'public sphere', has been the phrase most commonly used to ground a notion of public discursive culture and is most closely associated with Habermas:

> By 'the public sphere' we mean first of all a realm of our social life in which something approaching public opinion can be formed. Access is guaranteed to all citizens. A portion of the public sphere comes into being in every conversation in which private individuals assemble to form a public body.[25]

The very notion of 'public sphere' has come to be thought of as public spaces (coffee houses in the eighteenth century, or sites like 'speaker's corner' in London, or, as a favoured site for cultural-policy discussion, the museum), though it is worth remembering that with the German word *Öffentlicheit*, literally 'publicness', there is no necessary spatial association. And it is partly this notion of physical space which has made it difficult to think of the continuation of a public sphere into the present day.

Indeed there are two problems here which are germane to the discussion of publicness. One is the validity of imagining a notion of *the* public as a singular body of opinion-making (which tends to be the way that it is used) that is addressed and active in the production and consumption of, for instance, newspapers, and the second is the difficulty of transplanting that notion into a technologically new and distinct moment. On both accounts the prescient work of Oskar Negt and Alexander Kluge is very much to the point. In their 1972 book *Public Sphere and Experience*, which is a response, in part, to Habermas' work, the two pose the validity of a number of other publics beside the bourgeois public and put forward the idea of a proletarian public sphere as a counter public sphere. Alexander Kluge is also a filmmaker and novelist, who during the

---

[23] Jürgen Habermas, *The Structural Transformation of the Public Sphere: An Inquiry into a Category of Bourgeois Society*, translated by Thomas Burger, with Frederick Lawrence (Cambridge: Polity Press, 1989) – first published in Germany in 1962.

[24] Richard Sennett, *The Fall of Public Man* (London and Boston: Faber and Faber, 1986).

[25] Jürgen Habermas, 'The Public Sphere: An Encyclopedia Article' (1964) in Stephen Eric Bronner and Douglas MacKay Kellner, eds, *Critical Theory and Society: A Reader* (New York and London: Routledge, 1989), p. 136.

1970s (particularly) was instrumental in producing a critical-discursive form of filmmaking that conjoined activist cinema with documentary, drama and essayistic forms.[26] In his film of 1979 *The Patriot*, for instance, a schoolteacher takes her pupils out of the school to search for history, scouring official institutions, digging in the earth, pulling apart books, to analyse the recent history of Germany.[27] By working across various communicative forms, Kluge enacts the sort of flexible approach that is required to communicate 'publicly', when publicness has been scattered, fragmented, and where new technological forms have changed the nature of public production.

Kluge and Negt importantly foreground the way new forms of media production alter the very conditions of possibility for publicness:

> The classical public sphere of newspapers, chancellories, parliaments, clubs, parties, associations rests on a quasi-artisanal mode of production. By comparison, the industrialized public sphere of computers, the mass media, the media cartel, the combined public relations and legal departments of conglomerates and interest groups, and, finally, reality itself as a public sphere transformed by production, represent a superior and more highly organized level of production.[28]

The industrialization of publicness works dialectically to exert more control and regulation on media forms while also supplying the mechanisms for more fragmented, localized and culturally specific forms.

Yet, while Kluge and Negt usefully complicate notions of publicness and attempt to find an operational public forum for oppositional and proletarian politics in the present, they are still reliant on a communicative form that depends on singular, structural antagonisms (bourgeois versus proletarian). To get to a notion of a more heterogeneous sense of publicness, one more fitting for de Certeau's policy work, and more useable when antagonisms and connections are multiplying, the work of Michael Warner and Lauren Berlant is particularly useful. Writing from the position of queer theorists, Warner and Berlant multiply

[26] On Kluge's various activities and the links that can be made between them see the special issue of *October* (46) dedicated to his work, and in particular Stuart Liebman, 'Why Kluge?', *October* 46 (1988), pp. 5–22; and Fredric Jameson 'On Negt and Kluge', *October* 46 (1988), pp. 151–77. This issue also contains an interview with Kluge.

[27] See Thomas Elsaesser, *New German Cinema: A History* (Houndmills: Macmillan, 1989), pp. 258–64; and Alexander Kluge, 'On Film and the Public Sphere', *New German Critique*, 24–5 (1981–82), pp. 206–20.

[28] Oskar Negt and Alexander Kluge, *Public Sphere and Experience: Toward an Analysis of the Bourgeois and Proletarian Public Sphere*, translated by Peter Labanyi, Jamie Owen Daniel and Assenka Oksiloff (Minneapolis: University of Minnesota Press, 1993), p. 12 – first published in Germany in 1972.

the notion of a counter public and theorize it in a way that makes it both dialog-ically related to forms of dominant culture, but also generative and utopian in proposing other cultural forms. While their examples are mostly focused on les-bian and gay culture as a counter public sphere, how they figure this is relevant (potentially) to all sorts of other counter public spheres. What makes a counter public both public and 'counter' is crucial to their theory. On the one hand counter publics recognize that they are relationally subordinate to hegemonic cul-ture, thus: 'a counter public maintains at some level, conscious or not, an aware-ness of its subordinate status. The cultural horizon against which it marks itself off is not just a general or a wider public but a dominant one.'[29] And it is the 'marking itself off' that is also crucial: this counter public is not 'a lifestyle choice', it is a response to an act of epistemological violence on behalf of the dominant culture. Thus one of the most productive aspects of Warner's (and Berlant's) work is the way that they take a discussion that can seem abstract and ideational, and insist on the visceral, affective and emotional economies that it relates to:

> Often the impression seems to be that public and private are abstract cat-egories for thinking about law, politics, and economics. And so they are. But their power, as feminism and queer theory have had to insist, goes much deeper. A child's earliest education in shame, deportment, and cleaning is an initiation into the prevailing meaning of public and private, as when he or she locates his or her 'privates' or is trained to visit the 'privy'.[30]

When mentioning feminism and queer theory Warner could have also included a range of other studies, including one of the foundational texts of critical race studies, Frantz Fanon's *Black Skin, White Masks* – with its crucial discussions of public shame around the 'fact of blackness'.[31]

The other aspect of their approach to publicness that is important is the recognition that counter public spheres aren't simply 'reaction formations' but are, in their terms, world-making formations:

> By queer culture we mean a world-making project, where world, like public, differs from community or group because it necessarily includes more people that can be identified, more spaces than can be mapped beyond a few

---

[29] Michael Warner, *Publics and Counterpublics* (New York: Zone Books, 2002), p. 119.

[30] Warner, *Publics and Counterpublics*, p. 23.

[31] Frantz Fanon, *Black Skin, White Masks*, translated by Charles Lam Markmann (London and Sydney: Pluto Press, 1986), pp. 109–40. On class shame see for instance Carolyn Steedman, *Landscape for a Good Woman: The Story of Two Lives* (London: Virago Press, 1986). For a recent and crucial discussion of shame see Elspeth Probyn, *Blush: Faces of Shame* (Minneapolis: University of Minnesota Press, 2005).

reference points, modes of feeling that can be learned rather than experienced as birthright. The queer world is a space of entrances, exits, unsystematized lines of acquaintance, projected horizons, typifying examples, alternate routes, blockages, incommensurate geographies.[32]

It is partly this sense of world-making that gives a social group its publicness, rather than simply figuring it as a closed and 'private' community. For a social form to have publicness it must address not simply its 'members' but also its potential members: a counter public sphere includes invitations to participate. World-making addresses a potential participant not through persuasive argument, but through its practices of communication:

> There is no speech or performance addressed to a public that does not try to specify in advance, in countless highly condensed ways, the lifeworld of its circulation: not just through its discursive claims – of the kind that can be said to be oriented to understanding – but through the pragmatics of its speech genres, idioms, stylistic markers, address, temporality, mise-en-scène, citational field, interlocutory protocols, lexicon and so on.[33]

It is this aspect that shifts the notion of publics and counter publics beyond the discursive realm. Here, through a myriad of styles (ways of greeting, dress preferences, speech practices) a lifeworld is being both imagined and brought (partly) into being. This is not, then, just a site for the dissemination of ideas, of opinions – it is crucially cultural in that it is about forms of practice, forms of being and doing.

I think it is easy enough to see how Warner and Berlant's ideas about counter public spheres might be more conducive to the sort of radical social heterogeneity that Michel de Certeau seeks to foster. What I think is less clear is how this might find a practical form in cultural-policy debates. For de Certeau one of the key features of cultural policy was, as I've already mentioned, to establish the conditions for oral communication. For Ahearne this relates back to May 1968:

> A specifically oral exchange brings the speaker up more abruptly against the sense his or her speech can (or cannot) confer upon a given situation. It brings the cultural models informing that speech up against the social and political (micro-)structures with which they putatively engage. I want to suggest that this experience, cast into relief by the events of May 1968,

---

[32] Lauren Berlant and Michael Warner, 'Sex in Public' in Warner, *Publics and Counterpublics*, p. 198.
[33] Warner, *Publics and Counterpublics*, p. 114.

raked through the entire field of culture and transformed for Certeau the
key vectors of its development.[34]

One way that de Certeau sought to increase, in his cultural-policy research, oral
exchange was to promote the potential of electronic media forms for the proliferation of speech situations. For de Certeau and Giard it was radio that had the
potential to sustain radical heterogeneity rather than close it down:

> . . . Radio, whose richness, flexibility, and interest as a means of expression
> for different types of publics, have been underscored with the growth of free
> radio stations and local programming. They escape the influence of the state
> and the yoke of national cultural models as well as the commercial appetite
> of the radios on the outskirts of cities. These new programs constitute a free
> tool for experimentation, whereby groups that until now have been silent or
> without means can reappropriate for themselves the space of public speech,
> or at least a parcel of this space. If adolescents and young adults, as well as
> immigrants, are so interested in these free radio stations, it is because of their
> common situation of living on borderlines, at a point between two ages in
> life, two styles of behavior, two cultures. (CS: 123 with Giard)

The potential of electronic media has developed since de Certeau and Giard
wrote this, and now it is probably Internet technologies that provide the most
fertile ground for the proliferation of heterogeneous speech.

Examples of the kind of cultural initiative that could emerge out of de
Certeau's policy suggestions should include the work of the group Superflex.
Indeed, inasmuch as Superflex purposefully encourages communication specifically from immigrant groups and amateurs it may be seen as exemplary of de
Certeau's cultural policy. Superflex is a Danish art collaboration, that operates
across various fields, including engineering, TV production, global development and so on. Started in 1993 by Rasmus Nielsen, Jakob Fenger and
Bjørnstjerne Christiansen, Superflex has used various networks (including
financial ones) to establish technological and communicative initiatives across
the globe (mainly Europe, Africa and Asia). Rather than producing 'art' – products that can be consumed – it sees its role as the production of tools that other
people can use to make things with, but which also have a critical relationship
to the dominant networks of communication and material circulation:

> The starting point for creating a tool is a belief in a heterogeneous, complex
> society. . . Through the tools SUPERFLEX investigate communicative

---

[34] Ahearne, *Between Cultural Theory and Policy*, p. 29.

processes in which power, hegemony, assertion and oppression, the gain and loss of terrain become evident. . . . All tools share the aspect of empowerment: e.g. having their own energy supply, becoming an independent producer of energy, having their own Internet TV channel, joining a political/economic discussion. Taken in this sense, artistic praxis means a concrete cultural intervention that mediates between different interests or at least makes them visible. In their tools SUPERFLEX attempt to create conditions for the production of new ways of thinking, acting, speaking and imagining.[35]

One of its projects that is closest to de Certeau's policy suggestions is called Superchannel. Superchannel is Internet TV. Examples range from the channel '3M', situated near Turin in Italy and run by a group of young Moroccan immigrants (2M is the name of national Moroccan television) to 'Echigo-Tsumari Channel' in Tokamachi, Japan, used to promote regional cultures across Japan. Access to the programmes is via the Internet and while the initial programmes are streamed 'live' they are also retained as part of an archive which can be accessed even after the channel has 'gone to sleep'.

In Liverpool, England, Superchannel initially launched 'Coronation Court Channel' – hosted by the residents of Liverpool's oldest tower block. What followed was a series of channels based around resident groups, community groups, activists and so on – forming 'Tenantspin' (Liverpool High-Rise Tenants' Internet TV Channel) and then 'Common People Channel' – concentrated in Liverpool and neighbouring cities, with studios set up in high-rise tower blocks. The channels were run by residents who had been trained by Superflex workers, but who autonomously generated their own TV channel as a 'local network' available globally. The imbrications of place, culture, identity and accessibility produces new communicative forms that begin to alter the communicative landscape. Programmes produced for 'Common People', for instance, include 'African Hair Styles and Make-Up Tips' (28.10.2002 by the Nigerian Community Association, Liverpool); 'Sometimes Chicken Sometimes Dhal' (03.07.2002 by the Asian Women's Association in Trafford, Manchester); 'Sleeping Rough in Manchester' (23.09.2002 by *Big Issue* vendors – a homeless activism organization).

But giving just the titles and the names of the associations producing the material doesn't really provide a flavour of the programmes. 'A Short Drama in 3 Parts' was first streamed on 24.07.2002 and consists mainly of a video letter by a British Asian woman in England addressed to her daughter who might be

---

[35] Superflex, *Tools* (Köln: Verlag der Buchhandlung Walter König, 2003), p. 5. For an invaluable resource to all things Superflex, including streams of Superchannels, see www.superflex.dk.

about to get married and leave home. The video is the mother (who is billed in the opening credits as 'The Family Slave') giving instructions to the daughter (titled 'The Flirty One') who pops in and out of the kitchen where the programme is being videoed and where a number of friends and relatives congregate (variously titled 'The Old Biddies', 'The Nosey Neighbour', and so on). The video consists of a dhal being prepared as well as some chicken, and is designed to help the daughter in her (potential) new life. Intensely personal, culturally informative (the recipe not only gives you the ingredients but shows you how to make a family recipe of dhal), amateurishly informal (the 'family slave' answers the phone while making the food), it is also intimate diasporic communication available globally yet rooted in a small kitchen-diner in Northern England. The programme is a micro-communicative instance that can reverberate in unexpected places and which allows the receiver to 'listen in' – to the cooking and to the neighbourhood chat.

Such initiatives are in one sense 'minor' cultural forms; they are just the beginnings of new communicative networks. But in other ways they suggest a much more massive alteration of the communicative landscape. These initiatives re-direct the magical powers of technology, away from the monological tendencies of powerful networks, towards the interests of heteroglossia, towards the speech of others – amateurs and immigrants. They provide concrete examples of a slow emergence of the kind of voices that de Certeau thought he could hear in the streets in May 1968. They give vocal space to local associations, activist groups (for instance the 'Grey Panthers' – a group of pensioners proudly declaring their interests), young people, immigrant groups and so on. These groups are dynamic, mutable, adapting to changing cultural circumstances, but also 'world-making' with the resources at their disposal.

De Certeau's involvement in cultural policy clearly doesn't leave epistemology or ethics behind: it is fundamentally about providing spaces for the proliferation of knowledges under an obligation to the unmanageable heterogeneity of the everyday and the other. The involvement in cultural policy also maintains the commitment to the communicative potential of a psychoanalytic form of cultural practice.

CITIES OF GHOSTS

One book that de Certeau admired and often referred to was Karl Marx's *The Eighteenth Brumaire of Louis Bonaparte*.[36] This is in many ways the most

[36] Karl Marx, *The Eighteenth Brumaire of Louis Bonaparte* (1852) in Karl Marx and Friedrich Engels, *Selected Works in One Volume* (London: Lawrence and Wishart, 1980), pp. 98–179.

literary of Marx's historiographies, and, in an uncanny sense that echoes with de Certeau's approach to historiography, it is the book that can be most easily read as a form of psychoanalytic cultural historiography (in anticipation of psychoanalytic cultural historiography, of course).[37] *The Eighteenth Brumaire* is a form of historiography that is rich in figurations that suggest how historiography and psychoanalysis are imbricated: it would be hard, for instance, to imagine a text that is more evocative of the way that the past haunts the present:

> Men make their own history, but they do not make it just as they please; they do not make it under circumstances chosen by themselves, but under circumstances directly encountered, given and transmitted from the past. The tradition of all the dead generations weighs like a nightmare on the brain of the living. And just when they seemed engaged in revolutionizing themselves and things, in creating something that has never yet existed, precisely in such periods of revolutionary crisis they anxiously conjure up the spirits of the past to their service and borrow from them names, battle cries and costumes in order to present the new scene of world history in this time-honoured disguise and this borrowed language.[38]

This *pressing* of the past into the lives of the living is a theme that impacts on cultural policy in a number of ways, not least because culture (as a form of governance) always incorporates the activity of official memory (through monuments and museums).

In the first few pages of *The Eighteenth Brumaire* Marx raises what seems like an intractable problem: faced with the possibility of revolution, of liberating themselves from the shackles of the past, and about to launch into the future, what is it that people do? They cloak themselves in the clothes of the past; they drape themselves in the poetics of a past world. And yet what else could they do? For Marx's other point in these beginning pages is to categorically invoke the past as the determining condition of the present (their circumstances are directly transmitted from the past). History is, in a strong sense, determining of the future. We are limited in what we can think and know by the determining conditions of social being, which are already established. Yet alongside this is a utopian desire to remake the world, to remake

---

[37] For a reading of *The Eighteenth Brumaire* that is alert to its 'Freudian' themes, see Jeffrey Mehlman, *Revolution and Repetition: Marx/Hugo/Balzac* (Berkeley, Los Angeles and London: University of California Press, 1977). For recent commentary on *The Eighteenth Brumaire* (which includes a new translation of it) see Mark Cowling and James Martin, eds, *Marx's 'Eighteenth Brumaire': (Post)modern Interpretations* (London: Pluto Press, 2002).

[38] Marx, *The Eighteenth Brumaire*, p. 96.

practical life. This desire to shrug off the past will require a leap of faith, a leap into the unknown, and unknowable:

> The social revolution of the nineteenth century cannot draw its poetry from the past, but only from the future. It cannot begin with itself before it has stripped off all superstition in regard to the past. Earlier revolutions required recollections of past world history in order to drug themselves concerning their own content. In order to arrive at its own content, the revolution of the nineteenth century must let the dead bury their dead. There the phrase went beyond the content; here the content goes beyond the phrase.[39]

For a psychoanalytic historiography that is also interested in forming cultural policy, such sentiments are crucial but problematic (as they are for Marxism): how do you draw your poetry from the future? Doesn't the very act of 'drawing' suggest a returning to the past, to the available cultural resources? Yet there are also here some clear instructions: the only way forward is through reconciliation with the past.

For Marx, then, for revolution to succeed a relationship has to be established with death – with the dead. Looking around our cities we are continually faced with the figures of the dead: the officially mourned and celebrated figures of politicians, inventors, heroes, fighters and suchlike. There are also memorials to the dead who have died in wars. And yet the un-mourned, the un-acknowledged dead, the dead who might spoil the image of civic pride are absent – in the UK there is still no official monument to the slaves who died in transit or in captivity, and on whose backs the wealth of the nation partly rests. It would seem clear then that a cultural policy that was informed by cultural psychoanalysis and by its ethics and epistemology would find much to do in the work of memorializing. Yet there is also a way that psychoanalytically informed cultural policy is also directed to the practices of the present, to encouraging the proliferation of heterogeneity.

In an essay titled 'Ghosts in the City',[40] that is now included in the second volume of *The Practice of Everyday Life*, de Certeau works to describe a city (Paris) haunted by the past and filled with a radical heterogeneity. His implicit question is how this haunting and this heterogeneity could inform cultural policy and urban planning. To start with, de Certeau describes an uncanny urbanism:

[39] Marx, *The Eighteenth Brumaire*, p. 98.
[40] Michel de Certeau, 'Les revenants de la ville', *Architecture intérieure/Créé* 192–3, January–March 1983, pp. 98–101.

. . . urban planning destroyed even more than war had. Yet, some old buildings survived, even if they were caught in its nets. These seemingly sleepy, old-fashioned things, defaced houses, closed-down factories, the debris of shipwrecked histories still today raise up the ruins of an unknown, strange city. They burst forth within the modernist, massive, homogenous city like slips of the tongue from an unknown, perhaps unconscious language. . . . Heterogeneous references, ancient scars, they create bumps on the smooth utopias of the new Paris. Ancient things become remarkable. An uncanniness lurks there, in the everyday life of the city. It is a ghost that henceforth haunts urban planning. (PEL2: 133)

For de Certeau, then, the city is a place of radically divergent temporalities that will always refuse any attempt to unveil a homogenous façade of the city. The city is punctured by heterogeneity even if it is aiming towards smooth coherency. It is radical plurality that is the city's most valuable asset and the job of cultural policy is to allow this to flourish – to create situations where the unconscious language of difference can come to the foreground:

Gestures are the true archives of the city, if one understands by 'archives' the past that is selected and reused according to present custom. They remake the urban landscape every day. They sculpt a thousand pasts that are perhaps no longer nameable and that structure no less their experience of the city. Ways in which a North African moves into an HLM, in which a man from Rodez runs his bistro, in which a native of Malakoff walks in the subway, in which a passerby marks with graffiti his or her way of reading a poster. All of these practices of 'making do', polysemic customs of places and things, should be maintained by 'renovation'. How can the square, street, or building be offered up more to their inventions? This is a program for a renovation policy. (PEL2: 142)

The question facing cultural policy is how to remake the city, the nation, in the name of plurality, how to open it up to hospitality, how to make an un-homely (uncanny) home, where repressions reemerge into the open? The question isn't simply about facilitating the formation of 'free association' in communicative situations designed to be a practice of radical democracy. The ethical demand here is to recognize the repressions that are constitutive of the city and to allow space and situations for this repression to be articulated.

Again it is an artist who offers the most vivid indication of what this approach to urban cultural policy might involve. The title of 'artist as uncanny ethnographer' seems a fitting if awkward designation for Krzysztof Wodiczko. A Polish artist living and working mainly in the US, Wodiczko has become famous for his night projection of images (both still and moving) on to the sides of buildings, and for a range of urban vehicles and instruments, designed to address the ethical questions of democratic culture in the city:

> An intense presence of historic monuments, advertising, communication media and urban events merge with our daily personal performance into one uniform aesthetic practice dangerously securing the continuity of 'our' culture. Media art, performance art, performative design: they must inter-fere with these everyday aesthetics if they wish to contribute ethically to a democratic process. They must interrupt the continuity of existing social relations and perceptions well entrenched in the theatre of the city. Such arts, using the words of Simon Critchley in *Ethics of Deconstruction*, should 'interrupt the *polis* in the name of what it excludes and marginalises'. To preserve democracy one must challenge it; one must challenge its symmetry with an asymmetry of ethical responsibility.[41]

If the city is haunted by what it tries to exclude, then Wodiczko's work pur-posefully attempts to offer the ghosts a voice, and an image. And these aren't simply ghosts of the past, but people whose position in culture may appear to some as ghostly (asylum seekers, living in the half-light of non-citizenship, for instance). Wodiczko himself, as well as critics like Denis Hollier and Dick Hebdige, recognize the specific spectral condition that his projections and vehicles produce.[42] In a text from 1983 Wodiczko is explicit about the uncanny quality intended for his public projections (images projected on to the side of buildings and monuments):

> The attack [the projection] must be unexpected, frontal, and must come with the night, when the building, undisturbed by its daily func-tions, is asleep and when its body dreams of itself, when the architecture has its nightmares.

---

[41] Krzysztof Wodiczko, 'Open Transmission' in Alan Read, ed., *Architecturally Speaking: Practices of Art, Architecture and the Everyday* (London and New York: Routledge, 2000), pp. 87–8. The reference to Critchley is Simon Critchley, *The Ethics of Deconstruction: Derrida and Levinas* (Oxford: Basil Blackwell, 1992).

[42] Denis Hollier, 'While the City Sleeps: Mene, Mene, Tekel, Upharsin', *October* 64, 1993, pp. 3–15. Dick Hebdige, 'The Machine is *Unheimlich*. Wodiczko's Homeless Vehicle Project', *Public Address: Krzysztof Wodiczko*, Walker Art Centre, 1992, pp. 54–67. Dick Hebdige, 'Redeeming Witness: In the Tracks of the Homeless Vehicle Project', *Cultural Studies* 7: 2, 1993, pp. 173–223. Rosalyn Deutsche, 'Sharing Strangeness: Krzysztof Wodiczko's *Ægis* and the Question of Hospitality', *Grey Room* 6, 2002, pp. 26–43. See also Patricia C. Phillips, 'Creating Democracy: A Dialogue with Krzysztof Wodiczko', *Art Journal*, vol. 62, no. 4, 2003.

This will be a symbol-attack, a public psychoanalytical séance, unmasking and revealing the unconscious of the building, its body, the 'medium' of power.[43]

For Wodiczko the 'return of the repressed' is rendered both as an ideology critique of urban architecture and as a literal 'return of the oppressed'. City streets become haunted by giant images of what so often passes as invisible. Wodiczko has used his projections to turn public monuments into monuments of the homeless (or 'evicts' – his preferred term). He has projected massive chains and locks on the sides of empty buildings in New York. Weapons and money have appeared on war memorials, and famously in the 1980s a Swastika on the front of South Africa House in London. In one of his moving projections 'City Hall Tower Projection, Kraków' (1996), Wodiczko used video projection and sound to re-animate the Central Marketplace in Kraków. Thousands of people congregated in the Marketplace to watch as images of pairs of hands performing various gestures (making a hot drink, holding a candle, smoking a cigarette, etc.) were projected on to the tower. Stories accompanying the video projection were amplified across the square. These stories told of 'private' lives, of things that go on (mainly at night) 'behind closed doors'. A woman tells of her alcoholic husband and the way that he abuses her and their child. A young man tells of the night that his elder brother physically beat him when he found him in bed with another boy. A blind man talks of his son's embarrassment about being seen in the street with him.

These stories are both testimonies and ethnographies of the unseen city, but crucially they are not 'interpreted' by Wodiczko, rather they are sited. And it is the placing of such materials that is crucial. If the similarity between colonial ethnography and more recent cultural studies ethnography is often evident in the separation of the place of the ethnographic 'object' from the site of ethnographic production (from an 'over-there' to an 'over-here' – where the over-here might be seen as the West, or the Academy, etc.), then by situating the work in the street Wodiczko is doing something more than questioning the proper space of art. Such work intervenes in the field (the cardinal sin for forms of social science) as both an interruption in the urban environment and an interruption in the usual protocols of ethnography.

This uncanny ethnography is perhaps most evident in the various instruments that Wodiczko has been making since the early 1990s (mostly through the resources of the Massachusetts Institute of Technology's Media Lab, where Wodiczko is head of the Interrogative Design Group). These instruments are

---

[43] Krzysztof Wodiczko, *Critical Vehicles: Writings, Projects, Interviews* (Cambridge and London: The MIT Press, 1999), p. 47.

designed for communication, but under altered conditions (a theme begun with the Homeless Vehicle Project). From 1992 Wodiczko's work has been particularly focused on the experiences of migration. He has made a number of electronic instruments for people to use both to help tell their stories but also to give their stories a different visibility (to interrupt the invisibility of the migrant experience). The 'Alien Staff' (1992–96) is a rod with a video monitor at the top. In the central section, clear plastic cylinders can be filled with 'relics' of migrations (immigration papers, family photographs, etc.). The video monitor screens a testimony (an oral history) of migration. The migrant, who is also the user of the Staff, composes these testimonies and controls the 'play-back' when out on the street. A similar logic informs the 'Mouthpiece (Porte-Parole)' (1992–96), which Wodiczko describes as a 'cyborgian bandage'[44] – a video monitor of a mouth talking which is placed in front of the user's mouth thereby contesting the epistemological myth of 'direct address' (as unmediated communication). These instruments have been used in various cities across the world. In the US they were used by various groups to tell stories of what it means to be an immigrant, what it means not to have a 'green card' and to have to find the most poorly paid menial work.

Thus these instruments are not themselves messages, but tools for facilitating certain utterances. In this sense Wodiczko's practice is to facilitate the conditions of speech, to encourage oral exchange to take place where more often than not silence is the public discourse. In terms of cultural policy, Wodiczko's instruments contest the classic job of representation: his work doesn't represent homelessness or the homeless, for instance, or the immigrant experience; rather it alters the communicative economics and allows a space for self-presentation. Here, 'native informants' (and that means everybody) are invited to be their own ethnographers. Ethnographic 'objects' become subjects of their own ethnographies. Wodiczko's collected writing, *Critical Vehicles*, gives an account of the experience of using these devices: this is another turn in self-reflexivity and calls on the 'client-group' to give an account of the instruments' effects. In this sense these works would need to be judged (from the position of a cultural policy tuned to the ethical promotion of heterogeneity) for the different kinds of contact and communication they allow to take place. *Critical Vehicles* evidences a range of 'communication scenes', from the painful and self-conscious use of testimony (an almost confessional-therapeutic use) to their use as 'a starting point for . . . exchange and sharing'.[45] Ironically, perhaps, the most successful use of the instruments might come when they are abandoned: 'Conversation developed so well between the immigrants around the stick [the

Alien Staff] that they forgot about it. They ended up in a restaurant and the stick was just leaning against the wall.'[46]

Like de Certeau (whom Wodiczko acknowledges as a reference), this work privileges speech as the scene of otherness and everyday life. Wodiczko's instruments provide a way of operating that allows for the uncanny strangeness of geographical displacement to challenge the various discourses around migration (assimilation, for instance, as the neo-liberal dominant discourse) and allows for us (for those that stumble across these instruments) to become 'strangers to ourselves'.[47] In one way it is hard to imagine the social aesthetics being fostered by artists like Wodiczko and groups like Superflex, or the cultural-policy research of Michel de Certeau, being instituted on any large scale. As far as this goes the epigram that heads this chapter indicates how de Certeau understood his cultural-policy research: it would only be as an art of diversion, by diverting resources away from 'official' policy, that the task of proliferating heterogeneity would get done. What government would prioritize the orientation that de Certeau articulates? Yet the very fact that Wodiczko can engage public audiences, and that Internet TV stations facilitated by Superflex can operate to produce such democratic conditions, should offer concrete proof of the potential of such cultural policy. Perhaps, then, the fact that I find it hard to imagine a government adopting a cultural policy based on an ethics of hospitality to strangers, an ethics open to the heterogeneity of the everyday, says more about the cynicism of the times than the unfeasibility of such cultural policy. To live in a world where whole spheres of cultural work are simply given over to private enterprise (from the urban street furniture controlled by advertising companies, to the almost wholesale commercialization of TV and radio) has clearly worn away at our ability to imagine a time when things could be otherwise.

Michel de Certeau worked across a heterogeneous range of cultural arenas – political commentary, historiography, contemporary ethnology and cultural policy (to name the most obvious). Yet while the forms of practice differ from site to site – from dialogue with dusty documents to discussion with the living – there is a methodological core to this work which unites it. This methodology is forged from an analysis that recognizes that the social ordering (the spread of power) has epistemological consequences: what declares itself as transparent veils another reality, more heterogeneous, more unmanageable, that is constitutive of discourse but is not reducible to it. Looking forwards (cultural policy) or looking back (historiography), the challenge remains the

---

[46] Wodiczko, *Critical Vehicles*, p. 204.

[47] Kristeva's work on immigration and fear of otherness was also a resource for Wodiczko, see Julia Kristeva, *Strangers to Ourselves* (New York: Columbia University Press, 1991).

same: to fashion culture so that it is more open to a plurality of voices. Epistemological doubt is thereby always harnessed to the production of a more democratic culture. There is, though, no pure scene of free speech (not this side of a more fundamental revolution) that is being imagined: the nature of communication is compromised from the beginning. But the crucial point here is that epistemological doubt doesn't get in the way of communication, it actually provides the conditions and resources under which it can flourish – and this is because it is aligned to a poetics of heterogeneity that is ubiquitous and social: that is there, ready to spill out.

We have looked at the work of de Certeau alongside various other writers and I have focused on a number of disciplinary issues to do with colonial and sexual histories, the possibilities of psychoanalytic cultural analysis, a form of cultural policy that is born out of a recognition of alterity, and so on. What I claimed at the start was that these scenes were characterized by the meeting of varied cultural forms that are altered when they meet: thus as psychoanalysis and historiography meet something appears that is neither straightforwardly psychoanalytic nor historiographic. I think that when such practices meet in de Certeau's work each practice works to amplify in the other the potential it has for responding to heterogeneity in the face of epistemological critique. These scenes of disciplinary cross-pollination are galvanized by an ethical commitment which is also a political commitment to subjugated standpoints – both in looking to the past and in directing cultural work towards the future. That such an ethical commitment should find sustenance and 'resources of hope' in epistemological doubt is the central argument of this book.

CHAPTER 7

Cultural Studies: A Practitioner's Art
(Conclusion)

Practice is both the starting point and the testing ground of our conceptualisation of the world. What is needed is not so much the recovery of practical philosophy as the recovery of the philosophy of practice.[1]

MAKING CONTACT

The question I set out to address in this book was: what would cultural studies look like if it decided to engage with the work of Michel de Certeau? This question had a polemical edge to it – there are, after all, simply countless examples of citations of de Certeau's writing in work that purports to be cultural studies. What I was suggesting (implicitly) was that an engagement between cultural studies and de Certeau has yet to take place. Inasmuch as this book is a contribution to the debate about what cultural studies is, then it has tried to make its argument through substantive and generative work, by showing the kind of things that cultural studies, or cultural analysis, can do and has done, and how this doing can be considered in relation to the work of de Certeau.

For those who are familiar with de Certeau and with cultural studies this account might seem perverse in one specific detail: I have deliberately ignored several of the more famous formulations of de Certeau, specifically his account of tactics and strategy.[2] 'Strategies and tactics' has been de Certeau's biggest export: it has circulated in all sorts of disciplinary spaces (but most insistently in cultural studies) to the point where a theory of strategy and tactics is simply

---

[1] Ngũgĩ wa Thiong'o, *Moving the Centre: The Struggle for Cultural Freedoms* (Oxford: James Currey, 1993), p. 26.

[2] The chapter on de Certeau in my *Everyday Life and Cultural Theory: An Introduction* (London and New York: Routledge, 2002) concerns itself with strategies and tactics. For a subtle and useful account of the differences between strategy and tactics that stretches the cultural studies' account of these terms see both Jeremy Ahearne, *Michel de Certeau: Interpretation and its Other* (Cambridge: Polity Press, 1995) and Ian Buchanan, *Michel de Certeau: Cultural Theorist* (London: Thousand Oaks and New Delhi: Sage, 2000).

what de Certeau stands for. My implicit argument here has been that this is a mistake: or rather, it has allowed a number of disciplinary and sub-disciplinary paradigms to simply carry on as before, unaltered, conducting business as usual. In contrast, the active methodological imagination that de Certeau can provide, with its power to alter the very ground of cultural analysis, has generally failed to make contact (at all) with the project of cultural studies. Contact would entail the necessary alteration of cultural studies as an ongoing condition of its continued engagement with the world. My argument, then, is that if cultural studies wanted to be a form of cultural analysis that isn't based on the application of various 'off-the-shelf' explanations and operations (which fit where they touch), or a form of analysis that isn't performed with a tool-kit where the possible results are known in advance, then making contact with de Certeau can provide fertile ground for rethinking the business of cultural studies and cultural analysis.

Because cultural studies has remained relatively uninterested in establishing a methodological or meta-methodological base (an ethics, an epistemology),[3] it can appear (in worst light) either vague and platitudinous, or else a mirror image of what it set out to displace (the swapping of skateboarding for Wordsworth, so to speak, doesn't protect a form of inquiry from being divorced from daily life, or from congregating around a canon of set texts in acts of quasi-religious veneration). The general vagueness of cultural studies is well-described by Tony Bennett even though he is trying to suggest a common purpose to it:

> [The term 'cultural studies'] now functions largely as a term of convenience for a fairly dispersed array of theoretical and political positions which, however widely divergent they may be in other respects, share a commitment to examining cultural practices from the point of view of their intrication with, and within, relations of power.[4]

A nebulous statement such as 'intrication with, and within, relations of power' might point to a set of intentions of a vaguely post-Marxist flavour, yet not only does it lack any sort of material specificity with regard to practice, it simply describes the legitimating language common to nearly everyone in the human sciences who wants their work to have social resonance. Thus it is easy to imagine the same statement being made by historians, anthropologists, geographers,

---

[3] There is, I think, clear indication that this is changing: see for example Nick Couldry, *Inside Culture: Re-Imagining the Method of Cultural Studies* (London: Sage, 2000) and Joanna Zylinska, *The Ethics of Cultural Studies* (London and New York: Continuum Books, 2005).

[4] Tony Bennett, 'Putting Policy into Cultural Studies' in Lawrence Grossberg, Cary Nelson and Paula Treichler, eds, *Cultural Studies* (London and New York: Routledge, 1992), p. 23.

sociologists, political scientists and so on. In fact it may be that such definitions have traditionally related much more closely to these other fields of inquiry, and that these other disciplines would have a more substantial claim to this as an adequate description of their field.

Similarly when critics championing de Certeau want to align him with a form of cultural studies interested in tracking forms of social resistance, cultural studies appears simply to be the flip side of 'power studies':

> Of all the important theoretical writings in France in the 1970s and 1980s, Michel de Certeau's is most germane to cultural studies. Cultural studies may be defined as an interdisciplinary, critical, historical investigation of aspects of everyday life, with a particular emphasis on the problem of resistance, that is, the way that individuals and groups practice a strategy of appropriation in response to structures of domination.[5]

Just to be clear about this: I see no problem with the idea of being interested in forms of resistance, or in forms of power (how could you not be?); I just think that for cultural studies to constantly define itself in these terms (and to limit itself to these terms) is simply to concede that it is nothing more than a vague set of intentions (in a disciplinary context it describes cultural studies with mirrors and smoke). There might also be dishonesty in such a description – or rather a lack of fit between intention and practice. If 'power and resistance' were the grounding impulses for a disciplinary field then mightn't the following be unavoidable: judgements of efficacy (how successful is a form of resistance?); comparative studies (tracking power and resistance in relation to different forms of social organization); the organization of social movements; and so on? And yet, these are aspects of analysis that cultural studies seems to have studiously avoided; or else they are ways of operating that are generally outside of cultural studies' competence. Indeed if it is 'power and resistance' that is being sought, wouldn't you opt for a form of attention that is most visibly present in forms of political anthropology? Thus the work undertaken by James C. Scott, for instance, in his account of struggles in Malaysia and elsewhere, might answer Bennett and Poster's description of cultural studies much more effectively than work that purports to be cultural studies. Scott's realm of investigation includes a whole panoply of social and cultural forms:

> We might interpret the rumors, gossip, folktales, songs, gestures, jokes, and the theatre of the powerless as vehicles by which, amongst other things, they

---

[5] Mark Poster, *Cultural History and Postmodernity: Disciplinary Readings and Challenges* (New York: Columbia University Press, 1997), p. 108.

insinuate a critique of power while hiding behind anonymity or behind
innocuous understandings of their conduct. These patterns of disguising *ideological* insubordination are somewhat analogous to the patterns by which, in
my experience, peasants and slaves have disguised their efforts to thwart
material appropriation of their labor, their production, and their property: for
example, poaching, foot-dragging, pilfering, dissimulation, flight. Together,
these forms of insubordination might suitably be called the infrapolitics of the
powerless.[6]

Scott's work is not a world away from cultural studies, yet it is easily understood
within the terms of political anthropology: it doesn't need cultural studies to
function.

It would seem that cultural studies has, at times, a self-perception that presents it as a large-scale audit of good and bad objects and practices: in one
column go all the examples of transgression, subversion, resistance; in another
column are the networks of power, the examples of normativity. No doubt such
self-perception is inevitable when what you are doing is trying to persuade yourself and others that your work has important social consequences. Yet to look at
most examples of *actual cultural studies practice* (including work by Bennett and
Poster), what seems most evident (and vibrant) is the way that various forms of
attention (methods) struggle to engage with cultural objects and practices. This
struggling has been the lifeblood of cultural studies. It may seem odd, therefore,
that cultural studies has been content (or so it seems) to inhabit a position as a
methodological bricoleur and bricoleuse – melding empirical methods with
more speculative forms of social theory, for instance. In this context Mieke Bal's
assessment of cultural studies is apposite:

> While one of cultural studies' major innovations has been to pay attention to
> a different kind of object, as a new field averse to traditional approaches it has
> not been successful (enough) in developing a methodology to counter the
> exclusionary methods of the separate disciplines. More often than not, the
> methods have not changed. While the object – *what* you study – has changed,
> the method – *how* you do it – has not. But without the admittedly rigid
> methodologies of the disciplines, how do you keep analysis from floundering
> into sheer partisanship or being perceived as floundering?[7]

---

[6] James C. Scott, *Domination and the Arts of Resistance: Hidden Transcripts* (New Haven and
London: Yale University Press, 1990), p. xii.
[7] Mieke Bal, 'From Cultural Studies to Cultural Analysis: "A Controlled Reflection on the
Formation of Method"' in Paul Bowman, ed., *Interrogating Cultural Studies: Theory, Politics
and Practice* (London: Pluto, 2003), p. 30.

I think that unless Bal's point is heeded, cultural studies may well become a mirage – it will simply become the empty place where the human sciences fail to come together.

I am not suggesting that Michel de Certeau provides the 'true' distinctive methodology that cultural studies or cultural analysis (the latter is Bal's preferred term) might require to give itself substance; merely that de Certeau provides an example of someone who recognizes that 'method' is not simply fundamental but needs to be underwritten by metamethodological reflection.[8] In this way epistemology isn't an overly-specialized theoretical field that has little to say about the practicalities of doing cultural studies: critical epistemology becomes the very source of what is most inventive, most distinctive and most transformative in cultural studies' commerce with the world. Likewise, ethics isn't an abstraction which ignores the realities and urgency of politics; it is the *practical commitment* (to change, to heterogeneity, to hospitality) that directs cultural studies' inquiries, that generates its forms of attention, and allows it to pursue political and cultural objectives. Finally, and perhaps most crucially, methodology isn't a domain of expertise, only of interest to insiders. Methodology, to refer back to Michael Warner's notion of the counter public sphere, is a way of 'world-making' – in all its operational values (free association, listening for the unmanageable remainder and so on) a social world is being imagined (one hospitable to otherness, fashioned out of radically democratic practices and so on). And it is methodology that makes cultural studies an invitation to participate in world-making.

---

[8] An account of another 'metamethodology' is supplied by Gary Genosko, 'Félix Guattari: Towards a Transdisciplinary Metamethodology', *Angelaki: Journal of the Theoretical Humanities*, 8:1, 2003, p. 133.

Index

CPSIA information can be obtained at www.ICGtesting.com
Printed in the USA
LVOW11s1711140415

434560LV00003B/110/P